Liberalization
and Democratization

Liberalization and Democratization

Change in the Soviet Union and Eastern Europe

Edited by
NANCY BERMEO

The Johns Hopkins University Press

BALTIMORE AND LONDON

This book was brought to publication with the generous assistance of the Center of International Studies at Princeton University.

This book, with the exception of the last chapter, appeared as the October 1991 issue of *World Politics: A Journal of International Relations*, vol. 44, no. 1.

The Johns Hopkins University Press
701 West 40th Street
Baltimore, Maryland 21211-2190
The Johns Hopkins Press Ltd., London

Library of Congress Cataloging-in-Publication Data

Liberalization and democratization : change in the Soviet Union and Eastern
  Europe / edited by Nancy Bermeo.
     p.   cm.
  "This book, with the exception of the last chapter, appeared as the October 1991
issue of World politics: a journal of international relations, vol. 44, no. 1"—T.p.
verso.
  Includes bibliographical references and index.
  ISBN 0-8018-4417-7 (acid-free). — ISBN 0-8018-4418-5 (pbk. : acid-free)
  1. Europe, Eastern—Politics and government—1989–   2. Soviet Union—
Politics and government—1985–   I. Bermeo, Nancy Gina, 1951–   .
JN96.A2L53   1992
320.947—dc20   92-3068

CONTENTS

CONTRIBUTORS

NANCY BERMEO is Associate Professor of Politics at Princeton University and an Editor of *World Politics*. She is the author of *The Revolution within the Revolution* (1986), a study of redemocratization in Portugal, and has written several articles on the causes and effects of regime change in Europe and Latin America. She is currently preparing a broad comparative study titled *Democracy and the Legacies of Dictatorship*.

TIMUR KURAN is Associate Professor of Economics at the University of Southern California. His research focuses on the evolution of values and institutions. He is completing a book on the cognitive, social, political, and economic consequences of preference falsification—the act of concealing one's wants under social pressure.

GIUSEPPE DI PALMA is Professor of Political Science at the University of California, Berkeley. He is coeditor, with Laurence Whitehead, of *The Central American Impasse* (1986) and author of *To Craft Democracies: An Essay on Democratic Transitions* (1990).

ANDREW C. JANOS is Professor of Political Science at the University of California, Berkeley, in the fields of comparative politics and East European studies. His publications include *The Politics of Backwardness in Hungary* (1982) and *Politics and Paradigms* (1986).

RUSSELL BOVA is Associate Professor of Political Science and former Director of the Russian and Soviet Area Studies Program at Dickinson College, Carlisle, Pennsylvania. He is the author of numerous articles on Gorbachev-era Soviet politics and is currently working on a book dealing with the political dynamics of Soviet reform.

DAVID D. LAITIN is Professor of Political Science and Director of the Center for the Study of Politics, History and Culture (Wilder House) at the University of Chicago. He is the author of *Hegemony and Culture* (1986) and *Language Repertoires and State Construction in Africa* (forthcoming).

Liberalization
and Democratization

INTRODUCTION

By NANCY BERMEO

POLITICAL surprise provides a double stimulus for social scientists. An unexpected regime change, an unanticipated revolution—indeed, any political event that is both dramatic and unforeseen—forces us to analyze not just the origins of the change itself but the origins of our own amazement. The political surprises that emerged in the Soviet Union and Eastern Europe in the late 1980s have, accordingly, compelled us to ask not simply why events unfolded as they did but why our predictive theories left us unprepared. The five essays collected here address both of these questions and therefore offer insights about both politics and scholarship.

Whether shared or conflicting, the insights of these authors are not the product of editorial orchestration. With the exception of David Laitin's review article, none of these essays was commissioned. Each was written independently (though more or less simultaneously) as an individual response to the dramatic changes in what used to be called the Soviet bloc. This special issue of *World Politics* thus emerged quite naturally from special events.

Although each author fastens on a different piece of the intellectual puzzle, all of the essays collected here offer explanations for the disintegration of communist rule. Timur Kuran and Giuseppe Di Palma focus on what the former calls the East European Revolution; Russell Bova and David Laitin focus on liberalization in the Soviet Union; and Andrew Janos focuses on the dynamics of political change in Eastern Europe, the Soviet Union, and China.

How do they explain the challenges and changes we have found so surprising? Kuran reminds us that any "mass uprising results from multitudes of individual choices" (p. 16); accordingly, his argument derives from a focus on the individual citizen. He cautions that individual choices are always a complex amalgam of *observable public preferences* and *hidden private preferences*. Scholars, government officials, even opposition leaders are inevitably surprised by revolutions because they have little insight into what people's private preferences really are. Motivated by fear and, to a lesser extent, ignorance, most oppressed people engage in what Kuran calls "preference falsification." They hide their opposition to the government and live a lie, simply to live in peace.

Revolutions break out only when living a lie becomes intolerable or unnecessary. In the first case, citizens act against the state because their hostility to the existing order has grown so intense that it overpowers their fear of retribution. In the second case, it is the weight of fear itself that changes. After a few brave individuals dare to act on their private preferences and survive, lying seems less necessary and thousands of citizens, finally able to be true to themselves, jump on the revolutionary bandwagon.

What causes an individual's revolutionary threshold to change? Answering this question, Kuran consciously adopts a structuralist perspective. Private preferences can shift, he tells us, because of "economic recession, contacts with other societies, or intergenerational replacement" (p. 21). In the case of Eastern Europe, the Soviet reform movement reduced "the perceived risk of challenging the status quo." But he maintains that no one—not even Gorbachev—"could see that a revolution was in the making." Searching for the single factor that triggered this (or any other) revolution is "akin to trying to identify the spark that ignited a forest fire" (p. 37). Kuran's message is clear but sobering: preference falsification renders revolutions intrinsically unpredictable.

Though both Kuran and Di Palma devote a good deal of attention to the implications of lying and falsification, their messages and methods differ in important ways. Whereas Kuran focuses on the falsities of the powerless, Di Palma labors with the lies of the powerful. Di Palma makes a convincing case for the resilience of civil society under dictatorship but insists that "the surge in mobilization was not the sufficient or main cause" (p. 75) of East European regime collapse. "Communist regimes lost their will to rule" (p. 73), he tells us, because regime elites experienced a collective "crisis of faith" (p. 50). East European dictatorships were sustained by what Di Palma (following Maria Marcus) calls "legitimation from the top" (p. 55). Rulers ruled not because civil society thought them just but because they were convinced of their own superiority. Communism gave them an "ideology that could interpret reality and . . . reinvent it, even, if facts proved stubborn" (p. 56). Though some scholars argue that the changes in the Eastern bloc are rooted in a "convergence" with the West, Di Palma locates the change in "obdurate and insulating *divergence*" (p. 50; emphasis added). Communism's manifest inability to match the West in material terms or to provide anything approaching social equality strained the structure of legitimating lies for years until the "physical and ideological desertion" of the Soviet Union precipitated its final collapse (p. 49).

Di Palma's message to social scientists is no more sanguine than Kuran's. He wonders whether "we are theoretically equipped to accommodate the novelty of events in Eastern Europe" and cautions against any theories that stress "structural preconditions" and thus "underplay the role of choice" (p. 79). Nevertheless, this pessimism about existing theory is accompanied (happily) by optimism about the future of East European democracies. Di Palma concludes with the suggestion that a new zeitgeist is being born alongside a "new civic culture" that denies "the historical prophecies that stem from regional retardation and fragmentation" (p. 80).

Laitin, in his review article on national uprisings in the Soviet Union, also challenges a major historical prophecy—that empires inevitably disintegrate. Likening the Soviet Union to an "empire" is misleading, he argues, for it allows us to assume its "ultimate decomposition" (p. 143). Rather, the key to understanding the long-term implications of subnationalisms lies in a better understanding of "elite incorporation." Those who have observed the national uprisings in the Soviet Union and "envisioned an empire rotting from within" (p. 142) have failed to appreciate how different patterns of elite incorporation affect both the nature of nationalist struggles and the ability of the central authority to cope with nationalist conflict.

Di Palma's insistence that the "decisive operative relationship is not . . . between rulers and people" (p. 57) but between groups within the ruling elite fits well with Laitin's theory. The latter argues that where some significant sector of a regional elite has successfully assimilated Russian culture, the Soviet center can defend itself by exploiting elite divisions within the camp of the titular nationals. In regions where little assimilation of local elites has occurred, the center will find its allies among local minorities instead. Different patterns of elite incorporation create "different sorts of political cleavages [in which] the unfolding of national dramas will have distinct plots" (p. 174).

Laitin's study of patterns of elite incorporation in the various regions of the Soviet Union has led him to conclude that "the center will hold." Whether this judgment is viewed as optimistic or pessimistic depends on one's sympathies for the nationalist groups involved—but Laitin is unambiguously optimistic in his message to social scientists. "Whatever else these nationality movements have given us," he writes, they provide "social scientists with a sufficient range of cases to enable them to do their science better" (p. 142). Whereas Kuran stresses what we cannot know and Di Palma reminds us of what we do not know, Laitin focuses on what we might still learn.

Russell Bova argues that there is much to be learned from studying

Gorbachev's liberalization in the context of the larger literature on transitions from right-wing authoritarian rule. Where Kuran, Di Palma, and Janos draw parallels between communist rule and early absolutism, Bova strives to demonstrate the resemblance between liberalization in the Soviet Union and liberalization (and democratization) in Southern Europe and Latin America. His analysis of the conflicts between reformers and hardliners and of the many structural impediments to more rapid political change illustrates how the "dynamics of the liberalization process in the USSR adhere to a model of political change previously manifested in other parts of the world" (p. 137).

Though Bova is less concerned with the initiation of regime change than with the dynamics of a process already in motion, he nonetheless offers some insights into the question of what started the system change in the first place. He argues that in the USSR (as in Portugal, Spain, and Brazil) there were no "significant prior threats to authoritarian rule" outside the dictatorial regime. Change "had to be initiated from within the regime itself" (p. 123). For the Soviets, liberalization began, as it "invariably" does, with a split between reformers and conservatives in the dictatorial elite (p. 119). Bova explains the cause of the split with a variant of the convergence theory rejected by Di Palma. Citing Jerry Hough (who was apparently not surprised by liberalization), Bova writes that "the root of recent reform efforts" lies in the "increased education, urbanization, and stratification" produced by economic development (p. 133). He repeatedly challenges the received wisdom about Soviet exceptionalism and in so doing enlarges the set of theoretical lenses available for the study of the Soviet case.

Janos uses other theoretical lenses for the study of political change in communist regimes and thus expands our options even further. He suggests that we study contemporary Soviet and East European states not as cases of authoritarian regimes in transition but as cases of transitional *military societies* instead. Janos borrows the term from Herbert Spencer, who defined military societies as those in which industry is " 'essentially a permanent commissariat, existing solely to supply the needs of governmental-military structures' " (p. 94).

The recent changes in the Soviet Union and Eastern Europe were, according to Janos, brought on by a delayed but "genuine shift" from the principles of a military society to the principles of true and competitive industrialism. This shift, coupled with Gorbachev's "common [European] home strategy," forced the Soviet Union to abandon its claims on Eastern Europe and to adopt what Janos describes as a "Western democratic veneer" for its political institutions (p. 101).

Janos agrees with convergence theorists that communist regimes did industrialize and that as a result their societies became more complex and differentiated (p. 109). He goes so far as to argue that the impact of technological innovation "represents the only logical point of departure for the study of . . . political change" (p. 104). But his argument is ultimately not about convergence. Rather, it emphasizes international differences. He cautions social scientists not to expect "social processes like industrialization" to repeat themselves "from society to society" with the same effects (p. 104). In the West, with its models of true, competitive industrialism, "complexity and material abundance went hand in hand" (p. 109), whereas in Soviet-type regimes, industrialism brought "complexity cum scarcity" instead (p. 109).

In the context of a highly internationalized economic order, this combination of scarcity and complexity had powerful effects. Looking outward at what true industrialization brought to other states and looking upward at what became an increasingly affluent and corrupt communist political class, citizens of communist regimes "suffered a twofold effect of relative deprivation" (p. 108). This double deprivation led first to a legitimation crisis, then to the adoption of true industrialism, and finally to liberalization.

This brief comparative introduction outlines only the basic components of each author's argument. All five articles deserve much more attention. Fortunately, they are likely to receive this attention, for they are both timely and bold. Most provide fresh empirical material about unfolding events that are still difficult to describe much less understand. All provide a variety of theoretical insights into how our current and future understandings might be improved.

Taken as a whole, this collection raises many intriguing questions for future research and debate. Some scholars will cite the work of Brzezinski, Hough, and others and suggest that we were neither as surprised nor as theoretically ill prepared as some of these essays contend. Scholars will also scurry to illuminate and explain the many differences between transitions *within* Eastern Europe. Agnes Heller and Ferenc Fehér have argued that the term Eastern Europe itself is "a codeword for a region homogenized by sheer violence."[1] Future research on this region will likely underscore its heterogeneity and spark a debate about whether there was a singular East European revolution at all.

Debates about the explanatory weight of mass mobilization, elite disaffection, and the effects of the Gorbachev reforms abroad will occupy

[1] Heller and Fehér, *From Yalta to Glasnost: The Dismantling of Stalin's Empire* (London: Basil Blackwell, 1990), 281.

our time as well. The authors in this volume take different positions on each of these issues and provide a good foundation for future discussion.

They also offer us different forecasts about the fate of the changes that have already occurred. Janos is probably the most pessimistic. He writes that "the major nations of the former communist world may simply be too big to salvage" and that "in many of these countries, democracy may well remain a dream, or mere facade" (p. 111). Bova is cautious but, like Di Palma, guardedly optimistic. Writing of the long-term prospects for democracy in the Soviet Union, Bova ventures that it "is at least possible, if not probable, that a combination of skillful political leadership, external support, and good fortune may [come] to surprise the most pessimistic observers" (p. 136). This is a surprise that most of us would welcome, whether our predictive theories serve us well or not.

NOW OUT OF NEVER
The Element of Surprise in the East
European Revolution of 1989

By TIMUR KURAN*

I. United in Amazement

" **O**UR jaws cannot drop any lower," exclaimed Radio Free Europe one day in late 1989. It was commenting on the electrifying collapse of Eastern Europe's communist regimes.[1] The political landscape of the entire region changed suddenly, astonishing even the most seasoned political observers. In a matter of weeks entrenched leaders were overthrown, the communist monopoly on power was abrogated in one country after another, and persecuted critics of the communist system were catapulted into high office.

In the West the ranks of the stunned included champions of the view that communist totalitarianism is substantially more stable than ordinary authoritarianism.[2] "It has to be conceded," wrote a leading proponent of this view in early 1990, "that those of us who distinguish between the two non-democratic types of government underestimated the decay of Communist countries and expected the collapse of totalitarianism to take longer than has actually turned out to be the case."[3] Another acknowledged her bewilderment through the title of a new book: *The Withering Away of the Totalitarian State . . . And Other Surprises*.[4]

* This research was supported by the National Science Foundation under grant no. SES-8808031. A segment of the paper was drafted during a sabbatical, financed partly by a fellowship from the National Endowment for the Humanities, at the Institute for Advanced Study in Princeton. I am indebted to Wolfgang Fach, Helena Plain, Jack Goldstone, Kenneth Koford, Pavel Pelikan, Jean-Philippe Platteau, Wolfgang Seibel, Ulrich Witt, and three anonymous readers for helpful comments.

[1] Bernard Gwertzman and Michael T. Kaufman, eds., *The Collapse of Communism, by the Correspondents of "The New York Times"* (New York: Times Books, 1990), vii.

[2] For an early statement of this thesis, see Hannah Arendt, *The Origins of Totalitarianism*, 2d ed. (1951; reprint, New York: World Publishing, 1958), pt. 3. Arendt suggested that communism weakens interpersonal bonds rooted in family, community, religion, and profession, a situation that makes individuals terribly dependent on the goodwill of the state and thus blocks the mobilization of an anticommunist revolt.

[3] Richard Pipes, "Gorbachev's Russia: Breakdown or Crackdown?" *Commentary*, March 1990, p. 16.

[4] Jeane J. Kirkpatrick, *The Withering Away of the Totalitarian State . . . And Other Surprises* (Washington, D.C.: AEI Press, 1990). A decade earlier Kirkpatrick had articulated a variant of Arendt's thesis, insisting that the communist system is incapable of self-propelled evolu-

Even scholars who had rejected the concept of a frozen and immobile region were amazed by the events of 1989. In 1987 the American Academy of Arts and Sciences invited a dozen specialists, including several living in Eastern Europe, to prepare interpretive essays on East European developments. As the *Daedalus* issue featuring these essays went to press, the uprisings took off, prompting many authors to change "whole sentences and paragraphs in what were once thought to be completed essays." *Daedalus* editor Stephen Graubard remarks in his preface to the issue: "A quarterly journal has been obliged to adapt, inconveniently, but in some measure necessarily, the techniques of a weekly or even a daily newspaper."[5] Graubard proudly points out that even before the last-minute revisions the essays offered remarkable insights into the intellectual, social, and political stirrings that were transforming the region. But he concedes that neither he nor his essayists foresaw what was to happen. Recalling that in a planning session he had asked whether anything could be done to avoid publishing "an issue that will seem 'dated' three years after publication," he continues: "Was this passage a premonition of all that was to follow? One wishes that one could claim such extraordinary prescience. Regrettably, it did not really exist."[6]

Wise statesmen, discerning diplomats, and gifted journalists were also caught off guard. So too were futurologists. John Naisbitt's celebrated *Megatrends*, which sold eight million copies in the early 1980s, does not predict the fall of communism.[7] As the *Economist* observed even before the East European Revolution had run its course, 1989 turned out to be a year when "the most quixotic optimists" were repeatedly "proved too cautious."[8]

Within Eastern Europe itself the revolution came as a surprise even to leading "dissidents." In a 1979 essay, "The Power of the Powerless," Václav Havel recognized that the regimes of Eastern Europe were anything but invincible. They might be toppled, he wrote, by a "social movement," an "explosion of civil unrest," or a "sharp conflict inside an ap-

---

tion. See Kirkpatrick, "Dictatorships and Double Standards," *Commentary*, November 1979, pp. 34–45.

[5] Graubard, "Preface to the Issue 'Eastern Europe . . . Central Europe . . . Europe,' " *Daedalus* 119 (Winter 1990), vi.

[6] Ibid., ii.

[7] Naisbitt, *Megatrends: Ten New Directions Transforming Our Lives* (New York: Warner Books, 1982). The months following the East European Revolution saw the appearance of John Naisbitt and Patricia Aburdene, *Megatrends 2000: Ten New Directions for the 1990's* (New York: William Morrow, 1990). This sequel characterizes the East European developments of the late 1980s as an unforeseen "political earthquake" and then *predicts* that the 1990s will witness the further erosion of communism (chap. 3).

[8] *Economist*, November 18, 1989, p. 13.

parently monolithic power structure," among other possibilities.[9] This essay is at once a brilliant probe into the communist system's stability and a penetrating prognosis of its ultimate demise. Yet it steers clear of speculation on the timing of the collapse. It is replete with statements such as "we must see the hopelessness of trying to make long-range predictions" and "far-reaching political change is utterly unforeseeable," although it ends on a cautiously optimistic note: "What if [the 'brighter future'] has been here for a long time already, and only our own blindness and weakness has prevented us from seeing it around us and within us, and kept us from developing it?"[10]

Eight years later Havel himself would exhibit "blindness" to events that were ushering in a "brighter future." Less than three years before the revolution he commented as follows on the rousing welcome given by a Prague crowd to visiting Soviet leader Mikhail Gorbachev:

> I feel sad; this nation of ours never learns. How many times has it put all its faith in some external force which, it believed, would solve its problems? . . . And yet here we are again, making exactly the same mistake. They seem to think that Gorbachev has come to liberate them from Husák![11]

In late 1988, with less than a year to go, Havel was still unsure about the direction of events:

> Maybe [the Movement for Civil Liberties] will quickly become an integral feature of our country's life, albeit one not particularly beloved of the regime. . . . Perhaps it will remain for the time being merely the seed of something that will bear fruit in the dim and distant future. It is equally possible that the entire "matter" will be stamped on hard.[12]

Other Czechoslovak dissidents were just as unprepared for the revolution. In November 1989 Jan Urban suggested that the opposition contest the national elections scheduled for June 1991—only to be ridiculed by his friends for making a hopelessly utopian proposal.[13] Within a matter of days, they were all celebrating the fall of Czechoslovakia's communist dictatorship.

[9] Havel, "The Power of the Powerless" (1979), in Havel et al., *The Power of the Powerless: Citizens against the State in Central-Eastern Europe*, ed. John Keane and trans. Paul Wilson (Armonk, N.Y.: M. E. Sharpe, 1985), 42.

[10] Ibid., 87, 89, 96.

[11] Havel, "Meeting Gorbachev" (1987), in William M. Brinton and Alan Rinzler, eds., *Without Force or Lies: Voices from the Revolution of Central Europe in 1989–90* (San Francisco: Mercury House, 1990), 266.

[12] Havel, "Cards on the Table" (1988), in Brinton and Rinzler (fn. 11), 270–71.

[13] Sidney Tarrow, " 'Aiming at a Moving Target': Social Science and the Recent Rebellions in Eastern Europe," *PS: Political Science and Politics* 24 (March 1991), 12.

A few months before the revolution, in neighboring Poland negotiations were under way between the communist regime and Solidarity, the trade union that for years had been demanding political pluralism. To the surprise of almost everyone, the regime agreed in April 1989 to hold open elections for a pluralistic parliament. In elections scheduled for June all 100 Senate seats and 161 of the 460 Assembly seats would be contestable. Exceeding the wildest expectations, Solidarity won all but one of the Senate seats in addition to all of the Assembly seats it was allowed to contest. Stunned by the enormity of this success, Solidarity officials worried that the electorate had gone too far, that victory would force Solidarity into making bold political moves simply to satisfy raised hopes. They feared that such moves would provoke a communist crackdown. The significant point is that neither the government nor Solidarity was prepared for such a lopsided result. The April accord was designed to give Solidarity a voice in Parliament, not to substantiate and legitimate its claim to being *the* voice of the Polish people.[14]

We will never know how many East Europeans foresaw the events of 1989—or at least the impending changes in their own countries. But at each step, journalistic accounts invariably painted a picture of a stunned public. For example, two days after the breaching of the Berlin Wall, the *New York Times* carried an article in which an East German remarks: "It's unfathomable. If you had told me that one week ago, I wouldn't have believed it. Mentally, I still can't. It will take a few days before what this means sinks in."[15]

I know of only one systematic study of relevance. Four months after the fall of communism in East Germany, the Allensbach Institute asked a broad sample of East Germans: "A year ago did you expect such a peaceful revolution?" Only 5 percent answered in the affirmative, although 18 percent answered "yes, but not that fast." Fully 76 percent indicated that the revolution had totally surprised them.[16] These figures are all the more remarkable given the "I knew it would happen" fal-

---

[14] On the elections and the reactions they generated, see the reports of John Taglibue, *New York Times*, June 3–6, 1989. The events leading up to the April accord have been chronicled and interpreted by Timothy Garton Ash, "Refolution: The Springtime of Two Nations," *New York Review of Books*, June 15, 1989, pp. 3–10. He observed: "Almost no one imagined that the great gulf between 'the power' and 'the society,' between Jaruzelski and Walesa, could be so swiftly bridged" (p. 6). For another informative account of Poland's political transformation, see Elie Abel, *The Shattered Bloc: Behind the Upheaval in Eastern Europe* (Boston: Houghton Mifflin, 1990), chap. 4.

[15] *New York Times*, November 12, 1989, p. 1.

[16] Question 36 on the East German Survey of the Institut für Demoskopie Allensbach, February 17–March 15, 1990, Archive no. 4195 GEW. I am indebted to Elisabeth Noelle-Neumann, director of the institute, for agreeing to insert this question into a broader survey on East German political opinions.

lacy—the human tendency to exaggerate foreknowledge.[17] Even trained historians succumb to this fallacy, portraying unanticipated events as inevitable, foreseeable, and actually foreseen.[18] In view of this fallacy, if East Germans had been asked a year before the revolution, "Do you expect a revolution in a year's time?" the percentage of unqualified negative answers would undoubtedly have been even higher.

The events that sealed the fate of East Germany's communist regime took off in the final days of summer, when thousands of East German vacationers in Hungary took advantage of relaxed border controls to turn their trips into permanent departures for West Germany. The East German government responded by restricting its citizens' access to Hungary, only to see thousands show up at the West German embassy in Prague. In the ensuing days it acceded to a series of face-saving arrangements by which the vacationers could depart for the West, but only after first returning home. Each new concession prompted further waves of emigrants, however, confuting the government's expectation that the exodus would taper off quickly.[19] The government was not alone in failing to anticipate where events were headed. Thousands of East German citizens rushed to join the exodus precisely because they felt their chances of reaching the West would never again be so good. Had they known that the Berlin Wall was about to come down, few would have left in such haste, leaving behind almost all their possessions, including their cars.

It might be said that some very knowledgeable observers of the communist bloc *had* predicted its disintegration before the century was out. As early as 1969, for instance, the Soviet dissident Andrei Amalrik wrote that the Russian Empire would break up within a decade and a half. Although it is tempting to credit Amalrik with exemplary foresight, a rereading of his famous essay shows that he expected the Soviet Empire to meet its end following a protracted and devastating war with China, not through a string of popular upheavals. In fact, he explicitly stated that the Soviet system of government had left people too demoralized

[17] Baruch Fischhoff, "Hindsight ≠ Foresight: The Effect of Outcome Knowledge on Judgment under Uncertainty," *Journal of Experimental Psychology: Human Perception and Performance* 1 (August 1975), 288–99; and Baruch Fischhoff and Ruth Beyth, " 'I Knew It Would Happen'—Remembered Probabilities of Once-Future Things," *Organizational Behavior and Human Performance* 13 (February 1975), 1–16.

[18] David Hackett Fischer, *Historians' Fallacies: Toward a Logic of Historical Thought* (London: Routledge and Kegan Paul, 1971), chaps. 6–8.

[19] For a compilation of pertinent reports from the *New York Times*, see Gwertzman and Kaufman (fn. 1), 153–84. Superb eyewitness accounts include Timothy Garton Ash, "The German Revolution," *New York Review of Books*, December 21, 1989, pp. 14–19; and George Paul Csicsery, "The Siege of Nógrádi Street, Budapest, 1989," in Brinton and Rinzler (fn. 11), 289–302.

and too dependent on authority to participate in a spontaneous uprising.[20] So Amalrik did not really foresee the events of 1989. Like a broken watch that tells the correct time every twelve hours, he got the timing of the first crack in the empire essentially right, but on the basis of a spurious forecast of events.

This is not to suggest that the East European explosion came as *total* surprise to everyone. Though most were astonished when it happened, and though few who saw it coming expected it to be so peaceful, a small number of commentators had prophesied that the revolution would be swift and remarkably bloodless. Havel, despite his above-quoted remarks, is one of these. And Vladimir Tismaneanu, a Romanian émigré living in the United States, came close to predicting major change. About a year before the collapse of the Romanian regime, he depicted it as "probably the most vulnerable" in Eastern Europe. Sensing an "all-pervasive discontent," he observed that "the Braşov riots in November 1987, when thousands of citizens took to the streets, chanted anti-Ceauşescu slogans and burned the dictator's portraits, represent an unmistakable signal for Moscow that uncontrollable violence may flare up in Romania."[21] Tismaneanu failed to place the Romanian uprising in the context of an upheaval spanning all of the Soviet Union's Warsaw Pact allies. Nor did he predict that Romania would be the last Soviet satellite to overthrow its government. It is remarkable nonetheless that he diagnosed the Romanian regime's vulnerability. Like Havel, he succeeded where many Western observers failed, because he understood the weaknesses that underlay the apparent stability of the communist system. This understanding prepared him for the type of explosion that eventually occurred, although, as discussed further on, it did not endow him with the ability to predict when the revolution would break out.

While the collapse of the post–World War II political order of Eastern Europe stunned the world, in retrospect it appears as the inevitable consequence of a multitude of factors. In each of the six countries the leadership was generally despised, lofty economic promises remained unfulfilled, and freedoms taken for granted elsewhere existed only on paper. But if the revolution was indeed inevitable, why was it not foreseen? Why did people overlook signs that are clearly visible after the fact? One of the central arguments of this essay is precisely that interacting social and psychological factors make it inherently difficult to predict the out-

[20] Amalrik, *Will the Soviet Union Survive until 1984?* (1969) (New York: Harper and Row, 1970), esp. 36–44.
[21] Tismaneanu, "Personal Power and Political Crisis in Romania," *Government and Opposition* 24 (Spring 1989), 193–94.

come of political competition. I shall argue that the East European Revolution was by no means inevitable. What *was* inevitable is that we would be astounded if and when it arrived.

"The victim of today is the victor of tomorrow, / And out of Never grows Now!"[22] Brecht's couplet captures perfectly our central paradox: seemingly unshakable regimes saw public sentiment turn against them with astonishing rapidity, as tiny oppositions mushroomed into crushing majorities. Currently popular theories of revolution offer little insight into this stunning pace; nor for that matter do they shed light on the element of surprise in previous revolutions. All lay claim to predictive power, yet none has a track record at veritable prediction. The next section briefly critiques the pertinent scholarly literature. Without denying the usefulness of some received theories at explaining revolutions of the past, I go on to present a theory that illuminates both the process of revolutionary mobilization and the limits of our ability to predict where and when mobilizations will occur. Subsequent sections apply this argument to the case at hand.

The term *revolution* is used here in a narrow sense to denote a mass-supported seizure of political power that aims to transform the social order. By this definition it is immaterial whether the accomplished transfer of power brings about significant social change. With regard to the East European Revolution, it is too early to tell whether the postrevolutionary regimes will succeed in reshaping the economy, the legal system, international relations, and individual rights—to mention just some of the domains on the reformist agenda. But even if the ongoing reforms all end in failure, the upheavals of 1989 can continue to be characterized as a regionwide revolution.

II. Received Theories of Revolution and Their Predictive Weaknesses

In her acclaimed book *States and Social Revolutions*, Theda Skocpol treats social revolutions as the product of structural and situational conditions.[23] Specifically, she argues that a revolution occurs when two conditions coalesce: (1) a state's evolving relations with other states and local classes weaken its ability to maintain law and order, and (2) the elites harmed by this situation are powerless to restore the status quo ante yet

---

[22] Bertolt Brecht, "Lob der Dialectic" (In praise of dialectics, 1933), in *Gedichte* (Frankfurt: Suhrkamp Verlag, 1961), 3:73; poem translated by Edith Anderson.

[23] Skocpol, *States and Social Revolutions: A Comparative Analysis of France, Russia, and China* (Cambridge: Cambridge University Press, 1979).

strong enough to paralyze the government. Through their obstruction-ism the elites generate a burst of antielite sentiment, which sets in motion an uprising aimed at transforming the social order. The appeal of Skoc-pol's theory lies in its invocation of structural causes to explain shifts in the structure of political power. It does not depend on such "subjective" factors as beliefs, expectations, attitudes, preferences, intentions, and goals, although these do creep into structuralist case studies, including those of Skocpol herself.

Tracking emotions and mental states is a treacherous business, which is why the structuralist school considers it a virtue to refrain from ap-pealing to them. Social structures are ostensibly easier to identify, which would seem to endow the structuralist theory with predictive superiority over "voluntarist" theories based on "rational choice." Theories that fall under the rubric of rational choice have certainly been unsuccessful at predicting mass upheavals. What they explain well is the rarity of pop-ular uprisings.[24] The crucial insight of the rational-choice school is that an individual opposed to the incumbent regime is unlikely to participate in efforts to remove it, since the personal risk of joining a revolutionary movement could outweigh the personal benefit that would accrue were the movement a success. It is generally in a person's self-interest to let others make the sacrifices required to secure the regime's downfall, for a revolution constitutes a "collective good"—a good he can enjoy whether or not he has contributed to its realization. With most of the regime's opponents choosing to free ride, an upheaval may fail to mate-rialize even if the potential revolutionaries constitute a substantial ma-jority. Yet from time to time revolution does break out, and this presents a puzzle that the standard theory of rational choice cannot solve. The standard theory simply fails to make sense of why the first people to challenge the regime choose selflessly to gamble with their lives.[25]

With respect to the East European Revolution in particular, the stan-dard theory illuminates why, for all their grievances, the nations of the region were remarkably quiescent for so many years. It does not explain why in 1989 their docility suddenly gave way to an explosive demand for change. For its part, the structuralist theory elucidates why the revolu-tion broke out at a time when the Soviet Union was emitting increasingly convincing signals that it would not use force to try to preserve the East

---

[24] The seminal contribution is Mancur Olson, *The Logic of Collective Action: Public Goods and the Theory of Groups* (1965; rev. ed., Cambridge: Harvard University Press, 1971).

[25] This point is developed by Michael Taylor, "Rationality and Revolutionary Action," in Taylor, ed., *Rationality and Revolution* (Cambridge: Cambridge University Press, 1988), 63–97. Taylor also offers an illuminating critique of structuralism.

European status quo. But it explains neither why the old order collapsed so suddenly in several countries at once nor why the events of 1989 outdistanced all expectations.

Neither school has come to terms with its predictive weaknesses. That granted, can the deficiencies in question be overcome by incorporating additional relationships into these theories? It would seem, on the basis of reasons developed below, that perfect predictability is an unachievable objective. The theory developed here accommodates some of the major features and implications of these two theories, with the added virtue, however, of illuminating why major revolutions come as a surprise and why, even so, they are quite easily explained *after the fact*.

Like all unanticipated revolutions, the East European Revolution is generating multitudes of retrospective explanations that draw attention to its diverse causes and warning signs. To cite just one example, an essay written shortly after the fall of the East German regime begins with a flashback to April 1989: two passengers on an East German train, mutual strangers, share with each other their negative feelings about the regime, within earshot of others—a highly uncommon event, because of the ubiquity of informants. This opening gives the impression that East Germany was *obviously* reaching its boiling point, although the rest of the essay makes clear that the East German uprising was in fact scarcely anticipated.[26] Like so much else now rolling off the presses, this essay leaves unexplained why events seen in retrospect as harbingers of an imminent upheaval were not seen as such before the actual revolution.

Not that signs noticed in retrospect are necessarily fabrications. The *availability heuristic*, a mental shortcut we use to compensate for our cognitive limitations, highlights information consistent with actual events at the expense of information inconsistent with them.[27] Accordingly, events considered insignificant while the regime looked stable may suddenly gain enormous significance after it falls. Among all the events that are consistent with a particular outcome, those that fit into the models at our disposal will be the ones that attract attention. Thus, a structuralist will be predisposed to treat as significant the structural signs of the coming revolution. These signs need not be imaginary, but there is nothing in

[26] Edith Anderson, "Town Mice and Country Mice: The East German Revolution," in Brinton and Rinzler (fn. 11), 170–92.

[27] On the availability heuristic, see Amos Tversky and Daniel Kahneman, "Availability: A Heuristic for Judging Frequency and Probability," *Cognitive Psychology* 5 (September 1973), 207–32. The biases that this heuristic imparts to the use of historical knowledge are discussed by Shelley E. Taylor, "The Availability Bias in Social Perception and Interaction," in Daniel Kahneman, Paul Slovic, and Amos Tversky, eds., *Judgment under Uncertainty: Heuristics and Biases* (Cambridge: Cambridge University Press, 1982), 190–200.

the structuralist theory—or, for that matter, in the standard theory of rational choice—that explains why it is better at explanation than at prediction. This paradox is seldom appreciated, partly because the authors of retrospective accounts do not always concede *their own* bafflement. They generally write as though their favored theory shows the revolution to have been inevitable, seldom pausing to explain why, if this is so, they themselves had not offered unambiguous, unequivocal forecasts.

If one bête noire of the structuralist school is the rational-choice approach to the study of revolutions, another is the relative-deprivation approach. According to this third approach revolutions are propelled by economic disappointments, that is, by outcomes that fall short of expectations. If the consequent discontent becomes sufficiently widespread, the result is a revolt.[28] With respect to the major revolutions she investigates, Skocpol correctly observes that they began at times when levels of discontent were by historical standards not unusual. More evidence against the relative-deprivation theory comes from Charles Tilly and his associates, who find that in France the level of collective violence has been uncorrelated with the degree of mass discontent.[29] Thus, the relative-deprivation theory neither predicts nor explains. The reason is simple. While relative deprivation is doubtless a factor in every revolution in history, it is too common in politically stable societies to provide a complete explanation for every observed instability. By implication, to treat relative deprivation as an unmistakable sign of impending revolution is to subject oneself to a continuous string of alarms, mostly false.

III. Preference Falsification and Revolutionary Bandwagons

So mass discontent does not necessarily generate a popular uprising against the political status quo. To understand when it does, we need to identify the conditions under which individuals will display antagonism toward the regime under which they live. After all, a mass uprising results from multitudes of individual choices to participate in a movement for change; there is no actor named "the crowd" or "the opposition."

[28] For two of the major contributions to this approach, see James C. Davies, "Toward a Theory of Revolution," *American Sociological Review* 27 (February 1962), 5–19; and Ted R. Gurr, *Why Men Rebel* (Princeton: Princeton University Press, 1970).

[29] David Snyder and Charles Tilly, "Hardship and Collective Violence in France, 1830 to 1960," *American Sociological Review* 37 (October 1972), 520–32; and Charles Tilly, Louise Tilly, and Richard Tilly, *The Rebellious Century: 1830–1930* (Cambridge: Harvard University Press, 1975). For much additional evidence against the theory of relative deprivation, see Steven E. Finkel and James B. Rule, "Relative Deprivation and Related Psychological Theories of Civil Violence: A Critical Review," in Louis Kriesberg, ed., *Research in Social Movements, Conflicts and Change* (Greenwich, Conn.: JAI Press, 1986), 9:47–69.

The model presented here is in agreement with the rational-choice school on this basic methodological point, although it departs in important ways from the standard fare in rational-choice modeling.

Consider a society whose members are indexed by i. Each individual member must choose whether to support the government in public or oppose it; depending on his public acts and statements, each person is perceived as either a friend of the government or an enemy, for the political status quo or against. In private, of course, a person may feel torn between the government and the opposition, seeing both advantages and disadvantages to the existing regime. I am thus distinguishing between an individual's *private preference* and *public preference*. The former is effectively fixed at any given instant, the latter a variable under his control. Insofar as his two preferences differ—that is, the preference he expresses in public diverges from that he holds in private—the individual is engaged in *preference falsification*.

Let S represent the size of the public opposition, expressed as a percentage of the population. Initially it is near 0, implying that the government commands almost unanimous public support. A revolution, as a mass-supported seizure of political power, may be treated as an enormous jump in S.

Now take a citizen who wants the government overthrown. The likely impact of his own public preference on the fate of the government is negligible: it is unlikely to be a decisive factor in whether the government stands or falls. But it may bring him personal rewards and impose on him personal punishments. If he chooses to oppose the government, for instance, he is likely to face persecution, though in the event the government falls his outspokenness may be rewarded handsomely. Does this mean that our individual will base his public preference solely on the potential rewards and punishments flowing from the two rival camps? Will his private antipathy to the regime play no role whatsoever in his decision? This does not seem reasonable, for history offers countless examples of brave individuals who stood up for a cause in the face of the severest pressures, including torture.

On what, then, will our disaffected individual's choice depend? I submit that it will depend on a trade-off between two payoffs, one external and the other internal.[30]

The external payoff to siding with the opposition consists of the just-discussed personal rewards and punishments. In net terms, this payoff is apt to become increasingly favorable (or increasingly less unfavorable)

---

[30] For a detailed analysis of this trade-off, see Timur Kuran, "Private and Public Preferences," *Economics and Philosophy* 6 (April 1990), 1–26.

with S. The larger S, the smaller the individual dissenter's chances of being persecuted for his identification with the opposition and the fewer hostile supporters of the government he has to face. The latter relationship reflects the fact that government supporters, even ones privately sympathetic to the opposition, participate in the persecution of the government's opponents, as part of their personal efforts to establish convincing progovernment credentials. This relationship implies that a rise in S leaves fewer people seeking to penalize members of the public opposition.

The internal payoff is rooted in the psychological cost of preference falsification. The suppression of one's wants entails a loss of personal autonomy, a sacrifice of personal integrity. It thus generates lasting discomfort, the more so the greater the lie. This relationship may be captured by postulating that person i's internal payoff for supporting the opposition varies positively with his private preference, x^i. The higher x^i, the more costly he finds it to suppress his antigovernment feelings.

So i's public preference depends on S and x^i. As the public opposition grows, with his private preference constant, there comes a point where his external cost of joining the opposition falls below his internal cost of preference falsification. This switching point may be called his *revolutionary threshold, T^i*. Since a threshold represents a value of S, it is a number between 0 and 100.

If x^i should rise, T^i will fall. In other words, if the individual becomes more sympathetic to the opposition, it will take a smaller public opposition to make him take a stand against the government. The same will be true if the government becomes less efficient, or the opposition becomes more efficient, at rewarding its supporters and punishing its rivals. In fact, anything that affects the relationship between S and the individual's external payoff for supporting the opposition will change his revolutionary threshold. Finally, T^i will fall if i develops a greater need to stand up and be counted, for the internal cost of preference falsification will then come to dominate the external benefit at a lower S.[31]

This simple framework offers a reason why a person may choose to voice a demand for change even when the price of dissent is very high and the chances of a successful uprising very low. If his private opposi-

[31] The theory outlined in this section is developed more fully in Timur Kuran, "Sparks and Prairie Fires: A Theory of Unanticipated Political Revolution," *Public Choice* 61 (April 1989), 41–74. A summary of the present formulation was delivered at the annual convention of the American Economic Association, Washington, D.C., December 28–30, 1990. This presentation appeared under the title "The East European Revolution of 1989: Is It Surprising That We Were Surprised?" in the *American Economic Review, Papers and Proceedings* 81 (May 1991), 121–25.

tion to the existing order is intense and/or his need for integrity is quite strong, the suffering he incurs for dissent may be outweighed by the satisfaction he derives from being true to himself. In every society, of course, there are people who go against the social order of the day. Joseph Schumpeter once observed that in capitalist societies this group is dominated by intellectuals. Their position as "onlookers" and "outsiders" with much time for deep reflection causes them to develop a "critical attitude" toward the status quo. And because of the high value they attach to self-expression, they are relatively unsusceptible to social pressures.[32] The same argument applies to noncapitalist societies. As a case in point, a disproportionately large share of the East European dissidents were intellectuals.

Returning to the general model, we can observe that individuals with different private preferences and psychological constitutions will have different revolutionary thresholds. Imagine a ten-person society featuring the *threshold sequence*

$$A = \{0, 20, 20, 30, 40, 50, 60, 70, 80, 100\}.$$

Person 1 ($T^1 = 0$) supports the opposition regardless of its size, just as person 10 ($T^{10} = 100$) always supports the government. The remaining eight people's preferences are sensitive to S: depending on its level, they opt for one camp or the other. For instance, person 5 ($T^5 = 40$) supports the government if $0 \leq S < 40$ but joins the opposition if $40 \leq S \leq 100$. Let us assume that the opposition consists initially of a single person, or 10 percent of the population, so $S = 10$. Because the nine other individuals have thresholds above 10, this S is self-sustaining; that is, it constitutes an *equilibrium*.

This equilibrium happens to be vulnerable to a minor change in A. Suppose that person 2 has an unpleasant encounter at some government ministry. Her alienation from the regime rises, pushing her threshold down from 20 to 10. The new threshold sequence is

$$A' = \{0, 10, 20, 30, 40, 50, 60, 70, 80, 100\}.$$

Person 2's new threshold happens to equal the existing S of 10, so she switches sides, and S becomes 20. Her move into the opposition takes the form of tossing an egg at the country's long-standing leader during a government-organized rally. The new S of 20 is not self-sustaining but self-augmenting, as it drives person 3 into the opposition. The higher S of 30 then triggers a fourth defection, raising S to 40, and this process

[32] Schumpeter, *Capitalism, Socialism and Democracy*, 3d ed. (1950; reprint, New York: Harper Torchbooks, 1962), chap. 13.

continues until S reaches 90—a new equilibrium. Now the first nine individuals are in opposition, with only the tenth supporting the government. A slight shift in one individual's threshold has thus generated a *revolutionary bandwagon*, an explosive growth in public opposition.[33]

Now consider the sequence

$$B = \{0, 20, 30, 30, 40, 50, 60, 70, 80, 100\},$$

which differs from A only in its third element: 30 as opposed to 20. As in the previous illustration, let T^2 fall from 20 to 10. The resulting sequence is

$$B' = \{0, 10, 30, 30, 40, 50, 60, 70, 80, 100\}.$$

Once again, the incumbent equilibrium of 10 becomes unsustainable, and S rises to 20. But the opposition's growth stops there, for the new S *is* self-sustaining. Some government supporters privately enjoy the sight of the leader's egg-splattered face, but none follows the egg thrower into public opposition. We see that a minor variation in thresholds may drastically alter the effect of a given perturbation. And in particular, an event that causes a revolution in one setting may in a slightly different setting produce only a minor decline in the government's popularity.

Neither private preferences nor the corresponding thresholds are common knowledge. So a society can come to the brink of a revolution without anyone knowing this, not even those with the power to unleash it. In sequence A, for instance, person 2 need not recognize that she has the ability to set off a revolutionary bandwagon. Even if she senses the commonness of preference falsification, she simply cannot know whether the actual threshold sequence is A or B. Social psychologists use the term *pluralistic ignorance* to describe misperceptions concerning distributions of individual characteristics.[34] In principle, pluralistic ignorance can be mitigated through polls that accord individuals anonymity. But it is easier to offer people anonymity than to convince them that the preferences they reveal will remain anonymous and never be used against them. In any case, an outwardly popular government that knows preference falsification to be pervasive has no interest in publicizing the implied fra-

---

[33] Lucid analyses of bandwagon processes include Mark Granovetter, "Threshold Models of Collective Behavior," *American Journal of Sociology* 83 (May 1978), 1420–43; and Thomas C. Schelling, *Micromotives and Macrobehavior* (New York: W. W. Norton, 1978).

[34] Under the term *impression of universality*, the concept was introduced by Floyd H. Allport, *Social Psychology* (Boston: Houghton, Mifflin, 1924), 305–9. The term *pluralistic ignorance* was first used by Richard L. Schanck, "A Study of a Community and Its Groups and Institutions Conceived of as Behavior of Individuals," *Psychological Monographs* 43-2 (1932), 101.

gility of its support, because this might inspire the disaffected to bring their antigovernment feelings into the open. It has an incentive to discourage independent polling and discredit surveys that reveal unflattering information.

We have already seen that the threshold sequence is not fixed. Anything that affects the distribution of private preferences may alter it, for instance, an economic recession, contacts with other societies, or intergenerational replacement. But whatever the underlying reason, private preferences and, hence, the threshold sequence can move dramatically against the government without triggering a revolution. In the sequence

$$C = \{0, 20, 20, 20, 20, 20, 20, 20, 60, 100\}$$

the average threshold is 30, possibly because most people sympathize with the opposition. Yet $S = 10$ remains an equilibrium. It is true, of course, that a revolution is more likely under C than under A. C features seven individuals with thresholds of 20, A only one. A ten-unit fall in any one of the seven thresholds would trigger a revolution.

The point remains that widespread disapproval of the government is not sufficient to mobilize large numbers for revolutionary action. Antigovernment feelings can certainly bring a revolution within the realm of possibility, but other conditions must come together to set it off. By the same token, a revolution may break out in a society where private preferences, and therefore individual thresholds, tend to be relatively unfavorable to the opposition. Reconsider the sequence A', where the average threshold is 46, as opposed to 30 in C. Under A' public opposition darts from 10 to 90, whereas under C it remains stuck at 10. This simple comparison shows why the relative-deprivation theory of revolution has not held up under empirical testing. By treating the likelihood of revolution as the sum of the individual levels of discontent, the relative-deprivation theory overlooks the significance of the distribution of discontent. As our comparison between A' and C indicates, one sufficiently disaffected person with a threshold of 10 may do more for a revolution than seven individuals with thresholds of 20.

Imagine now that a superpower long committed to keeping the local government in power suddenly rescinds this commitment, declaring that it will cease meddling in the internal affairs of other countries. This is precisely the type of change to which the structuralist theory accords revolutionary significance. In the present framework, such a change will not necessarily ignite a revolution. The outcome depends on both the preexisting distribution of thresholds and the consequent shifts. Since the postulated change in international relations is likely to lower the expected cost of joining the opposition, people's thresholds are likely to fall. Let us say that every threshold between 10 and 90 drops by 10 units. If the preexisting threshold sequence were A, B, or C, the result would be an explosion in S from 10 to 90. But suppose that it were

$$D = \{0, 30, 30, 30, 30, 30, 30, 30, 30, 100\}.$$

The structural shock turns this sequence into

$$D' = \{0, 20, 20, 20, 20, 20, 20, 20, 20, 100\}.$$

Fully four-fifths of the population is now willing to switch over to the opposition but *only if someone else goes first*. No one does, leaving S at 10.

Structural factors are thus part of the story, yet by no means the whole story. While they certainly affect the likelihood of revolution, they cannot possibly deliver infallible predictions. A single person's reaction to an event of global importance may make all the difference between a massive uprising and a *latent bandwagon* that never takes off. So to suggest, as the structuralists do, that revolutions are brought about by deep historical forces with individuals simply the passive bearers of these forces is to overlook the potentially crucial importance of individual characteristics of little significance in and of themselves. It is always a conjunction of factors, many of them intrinsically unimportant and thus unobserved, if not unobservable, that determines the flow of events. A major global event can produce drastically different outcomes in two settings that differ trivially. Structuralism and individualism are not rival and mutually incompatible approaches to the study of revolution, as Skocpol would have it. They are essential components of a single story.

We can now turn to the question of why with hindsight an unanticipated revolution may appear as the inevitable consequence of monumental forces for change. A successful revolution brings into the open long-repressed grievances. Moreover, people who were relatively content with the old regime embrace the new regime, and they are apt to attribute their former public preferences to fears of persecution.

Reconsider the threshold sequence

$$A' = \{0, 10, 20, 30, 40, 50, 60, 70, 80, 100\}.$$

The relatively high thresholds in A' are likely to be associated with private preferences more favorable to the government than to the opposition.[35] Person 9 ($T^9 = 80$) is much more satisfied with the government than, say, person 3 ($T^3 = 20$). As such she has little desire to join a move-

---

[35] Relatively high thresholds may also be associated with relatively great vulnerability to social pressure.

ment aimed at toppling it. Remember that public opposition settles at 90, she being the last to jump on the revolutionary bandwagon. The important point is this: person 9 changes her public preference only after the opposition snowballs into a crushing majority, making it imprudent to remain a government supporter.

Having made the switch, she has every reason to feign a long-standing antipathy to the toppled government. She will not admit that she yearns for the status quo ante, because this would contradict her new public preference. Nor will she say that her change of heart followed the government's collapse, because this might render her declared sympathy for the revolution unconvincing. She will claim that she has long had serious misgivings about the old order and has sympathized with the objectives of the opposition. An unintended effect of this distortion is to make it seem as though the toppled government enjoyed even less genuine support than it actually did.

This illusion is rooted in the very phenomenon responsible for making the revolution a surprise: preference falsification. Having misled everyone into seeing a revolution as highly unlikely, preference falsification now conceals the forces that were working against it. One of the consequences of postrevolutionary preference falsification is thus to make even less comprehensible why the revolution was unforeseen.

The historians of a revolution may appreciate the biases that afflict people's postrevolutionary accounts of their prerevolutionary dispositions without being able to measure the significance of these biases. Consider the sequence

$$C' = \{0, 10, 20, 20, 20, 20, 20, 20, 60, 100\}.$$

Like A', this sequence drives S from 10 to 90, implying that nine out of ten individuals have an incentive to say that they despised the prerevolutionary regime. If thresholds below 50 reflect private support for a revolution, and those above 50 private satisfaction with the status quo, eight of the nine would be telling the truth, the one liar being person 9 ($T^9 = 60$). It follows from the same assumption that four of the nine would be lying if the threshold sequence were A'. But once again, because thresholds are not public knowledge, historians may have difficulty determining whether the prerevolutionary sequence was A or C—or for that matter, whether the postrevolutionary sequence is A' or C'.

Before moving to the East European Revolution, it may be useful to comment on how the foregoing argument relates to three sources of controversy in the literature on revolutions: the continuity of social change, the power of the individual, and the significance of unorganized crowds.

The proposed theory treats continuous and discontinuous change as a single, unified process. Private preferences and the corresponding thresholds may change gradually over a long period during which public opposition is more or less stable. If the cumulative movement establishes a latent bandwagon, a minor event may then precipitate an abrupt and sharp break in the size of the public opposition. This is not to say that private preferences change *only* in small increments. A major blunder on the part of the government may suddenly turn private preferences against it.

Such a shift could also occur in response to an initial, possibly modest, increase in public opposition. The underlying logic was expressed beautifully by Alexis de Tocqueville: "Patiently endured so long as it seemed beyond redress, a grievance comes to appear intolerable once the possibility of removing it crosses men's minds."[36] In terms of our model, Tocqueville suggests that the threshold sequence is itself dependent on the size of the public opposition. If so, a revolutionary bandwagon may come about as the joint outcome of two mutually reinforcing trends: a fall in thresholds and a rise in public opposition. Imagine that public opposition rises sufficiently to convince those privately sympathetic to the government that a revolution might be in the making. This realization induces many of them to think about possible alternatives to the status quo. Their thinking starts a chain reaction through which private preferences shift swiftly and dramatically against the government. The consequent changes in the threshold sequence cause the revolutionary bandwagon to accelerate.

The theory depicts the individual as both powerless and potentially very powerful. The individual is powerless because a revolution requires the mobilization of large numbers, but he is also potentially very powerful because under the right circumstances he may set off a chain reaction that generates the necessary mobilization. Not that the individual can know precisely when his own choice can make a difference. Although he may sense that his chances of sparking a wildfire are unusually great, he can never be certain about the consequences of his own opposition. What is certain is that the incumbent regime will remain in place unless someone takes the lead in moving into the opposition.

As we saw in the previous section, the standard theory of rational choice depicts the potential revolutionary as paralyzed by the realization of his powerlessness. Many social thinkers who, like the present author, accept the logic of collective action have struggled with the task of explaining how mass mobilizations get started. One of the proposed expla-

[36] Tocqueville, *The Old Régime and the French Revolution* (1856), trans. Stuart Gilbert (Garden City, N.Y.: Doubleday, 1955), 177.

nations rests on a cognitive illusion: the individual overestimates his personal political influence. Another invokes an ethical commitment: the individual feels compelled to do his fair share for the attainment of a jointly desired outcome.[37] The approach used here, which is not incompatible with these explanations, places the burden of sparking the mobilization process on the individual's need to be true to himself. This approach is consistent with the fact that revolutionary leaders tend to be surprised when their goals materialize. The cognitive-illusion explanation is not: people who challenge the government out of an overestimation of their personal ability to direct the course of history will not be surprised when their wishes come true. The approach of this essay is also consistent with the fact that some people risk their lives for a revolution even as the vast majority of the potential beneficiaries refrain from doing their own fair share.

Finally, the outlined theory accords organized pressure groups and unorganized crowds complementary roles in the overthrow of the government. Organized oppositions enhance the external payoff to dissent, both by providing the individual dissenter with a support network and by raising the likelihood of a successful revolution. They also help shatter the appearance of the invulnerability of the status quo, and through propaganda, they shift people's private preferences in favor of change. Charles Tilly is therefore right to draw attention to the structural and situational factors that govern a society's pattern of political organization.[38] But as Pamela Oliver warns, we must guard against overemphasizing the role of organization at the expense of the role of the unorganized crowd. A small difference in the resources at the disposal of an organized opposition may have a tremendous impact on the outcome of its efforts.[39] This observation makes perfect sense in the context of the theory developed here. Where a small pressure group fails to push a bandwagon into motion a *slightly better organized* or *slightly larger* one might.

IV. East European Communism and the Wellspring of Its Stability

Communist parties came to power in Russia, and then in Eastern Europe and elsewhere, with the promise that "scientific socialism" would pio-

[37] Each of these is developed by Steven E. Finkel, Edward N. Muller, and Karl-Dieter Opp, "Personal Influence, Collective Rationality, and Mass Political Action," *American Political Science Review* 83 (September 1989), 885–903.

[38] Tilly, *From Mobilization to Revolution* (Reading, Mass.: Addison-Wesley, 1978).

[39] Oliver, "Bringing the Crowd Back In: The Nonorganizational Elements of Social Movements," in Louis Kriesberg, ed., *Research in Social Movements, Conflict and Change* (Greenwich, Conn.: JAI Press, 1989): 11:1–30.

neer new dimensions of freedom, eliminate exploitation, vest political power in the masses, eradicate nationalism, and raise standards of living to unprecedented heights—all this, while the state was withering away. They did not deliver on any of these promises. Under their stewardship, communism came to symbolize repression, censorship, ethnic chauvinism, militarism, red tape, and economic backwardness.

The failures of communism prompted a tiny number of Soviet and East European citizens to criticize official policies and established institutions. Such dissidents expressed their frustrations through clandestine self-publications (*samizdat*) and writings published in the West (*tamizdat*). Given the chasm between the rhetoric of communism and its achievements, the existence of an opposition is easily understood. Less comprehensible is the rarity of public opposition—prior, that is, to 1989. The few uprisings that were crushed—notably, East Berlin in 1953, Hungary in 1956, and Czechoslovakia in 1968—are the exceptions that prove the rule. For most of several decades, most East Europeans displayed a remarkable tolerance for tyranny and inefficiency. They remained docile, submissive, and even outwardly supportive of the status quo.

This subservience is attributable partly to punishments meted out by the communist establishment to its actual and imagined opponents. In the heyday of communism a person speaking out against the leadership or in favor of some reform could expect to suffer harassment, lose his job, and face imprisonment—in short, he could expect to be denied the opportunity to lead a decent life. Even worse horrors befell millions of suspected opponents. Just think of the forced-labor camps of the Gulag Archipelago and of the liquidations carried out under the pretext of historical necessity. "We can only be right with and by the Party," wrote a leading theoretician of communism, "for history has provided no other way of being in the right."[40] Such thinking could, and did, serve to justify horrible crimes against nonconformists.

Yet official repression is only one factor in the endurance of communism. The system was sustained by a general willingness to support it in public: people routinely applauded speakers whose message they disliked, joined organizations whose mission they opposed, and signed defamatory letters against people they admired, among other manifestations of consent and accommodation. "The lie," wrote the Russian novelist Alexander Solzhenitsyn in the early 1970s, "has been incorporated into the state system as the vital link holding everything together,

[40] The words of Leon Trotsky, cited by Arendt (fn. 2), 307.

with billions of tiny fasteners, several dozen to each man."[41] If people stopped lying, he asserted, communist rule would break down instantly. He then asked rhetorically, "What does it mean, *not to lie?*" It means *"not saying what you don't think*, and that includes not whispering, not opening your mouth, not raising your hand, not casting your vote, not feigning a smile, not lending your presence, not standing up, and not cheering."[42]

In "The Power of the Powerless," Havel speaks of a greengrocer who places in his window, among the onions and carrots, the slogan "Workers of the World, Unite!" Why does the greengrocer do this, Havel wonders.

> Is he genuinely enthusiastic about the idea of unity among the workers of the world? Is his enthusiasm so great that he feels an irrepressible impulse to acquaint the public with his ideals? Has he really given more than a moment's thought to how such a unification might occur and what it would mean?

Havel's answer is worth quoting at length:

> The overwhelming majority of shopkeepers never think about the slogans they put in their windows, nor do they use them to express their real opinions. That poster was delivered to our greengrocer from the enterprise headquarters along with the onions and carrots. He put them all into the window simply because it has been done that way for years, because everyone does it, and because that is the way it has to be. If he were to refuse, there could be trouble. He could be reproached for not having the proper "decoration" in his window; someone might even accuse him of disloyalty. He does it because these things must be done if one is to get along in life. It is one of the thousands of details that guarantee him a relatively tranquil life in "harmony with society," as they say.[43]

So our greengrocer puts up the assigned slogan to communicate not a social ideal but his preparedness to conform. And the reason the display conveys a message of submission is that every submissive greengrocer has exhibited the same slogan for years. By removing the poster—or worse, replacing it with one that reads "Workers of the World, Eat Onions and Carrots!"—our greengrocer would expose himself to the charge of subversion. He therefore displays the required slogan faithfully and fends off trouble. In the process, he reinforces the perception that society is solidly behind the Party. His own prudence thus becomes a factor in the willingness of other greengrocers to promote the unity of the world's

---

[41] Solzhenitsyn, "The Smatterers" (1974), in Solzhenitsyn et al., *From under the Rubble*, trans. A. M. Brock et al. (Boston: Little, Brown, 1975), 275.

[42] Ibid., 276; emphasis in original.

[43] Havel (fn. 9), 27–28.

workers. Moreover, it pressures farmers, miners, bus drivers, artists, journalists, and bureaucrats to continue doing and saying the things expected of *them*.

Efforts to prove one's loyalty to the political status quo often took more tragic forms than a greengrocer's display of a well-worn Marxist slogan. People tattled on each other. And they ostracized and vilified nonconformists who were saying or doing things that they admired. The Romanian dissident Norman Manea writes of authors who "persecuted their colleagues on the 'blacklist' with tireless, diabolical energy."[44] In the same vein, the Polish dissident Piotr Wierzbicki writes about a famous composer who went out of his way to alert the government to an anti-Soviet insinuation on the sleeve of a record by a Pole living abroad. The squealing composer knew that this information was likely to block the local performance of his fellow Pole's music. He did it to prove his loyalty to the regime—to earn, as it were, a certificate of normalcy.[45]

In 1977 a group of Czechoslovak intellectuals established a loose association, Charter 77, dedicated to the basic human rights that Czechoslovakia agreed to respect by signing the Helsinki accords of 1975.[46] The government responded by detaining the spokesmen of Charter 77 and launching a nationwide campaign against the association.[47] In the course of this campaign millions of ordinary citizens expressed their opposition to Charter 77 by signing statements of condemnation, sending hate letters to newspapers, and ostracizing its signatories. Many an opponent of Charter 77 did so in betrayal of his conscience.

It is true of course that some who participated in this campaign saw Charter 77 as a menacing organization bent on tarnishing Czechoslovakia's image abroad. And the tale-bearing Polish composer may well have had motives other than a desire to please the regime, for instance, jealousy or professional competition. But East Europeans turned against each other routinely even in the absence of such motives.

Let us return to the story of the greengrocer. Havel asks us to "imagine that one day something in our greengrocer snaps and he stops putting up the slogans." The greengrocer also "stops voting in elections he knows are a farce"; he "begins to say what he really thinks at political meetings"; and he "even finds the strength in himself to express solidar-

---

[44] Manea, "Romania: Three Lines with Commentary," in Brinton and Rinzler (fn. 11), 327.
[45] Wierzbicki, "A Treatise on Ticks" (1979), in Abraham Brumberg, ed., *Poland: Genesis of a Revolution* (New York: Random House, 1983), 205.
[46] The Charter 77 declaration is reproduced in Havel et al. (fn. 9), 217–21.
[47] See Timothy Garton Ash, *The Uses of Adversity: Essays on the Fate of Central Europe* (1983–89) (New York: Random House, 1989), esp. 61–70.

ity with those whom his conscience commands him to support." In short, he makes "an attempt to *live within the truth*."[48] Here are the likely consequences of this revolt:

> [The greengrocer] will be relieved of his post as manager of the shop and transferred to the warehouse. His pay will be reduced. His hopes for a holiday in Bulgaria will evaporate. His children's access to higher education will be threatened. His superiors will harass him and his fellow workers will wonder about him. Most of those who apply these sanctions, however, will not do so from any authentic inner conviction but simply under pressure from conditions, the same conditions that once pressured the greengrocer to display the official slogans. They will persecute the greengrocer either because it is expected of them, or to demonstrate their loyalty, or simply as part of the general panorama, to which belongs an awareness that this is how situations of this sort are dealt with, that this, in fact, is how things are always done, particularly if one is not to become suspect oneself.[49]

The brilliance of this vignette lies in its insights into the pressures that kept East Europeans outwardly loyal to their inefficient, tyrannical regimes. Official repression met with the approval of ordinary citizens and indeed was predicated on their complicity. By falsifying their preferences and helping to discipline dissenters, citizens jointly sustained a system that many considered abominable. According to Havel, the crucial "line of conflict" ran not between the Party and the people but "through each person," for in one way or another everyone was "both a victim and a supporter of the system."[50]

The same idea found vivid expression in a banner hung above the altar in an East German church: "I am Cain *and* Abel."[51] The implied intrapersonal conflict is rooted of course in the clash between the individual's drive to exercise autonomy and his need for social acceptance. Until 1989 most East Europeans tended to resolve this chronic clash in favor of social acceptance. By thus avoiding an open battle with communism, they acquiesced to battle silently with themselves. In the process, most achieved a measure of outer security, though at the expense of inner peace.

Not that communist rule managed to do away altogether with the human propensity to protest. As Wierzbicki points out, newspapers received letters of complaint in abundance—about shabby housing, the neglected grave of some poet or other, and the sloppily painted fence of a

---

[48] Havel (fn. 9), 39; emphasis in original.
[49] Ibid., 39.
[50] Ibid., 37.
[51] Timothy Garton Ash, "Eastern Europe: The Year of Truth," *New York Review of Books*, February 15, 1990, p. 18; emphasis in original.

children's playground. Yet protesters tended to stay within a Party-defined zone of acceptability: they refrained from probing too deeply into issues and avoided challenging communism itself. A schoolteacher writing furious letters about a defective appliance would not bring herself to blame the system that produces useless appliances. Nor would she sign a letter expressing solidarity with dissidents or join a demonstration for freedom of speech.[52]

The typical East European feigned opposition to the few dissidents, though in private he applauded their mission. Havel suggests that this admiration was coupled with a resentment: people who lacked the courage to be true to themselves felt threatened by displays of integrity on the part of others. They thus treated open defiance "as an abnormality, as arrogance, as an attack on themselves, as a form of dropping out of society."[53] If it is true that the "iron in the soul" of another reminded a conformist of the lack of iron in his own, this would have served as an additional obstacle to overt opposition.[54]

Another such obstacle was pluralistic ignorance: people alienated from the communist regime did not know how widely their alienation was shared. They could sense the repressed discontent of their conformist relatives and close friends; they could observe the hardships in the lives of their fellow citizens; and they could intuit that past uprisings would not have occurred in the absence of substantial discontent. Still, they lacked reliable, current information on how many of their fellow citizens favored a change in regime. The government-controlled press exploited this ignorance by stressing the "unity of socialist society" and its "solidarity in supporting the Party." Insofar as such propaganda led potential revolutionaries to underestimate the prevalence of discontent, it weakened their incentives to join the minuscule opposition.

Governments throughout history have recognized the significance of preference falsification and out of self-interest have tried to keep themselves informed about the private preferences of their constituents. Louis XIV told his heir that "the art of governing" consists in "knowing the real thoughts of all the princes in Europe, knowing everything that people try to conceal from us, their secrets, and keeping close watch over them."[55] So it is that the communist governments of Eastern Europe conducted numerous surveys to find out the true thoughts and feelings

[52] Wierzbicki (fn. 45), 206–7.

[53] Havel (fn. 9), 37.

[54] The metaphor belongs to Barrington Moore, Jr., *Injustice: The Social Bases of Obedience and Revolt* (White Plains, N.Y.: M. E. Sharpe, 1978).

[55] Cited by Norbert Elias, *Power and Civility* (1939), trans. Edmund Jephcott (New York: Pantheon, 1982), 197.

of their subjects. If the fact that they kept the results secret is any indication, these were not entirely flattering to them or their policies. Information for publication "was checked beforehand and given the appropriate interpretation," to keep it from emboldening the regime's declared and potential opponents.[56]

It would be an exaggeration to suggest that *all* East European supporters of communist rule were privately opposed to the status quo. Some benefited handsomely from the system, and others felt threatened by major reform. Nor did those who became conscious of the failures of communism necessarily lose faith in official ideals. Even leading dissidents remained sympathetic to central planning and collective ownership and ever suspicious of the free-enterprise system.[57] By and large, they felt that communism was betrayed by self-serving leaders, not that it was inherently unworkable.

These observations are consistent with opinion polls of East Europeans traveling abroad conducted by Western organizations in the 1970s and early 1980s. With remarkable consistency and for each nation, the data showed that in free elections offering a full spectrum of choices, including a Democratic Socialist Party and a Christian Democratic Party, the Communist Party would receive at most a tenth of the vote, and the socialists would invariably be the winners.[58]

Further systematic evidence is contained in surveys conducted from 1970 onward for the benefit of the leadership by the Central Institute for Youth Development in Leipzig. Now being declassified, these surveys suggest that until the mid-1980s most East Germans accepted the official goals of socialism. In 1983, 46 percent of a sample of trade school students endorsed the statement "I am a devoted citizen of the German Democratic Republic," whereas 45 percent endorsed it with reservations and only 9 percent rejected it. And in 1984, 50 percent agreed that "socialism will triumph throughout the world," whereas 42 percent agreed with reservations and 8 percent disagreed. Between 1970 and 1985, the results showed little variation.[59] They may, of course, have been based on a

[56] Jiří Otava, "Public Opinion Research in Czechoslovakia," *Social Research* 55 (Spring–Summer 1988), 249. Every issue of the Czechoslovak government's official bulletin on public opinion stated: "We remind all researchers that this bulletin is not meant for the public, which means not even for your friends and acquaintances, but serves exclusively as internal material for poll-takers and those who collaborate with us" (p. 251 n. 2).

[57] See Vladimir Tismaneanu, *The Crisis of Marxist Ideology in Eastern Europe: The Poverty of Utopia* (London: Routledge, 1988), esp. chap. 4.

[58] Henry O. Hart, "The Tables Turned: If East Europeans Could Vote," *Public Opinion* 6 (October–November 1983), 53–57. The surveys reported by Hart cover Czechoslovakia, Hungary, Poland, Romania, and Bulgaria.

[59] "Daten des Zentralinstituts für Jugendforshung Leipzig" (Mimeograph), Tables 1 and 2. These tables were compiled by Walter Friedrich, the director of the institute, and distrib-

flawed methodology, as was much public opinion research done in Eastern Europe. But, as we shall see later, it is highly significant that after 1985 this same methodology registered a sustained deterioration both in the citizenry's attachment to the regime and in its faith in socialism.

It thus appears that while the East Europeans overwhelmingly disliked the regimes under which they were living, they were much less troubled by the principles of socialism—at least until the mid-1980s. To make sense of this finding, we need to touch on the cognitive implications of preference falsification. Disaffected citizens choosing to conform to the regime's demands typically paid lip service to official goals, used Marxist jargon, and made excuses for communism's shortcomings by pointing to the ostensibly worse failures of capitalism. In the process, they unavoidably kept their fellow citizens uninformed about those of their private beliefs that were inimical to the status quo. Worse, they knowingly exposed one another to false facts and misleading arguments. In short, they distorted public discourse. Since public discourse influences what is noticed and how events are interpreted, this distortion undoubtedly affected the evolution of East European private preferences. East Europeans subjected from early childhood to predictions of the imminent demise of capitalism and to theories of the incontrovertible superiority of communism must have become more or less conditioned to think in Marxist terms, developing some mental resistance to the fundamental flaws of their social order.[60]

If this reasoning is correct, Marxist discourse would also have blunted the ability of East Europeans to articulate an alternative economic order. Vladimir Shlapentokh points to a paradox here. The socialist worker mistrusts the market order, even though he obtains his treasured blue jeans through the only free market to which he has access—the *black* market. Likewise, the enterprise manager who turns regularly to the underground economy for vital spare parts dreads economic liberalization. Shlapentokh ascribes such inconsistencies to a disjunction between the "pragmatic" and "theoretical" layers of the individual mind.[61]

---

uted to the participants at a conference held in Ladenburg in February 1991, under the auspices of the Gottlieb Daimler and Karl Benz Foundation. Elisabeth Noelle-Neumann brought the document to my attention; John Ahouse translated it into English.

[60] For a fuller argument on how preference falsification distorts public discourse and how, in turn, this distortion warps the evolution of people's private preferences, see Timur Kuran, "The Role of Deception in Political Competition," in Albert Breton et al., eds., *The Competitive State* (Boston: Kluwer-Nijhoff, 1990), 71–95.

[61] Though Shlapentokh develops the argument with respect to the Soviet Union, it applies also to Eastern Europe. See Shlapentokh, *Soviet Public Opinion and Ideology: Mythology and Pragmatism in Interaction* (New York: Praeger, 1986); and idem, *Public and Private Life of the Soviet People: Changing Values in Post-Stalin Russia* (New York: Oxford University Press, 1989).

Known in cognitive psychology as *mental partitioning*, this phenomenon is an inevitable consequence of the mind's limitations in receiving, storing, retrieving, and processing information. People are simply unable to incorporate into a single, comprehensive model the multitudes of variables and relationships that bear on their happiness; they thus ignore many interconnections and treat closely related phenomena as unrelated.[62]

For our purposes, the important implication is this: an East European confronted daily with communism's shortcomings would not necessarily have taken them as a sign of the unworkability of the system. He could easily have turned against individual functionaries without losing faith in the system in which they operated. Some East Europeans did of course recognize that specific shortcomings were part of a general pattern of failure. Many were intellectuals with much time to think and thus to make the mental connections necessary for identifying the system's fundamental flaws. But many others did not make these connections, partly because the prevailing public discourse provided no help.

So processes rooted in preference falsification kept private opposition to communism far from unanimous. This does not negate the fact that vast numbers remained outwardly loyal to communist rule primarily out of fear. But for widespread preference falsification, the communist regimes of Eastern Europe would have faced severe public opposition, very possibly collapsing before 1989. In view of its profound impact on both private and public sentiment, preference falsification may be characterized as the wellspring of the communist system's stability.

V. The Revolution

The foregoing argument has two immediate implications. First, the regimes of Eastern Europe were substantially more vulnerable than the subservience and quiescence of their populations made them seem. Millions were prepared to stand up in defiance if ever they sensed that this was sufficiently safe. The people's solidarity with their leaders would then have been exposed as illusory, stripping the veneer of legitimacy from the communist monopoly on power. Second, even the support of those genuinely sympathetic to the status quo was rather thin. Though many saw no alternative to socialism, their many grievances predisposed them to the promise of fundamental change. Were public discourse

[62] See John H. Holland et al., *Induction: Processes of Inference, Learning, and Discovery* (Cambridge: MIT Press, 1986); and Amos Tversky and Daniel Kahneman, "The Framing of Decisions and the Rationality of Choice," *Science* 211 (January 1981), 453–58.

somehow to turn against socialism, they would probably awaken to the possibility that their lives could be improved.

But what would catalyze the process of revolutionary mobilization? With hindsight it appears that the push came from the Soviet Union. In the mid-1980s festering economic problems, until then officially denied, convinced the top Soviet leadership to call for *perestroika* (restructuring) and *glasnost* (public openness). Repressed grievances burst into the open, including dissatisfaction with communist rule itself. And with Mikhail Gorbachev's rise to the helm in 1985, the Soviet Union abandoned its long-standing policy of confrontation with the West, to seek accommodation and cooperation.[63] In Eastern Europe these changes kindled hopes of greater independence and meaningful social reform.

Lest it appear that these developments provided a clear signal of the coming revolution, remember that Havel dismissed a Czechoslovak crowd's jubilation over Gorbachev as a sign of naïveté. He was hardly alone in his pessimism. Even if Gorbachev wanted to liberate Eastern Europe, a popular argument went, it was anything but obvious that he could. Surely, the military and hard-line conservatives would insist on retaining the Soviet Union's strategic buffer against an attack from the West.

Nor was this the only obstacle to liberation. Economic and ethnic tensions within the Soviet Union could provide the pretext for a conservative coup. There was always the precedent of Khrushchev, toppled in 1964. About the time that Havel was exuding pessimism, a joke was making the rounds in Prague: "What is the difference between Gorbachev and Dubček [the deposed leader of the 1968 Prague Spring]?" The answer: "None—except Gorbachev doesn't know it yet."[64] Significantly, in the fall of 1989 Moscow was rife with rumors of an impending coup.[65] Some observers expected Gorbachev to survive but only by reversing course and becoming increasingly repressive.[66] An old Soviet joke expresses the underlying thinking. Stalin leaves his heirs in the Party two envelopes. One is labeled, "In case of trouble, open this." Trouble arises and the envelope is opened ceremoniously: "Blame me."

---

[63] For details, see Robert C. Tucker, *Political Culture and Leadership in Soviet Russia: From Lenin to Gorbachev* (New York: W. W. Norton, 1987), chap. 7.

[64] *Economist*, July 18, 1987, p. 45.

[65] Z [anonymous], "To the Stalin Mausoleum," *Daedalus* 119 (Winter 1990), 332.

[66] With the revolution, the notion that Gorbachev would turn to the army and the KGB in a bid to stay in power lost plausibility. It regained plausibility in late 1990 with the resignation of his foreign minister, Eduard Shevardnadze, who publicly accused Gorbachev of plotting with hard-liners to create a repressive dictatorship.

The other envelope is labeled, "In case of more trouble, open this." More trouble comes and the second envelope is opened: "Do as I did."[67]

In support of their prediction that the conservative elements in the leadership would prevail sooner or later, pessimists frequently invoked the conservatism of the Soviet people. In a widely discussed 1988 article, for instance, a Russian social scientist argued that seven decades of bureaucratic regimentation had suppressed individual creativity, reorienting the "Soviet value system away from revolutionary transformation to conservative immobility." Communism had quashed the very personal qualities on which the reformists were counting.[68] In June 1989 another Soviet observer would confess: "For three years I have tried to find out whether or not there is mass support for *perestroika*, and now I feel I can conclude that it does not exist." He blamed not only the individual citizen's fear of change but also the Soviet ethic that identifies social justice with economic equality.[69] The upshot of such comments, to which scores more from diverse sources could be added, was that Soviet citizens tended to be deeply suspicious of Gorbachev's intentions. Many commentators inferred that Gorbachev's reforms were doomed, reasoning that he could not rely on the masses for protection against a conservative challenger.

As Gorbachev was trying to restructure the Soviet Union, Poland was testing the limits of its freedom from Moscow. The struggle to legalize Solidarity had already given the country a taste of pluralism, and government censorship was being relaxed in fits and starts. Everyone recognized that this softening enjoyed Gorbachev's approval. Yet few informed people put much faith in Gorbachev's ability to push the liberation of Eastern Europe substantially forward, and once again it was not clear that he intended to try. "Dissidents throughout Europe," wrote the *Economist* in mid-1987, sound "sceptical" when talking about Gorbachev. "This is not because they question [his] reforming zeal. It is simply that many thinking people in Eastern Europe have come to believe that real change in Communist countries cannot be imposed from the top—or from outside—but must emerge from below."[70] Plenty of events lent credence to this reasoning. For instance, Gorbachev did not prevent

[67] Recorded by Daniel Bell, "As We Go into the Nineties: Some Outlines of the Twenty-first Century," *Dissent* 37 (Spring 1990), 173.

[68] Igor Kon, "The Psychology of Social Inertia" (1988), *Social Sciences* 20, no. 1 (1989), 60–74.

[69] Gennadii Batyagin, TASS, June 28, 1989, quoted by Elizabeth Teague, "Perestroika and the Soviet Worker," *Government and Opposition* 25 (Spring 1990), 192.

[70] *Economist*, July 18, 1987, p. 45.

the East German regime from falsifying the results of local elections held in the spring of 1989 or from endorsing China's massacre at Tiananmen Square that summer. Nor did he keep the East German regime from using force to disperse small demonstrations against these two acts.[71]

In sum, prior to the actual revolution it was not at all clear that the Soviet Union would sit back if its six Warsaw Pact allies tried to overthrow their communist regimes. Statements, events, and trends that in retrospect appear as unmistakable signs of an explosion in the making coexisted with many signs that pointed in the direction of inertia and continued stability. Some of Gorbachev's actions did indeed suggest that he wanted to institute fundamental reforms in many areas, including the Soviet Union's relationship with its East European satellites. But there were many reasons to expect his efforts to end in failure.

Yet since the revolution it has seemed as though Gorbachev *engineered* the liberation of Eastern Europe. In fact, he was a master at putting the best face on events that had pushed past him. In the fall of 1989 there were many reports that events were going much further and/or faster than Gorbachev wanted. He was reportedly willing to permit moves toward democracy, provided the communists were not humiliated and Eastern Europe's military ties to the Soviet Union were preserved. And like leaders in Washington, Paris, Bonn, and elsewhere, he was reluctant to support anything that might disturb Europe's hard-won peace. But when the peoples of Eastern Europe grabbed political power, pushed the communists aside, and proclaimed their intention to leave the Warsaw Pact, Gorbachev just accepted reality and gave his blessing to events generated by forces beyond his control. One is reminded of the horseman who, thrown from his horse, explains with a smile that he has "dismounted."

The point remains that the Soviet reform movement fueled expectations of a freer Eastern Europe, reducing for growing numbers the perceived risk of challenging the status quo. In terms of the model described in Section III, the movement lowered the revolutionary thresholds of East Europeans, making it increasingly easy to set in motion a revolutionary bandwagon. But no one could see that a revolution was in the making, not even the Soviet leader whose moves were helping to establish the still-latent bandwagon.

Recall that revolutionary thresholds are influenced also by people's private preferences. Since private preferences are governed to a considerable extent by public discourse, the dissent generated by Soviet glasnost

---

[71] Timothy Garton Ash, "Germany Unbound," *New York Review of Books*, November 22, 1990, p. 12.

probably pushed the private preferences of East Europeans against communism and communist rule. The East German surveys discussed above provide dramatic evidence to this effect. They show that after 1985 East German attachment to socialism steadily deteriorated. By October 1989 only 15 percent of the surveyed trade school students endorsed the statement "I am a devoted citizen of the German Democratic Republic," down from 46 percent in 1983. Fully 60 percent endorsed it with reservations and 25 percent rejected it. In the same month as few as 3 percent continued to believe that "socialism will triumph throughout the world," down from 50 percent in 1984. Just 27 percent agreed with reservations and a whopping 70 percent disagreed.[72] The contrast between the figures for 1989 and those for 1983–84 is striking. It points to a massive rise in discontent in the second half of the decade, a rise that must have lowered the revolutionary thresholds of millions of individual East Germans.

What specific events set the revolutionary bandwagon in motion? One must recognize that attempting to answer this question is akin to trying to identify the spark that ignited a forest fire or the cough responsible for a flu epidemic. There were many turning points in the East European Revolution, any one of which might have derailed it.

One turning point came in early October, when East German officials refused to carry out Party leader Honecker's order to open fire on street demonstrators. On October 7 Gorbachev was in Berlin for celebrations marking the fortieth anniversary of the German Democratic Republic. With scores of foreign reporters looking on, crowds took to the streets, chanting, "Gorby! Gorby!" And the police clubs went into action. West German television immediately played these events back to the rest of East Germany. The scenes alerted disgruntled citizens in every corner of the country to the pervasiveness of discontent, while the government's weak response revealed its vulnerability. A peaceful protest broke out in Leipzig on October 9. Honecker ordered the regional Party secretary to block the demonstration, by force if necessary. But bloodshed was averted when Egon Krenz, a Politburo member in charge of security, flew to Leipzig and encouraged the security forces to show restraint. Local leaders—some of whom had already appealed for restraint—accepted this contravention of Honecker's order, and tens of thousands marched without interference. Sensing the shifting political winds, more and more East Germans throughout the country took to the streets. The East German uprising was now in full swing. As the regime tried to stem the tide through a string of concessions, the swelling crowds began to

[72] "Daten des Zentralinstituts für Jugendforschung Leipzig" (fn. 59), Tables 1 and 2.

make increasingly bold demands. Within a month the Berlin Wall would be breached, and in less than a year the German Democratic Republic would become part of a unified, democratic Germany.[73]

Another turning point came on October 25, during Gorbachev's state visit to Finland. Two months earlier a Solidarity offical had formed Poland's first noncommunist government since the 1940s, following the Communist Party's stunning defeat at the polls. A legislative deputy to Gorbachev had declined detailed comment on the grounds that the developments were a domestic matter for the Poles.[74] The communists were in retreat in Hungary, too. In meetings with dissident groups the Hungarian Communist Party had endorsed free parliamentary elections. Then, in the belief that its candidates would do poorly running under the banner of communism, it had transformed itself into the Hungarian Socialist Party.[75] This was the first time that a ruling communist party had formally abandoned communism. With the world wondering whether the Soviet Union had reached the limits of its tolerance, Gorbachev declared in Finland that his country had no moral or political right to interfere in the affairs of its East European neighbors. Defining this position as "the Sinatra doctrine," his spokesman jokingly asked reporters whether they knew the Frank Sinatra song "I Did It My Way." He went on to say that "Hungary and Poland are doing it their way." Using the Western term for the previous Soviet policy of armed intervention to keep the governments of the Warsaw Pact in communist hands, he added, "I think the Brezhnev doctrine is dead."[76] Coming on the heels of major communist retreats in Poland and Hungary, these comments offered yet another indication that Gorbachev would not try to silence East European dissent.

If one effect of this signal was to embolden the opposition movements of Eastern Europe, another must have been to discourage the governments of Eastern Europe from resorting to violence unilaterally. This is not to say that Gorbachev enunciated his Sinatra doctrine with the intention of encouraging East European oppositions to grab for power. Nor is it to say that the revolution would have petered out in the absence of this move. By the time Gorbachev renounced the Soviet Union's right to intervene, opposition movements in Poland, East Germany, and Hungary already commanded mass support, and it is unlikely that anything

[73] This account draws on Ash (fn. 19); Anderson (fn. 26); and the *New York Times* reports compiled in Gwertzman and Kaufman (fn. 1), 158–60, 166–84, 216–22.

[74] *New York Times*, August 18, 1989, p. 1.

[75] Ibid., October 8, 1989, p. 1. For a fuller account of the transformation, see Abel (fn. 14), chap. 2.

[76] *New York Times*, October 26, 1989, p. 1.

short of massive brutality would have broken their momentum and restored the status quo ante. Nonetheless, some incumbent communist leaders were seriously considering a military solution, and the proclamation of the Sinatra doctrine may well have tipped the balance against the use of force. Had even one East European government resorted to force at this stage, the result may well have been a series of bloody and protracted civil wars.

Just as we cannot be certain that a delay in announcing the new Soviet doctrine would have altered the course of history, we will never know whether the contravention of Honecker's order to shoot had a significant impact on the subsequent flow of events. What can be said is this: had Honecker's subordinates enforced his order, the growth of the opposition would have slowed, and later demonstrations would probably not have stayed peaceful. The same historical significance can be attributed to the restraint shown by the individual soldiers on duty during the demonstration and by the individual demonstrators. In the tense atmosphere of the demonstration a shot fired in panic or a stone thrown in excitement could have sparked a violent confrontation. It was an extraordinary conjunction of individual decisions that kept the uprising peaceful and prevented the revolution from being sidetracked.

The success of antigovernment demonstrations in one country inspired demonstrations elsewhere. In early November, Sofia was shaken by its first demonstration in four decades as several thousand Bulgarians marched on the National Assembly. Within a week, on the very day throngs broke through the Berlin Wall, Todor Zhivkov's thirty-five-year leadership came to an end, and his successor began talking of radical reforms.

Up to that time Czechoslovakia's communist government had yielded little to its own opposition. Conscious of developments elsewhere, it had simply promised economic reforms and made minor concessions on travel and religion.[77] These retreats encouraged the swelling crowds to ask for more. On November 24, just hours after Alexander Dubček addressed a crowd of 350,000 in his first public speech since 1968, the Communist Party declared a shake-up in the leadership, only to face a much larger rally of people shouting, "Shame! Shame! Shame!" The new government tried to placate the demonstrators by vowing to punish the commandant of the paramilitary forces that had roughed up protestors a week earlier. Unimpressed, the opposition leaders labeled the announced changes "cosmetic" and promised to redouble their pressure. The success

[77] Ibid., November 16, 1989, p. 1.

of the general strike they called for November 27 led the Communist Party to capitulate within a matter of hours to their major demands, including an end to its monopoly on political power.[78] "Not since the Paris crowd discovered that the dreaded Bastille contained only a handful of prisoners and a few terrified soldiers has a citadel fallen with such ease," wrote the *Economist* a few days later. "They just had to say boo."[79]

This brings us back, for one last time, to Havel's brilliant 1979 essay. He predicted there that when the greengrocers decided they had had enough, communism would fall like a house of cards. So it turned out: when the masses took to the streets, the support for the Czechoslovak government just vanished. The mobilization process followed the patterns of East Germany and Bulgaria. Emboldened by signals from the Soviet Union and the successes of opposition movements in neighboring countries, a few thousand people stood up in defiance, joining the tiny core of long-persecuted activists. In so doing they encouraged additional citizens to drop their masks, which then impelled more onlookers to jump in. Before long fear changed sides: where people had been afraid to oppose the regime, they came to fear being caught defending it. Party members rushed to burn their cards, asserting they had always been reformists at heart. Top officials, sensing that they might be made to pay for standing in the way of change and for any violence, hastened to accept the opposition's demands, only to be confronted with bolder ones yet.

Had the civilian leadership or the top brass attempted to resist the opposition, the transfer of power would not have been so swift, and certainly not so peaceful. One of the most remarkable aspects of the East European Revolution is that, with the partial exception of Romania, the security forces and the bureaucracy just melted away in the face of growing public opposition. Not only did state officials shy away from putting up a fight, but many crossed over to the opposition as a transfer of power appeared increasingly likely. This is highly significant, for a defection from the inner establishment is an unusually good indicator of the prevailing political winds. A Politburo member distancing himself from the Party leader does more to expose the regime's vulnerability than a greengrocer who stops displaying the obligatory Marxist slogan. In turn, a defiant greengrocer does more harm to the regime's image than does an obstreperous prisoner in solitary confinement.

[78] For an eyewitness account of these events, see Timothy Garton Ash, "The Revolution of the Magic Lantern," *New York Review of Books*, January 18, 1990, 42–51. See also Abel (fn. 14), chap. 3.
[79] *Economist*, December 2, 1989, p. 55.

In the simple model of Section III the perceived strength of the public opposition is measured by S, the share of society publicly in opposition. This variable treats all individuals equally: with ten individuals, each individual carries a weight of 10 percent. But in reality, as I have argued, members of society differ in their contributions to the perceived strength of the opposition. So a more realistic measure of perceived strength would be some *unequally weighted* indicator of public opposition, where the weights correlate with levels of relative influence. Such a weighted measure would assign a Politburo member more weight than a greengrocer, and the latter more weight than a nameless prisoner. Were we to introduce this refinement into our model, the central argument would remain unaffected: with public preferences still interdependent, there would remain the possibility of a latent, unobserved bandwagon.[80] My reason for abstracting from this refinement in Section III was to keep the presentation simple.

Some of the officials who distanced themselves from the Party or even moved into the opposition as the uprisings took off may at heart have disliked the communist social order. Many others undoubtedly acted for opportunistic reasons rather than out of conviction. Sensing the imminent collapse of the old order, they abandoned it in hopes of finding a place in the order about to be born. A few chose to resist, but the speed of the anticommunist mobilization left most of them with insufficient time to plan and execute a coordinated response. Had the mobilization been slower, they might well have managed to mount a credible, effective response.[81]

Timothy Garton Ash, an eyewitness to the mobilizations in Hungary, Poland, East Germany, and Czechoslovakia, characterizes 1989 as Eastern Europe's "year of truth."[82] This designation is accurate insofar as it captures the end of feigned support for communism. But it conceals the push the revolution got from preference falsification on the part of those who sympathized with the status quo. As noncommunists threw off their masks in joy and relief, many genuine communists slipped on masks of their own—masks depicting them as the helpless functionaries of a repressive system, as former preference falsifiers thrilled to be speaking their minds after years of silent resentment. Yet Ash's label is meaningful in another sense as well. The flowering of anticommunist discourse has

---

[80] For a demonstration, see Kuran (fn. 31).
[81] The pace of events was undoubtedly a key factor also in the failure of conservative groups in the Soviet Union to block Eastern Europe's liberation. Had events proceeded more slowly, they might have had time to oust Gorbachev and order the Red Army into action.
[82] Ash (fn. 51).

exposed the official ideology more clearly than ever before as a heap of sophistry, distortion, and myth. It has awakened millions of dormant minds, confronting citizens resigned to the status quo with the conflicts between the pragmatic and theoretical layers of their beliefs. This is to say neither that the thoughts of every East European are now internally consistent nor that Marxist thinking has ceased. Rather, it is to suggest that the transformation of public discourse has opened many to new possibilities.

In the days following the fall of Czechoslovakia's communist regime, a banner in Prague read: "Poland—10 years, Hungary—10 months, East Germany—10 weeks, Czechoslovakia—10 days."[83] The implied acceleration reflects the fact that each successful challenge to communism lowered the perceived risk of dissent in the countries still under communist rule. In terms of our model, as revolutionary thresholds in neighboring countries fell, the revolution became increasingly contagious.

Had this banner been prepared a few weeks later, it might have added "Romania—10 hours." As the Czechoslovak uprising neared its climax, the executive committee of the Romanian Communist Party was busy reelecting Nicolae Ceauşescu as president and interrupting his acceptance speech with standing ovations. Three weeks later protests broke out in the western provinces, but they were brutally put down by the security forces. Confident of his ability to prevent a replay of the events that had brought down other communist regimes, Ceauşescu left for a state visit to Iran, but the protests intensified. Upon his return he organized a rally to denounce the "counterrevolutionaries," but when he started to speak he was booed. Television broadcast the look of shock on his face, and the Romanian revolt was on. The consequent change of regime turned out to be bloodier than the previous five, because the security forces responsible for the earlier massacre resisted the revolution. They caused hundreds of deaths before they were beaten by the army. Ceauşescu tried to escape but he was caught and summarily executed.[84]

Yet again, the world watched a nation jump with little warning from quiescence and subservience to turbulence and defiance. As the year went out, commentators were still marveling at the speed with which the political landscape of Eastern Europe had changed. Long-persecuted dissidents now occupied high government positions. In Czechoslovakia, for instance, Havel was president, Dubček, chairman of the Federal As-

[83] "Czechoslovakia: The Velvet Revolution," *Uncaptive Minds* 3 (January–February 1990), 11.
[84] For the *New York Times* reports of these events, see Gwertzman and Kaufman (fn. 1), 332–39.

sembly, and Jiří Dienstbier (a Charter 77 signatory serving time as a coal stoker), foreign minister. All six countries began planning free elections and committed themselves to economic liberalization. Some even moved to withdraw from the Warsaw Pact.

VI. The Predictability of Unpredictability

Unexpected as they were, these developments now seem as though they could easily have been predicted. Was it not obvious that the economic failures of communism had sown the seeds of a massive revolt? Was it not self-evident that the East Europeans were just waiting for an opportunity to topple their despised dictators? Did not the severe domestic problems of the Soviet Union necessitate its withdrawal from Eastern Europe, to concentrate its resources on economic reforms? Retrospective accounts of 1989 offer a panoply of such reasons why the East European Revolution was inevitable. "It is no accident that Mikhail Gorbachev declined to intervene," writes one commentator[85]—this, in a volume peppered with comments on how 1989 surprised one and all.

This essay has shown that the warning signs of the revolution remained cloudy until it was all over. Moreover, the unobservability of private preferences and revolutionary thresholds concealed the latent bandwagons in formation and also made it difficult to appreciate the significance of events that were pushing these into motion. The explanation for this predictive failure transcends the particularities of Eastern Europe: this is after all hardly the first time a major social uprising has come as a big surprise.

The French Revolution of 1789 shocked not only Louis XVI and his courtiers but also outside observers and the rioters who helped end his reign. Yet it had many deep causes—all expounded at great length in literally thousands of volumes. This paradox is one of the central themes of Tocqueville's *Old Régime and the French Revolution*. "Chance played no part whatever in the outbreak of the revolution," he observes. "Though it took the world by surprise, it was the inevitable outcome of a long period of gestation, the abrupt and violent conclusion of a process in which six generations played an intermittent part."[86]

In this century the Nazi takeover of Germany took place with astonishing speed. Within a few months entrenched political institutions were turned upside down, all democratic opposition was destroyed, and a la-

---

[85] William M. Brinton, "Gorbachev and the Revolution of 1989–90," in Brinton and Rinzler (fn. 11), 373.
[86] Tocqueville (fn. 36), 20.

bor movement with millions of members was driven underground.[87] Though it was not foreseen, there is no shortage of explanations for the rise of Nazism. The Iranian Revolution of 1979–80 offers yet another example of an unanticipated uprising. There now exists a panoply of competing explanations, including ones that invoke class conflicts, failures of governance, foreign exploitation, economic reversals, the disaffections of bazaar merchants, and Islamic ideology.[88] Yet for all their differences, students of this revolution agree that it stunned almost everyone—the Shah and the Ayatollah Khomeini, the CIA and the KGB, statesmen, diplomats, academics, and journalists.

The very revolution that prepared the ground for the first communist regime in history was an unforeseen event. Weeks before the Russian Revolution of February 1917 Lenin told an audience in Switzerland that Russia's great explosion lay in the distant future and that older men like himself would not live to see it.[89] And with just days to go, foreign observers in Petrograd were advising their capitals that the monarchy was stable and secure.[90] But the tsar fell, and before the year was over the communists had gained full control of the government. It has since been recognized that Marxist scholarship did not prepare us for the world's first successful communist revolution occurring in, of all places, backward, semifeudal Russia.[91]

Nor did Marxist scholarship—or for that matter, non-Marxist scholarship—anticipate the midcentury uprisings in the communist states of Eastern Europe. "The Hungarian uprising of October 1956 was a dramatic, sudden explosion, apparently not organized beforehand by a revolutionary center; neither outsiders nor the participants had anticipated anything like the irresistible revolutionary dynamism that would sweep the country." Thus begins *The Unexpected Revolution*, a monograph on this failed attempt to overthrow communism that is replete with evi-

---

[87] Detlev J. K. Peukert, *Inside Nazi Germany: Conformity, Opposition, and Racism in Everyday Life*, trans. Richard Deveson (New Haven: Yale University Press, 1987), 27–28 and passim.

[88] For a sample of explanations, see Hamid Algar, *The Islamic Revolution in Iran* (London: Muslim Institute, 1980); Said Amir Arjomand, "Iran's Islamic Revolution in Comparative Perspective," *World Politics* 38 (April 1986), 383–414; Shaul Bakhash, *The State and Revolution in Iran* (London: Croom Helm, 1984); Nikki R. Keddie, *Roots of Revolution* (New Haven: Yale University Press, 1981); and Robert Looney, *Economic Origins of the Iranian Revolution* (Boulder, Colo.: Westview Press, 1982).

[89] Leonard Schapiro, *The Russian Revolutions of 1917: The Origins of Modern Communism* (New York: Basic Books, 1984), 19.

[90] William H. Chamberlin, *The Russian Revolution, 1917–1921* (New York: Macmillan, 1935), 1:73–76.

[91] Further evidence concerning the element of surprise in the French, Russian, and Iranian revolutions may be found in Kuran (fn. 31), secs. 2, 6–7.

dence of widespread preference falsification right up to the uprising.[92] Prior to October 1956 writers who were to play leading roles gave not the slightest sign of opposition to the political status quo. For another example, clerical employees remained docile and submissive until the uprising in which they participated, often hiding their grievances even from family members.[93]

The Prague Spring of 1968 offers another example of an unforeseen attempt to crack the wall of communism. In a retrospective account, Havel writes that in 1967 the entire nation was behaving like the Good Soldier Švejk, accommodating itself to the regime's demands. "Who would have believed . . . that a year later this recently apathetic, skeptical, and demoralized society would stand up with such courage and intelligence to a foreign power!" "And," he continues, "who would have suspected that, after scarcely a year had gone by, this same society would, as swiftly as the wind blows, lapse back into a state of deep demoralization far worse than its original one!"[94]

This tally of unanticipated uprisings could be expanded, but the point has been made: the revolution of 1989 was not the first to surprise us. Time and again entrenched authority has vanished suddenly, leaving the victors astonished at their triumph and the vanquished, at their defeat.

Should we conclude, along with John Dunn, that revolutions are ineluctable "facts of nature," events that fail "to suggest the dominance of human reason in any form"?[95] In other words, is the culprit human irrationality? The argument developed in this paper does not point in this direction. It suggests, on the contrary, that predictive failure is entirely consistent with calculated, purposeful human action. Underlying an explosive shift in public sentiment are multitudes of individual decisions to switch political allegiance, each undertaken in response to changing incentives. So just as a failure to predict a rainstorm does not imply that the clouds obey no physical laws, a failure to predict some revolution does not imply individual irrationality.

Dunn also suggests that revolutions have too many determinants to make them amenable to a grand, comprehensive theory. Shunning the futile exercise of constructing a theory with universal applicability, we ought to focus, he says, on the particularities of each situation. Although

---

[92] Paul Kecskemeti, *The Unexpected Revolution: Social Forces in the Hungarian Uprising* (Stanford, Calif.: Stanford University Press, 1961), 1.

[93] Ibid., 60, 84–85.

[94] Havel, *Disturbing the Peace: A Conversation with Karel Hvížďala* (1986), trans. Paul Wilson (New York: Alfred A. Knopf, 1990), 109.

[95] Dunn, *Modern Revolutions: An Introduction to the Analysis of a Political Phenomenon*, 2d ed. (New York: Cambridge University Press, 1989), 2–3.

I agree that revolutions are complex events brought on by a symphony of interacting variables, I depart from Dunn on the usefulness of general theorizing: obstacles to forecasting particular revolutions do not preclude useful insights into the *process* of revolution. Even if we cannot predict the time and place of the next big uprising, we may prepare ourselves mentally for the mass mobilization that will bring it about. Equally important, we can understand why it may surprise us. There are other spheres of knowledge where highly useful theories preclude reliable predictions of specific outcomes. The Darwinian theory of biological evolution illuminates the process whereby species evolve but without enabling us to predict the future evolution of the gazelle. Sophisticated theories of the weather elucidate why it is in perpetual flux but without making it possible to say with much confidence whether it will rain in Rome a week from next Tuesday.

Such general theories have a common virtue: they reveal the source of their predictive limitations. The reason they cannot predict infallibly is not simply that they contain large numbers of variables. In each theory variables are related to one another *nonlinearly*; that is, a *small* perturbation in one variable, which normally produces *small* changes in other variables, may under the right set of circumstances have *large* consequences. Consider the theory of climatic turbulence developed by Edward Lorenz. It shows that a sparrow flapping its wings in Istanbul—an intrinsically insignificant event—can generate a hurricane in the Gulf of Mexico. This is because the weather at any given location is related to its determinants nonlinearly. In other words, its sensitivity to other variables, and their sensitivities to one another, are themselves *variable*. Accordingly, variable x may be impervious to a jump in y from 20 to 200, yet exhibit hypersensitivity if y rises a bit higher, say, to 202. It may then start to grow explosively, effectively feeding on itself. The notion that small events may unleash huge forces goes against much of twentieth-century social thought, with its emphasis on linearity, continuity, and gradualism. But in contexts as different as technological diffusion and cognitive development it is the key to understanding a host of otherwise inexplicable phenomena.

What endows intrinsically insignificant events with potentially explosive power in the context of political change is that public preferences are interdependent. Because of this interdependence, the equilibrium levels of the public opposition are related to the underlying individual characteristics nonlinearly. A massive change in private preferences may leave the incumbent equilibrium undisturbed, only to be followed by a tiny change that destroys the status quo, setting off a bandwagon that will culminate in a very different equilibrium. Partly because of preference falsification, the nature of the interdependence is *imperfectly observable*. This is why a massive rise in public opposition may catch everyone by surprise.

Because preference falsification afflicts politics in every society, major revolutions are likely to come again and again as a surprise. This is not to assert the impossibility of accurate prediction. If we possessed a reliable technique for measuring people's revolutionary thresholds, we would see what it would take to get a revolution started. And if we understood the determinants of these thresholds, we would know when the required conditions were about to be met. For all practical purposes, however, such information is available only in highly incomplete form. In any case, there is an irremovable political obstacle to becoming sufficiently knowledgeable: vulnerable regimes can block the production and dissemination of information potentially harmful to their own survival. Censorship and the regulation of opinion surveys—both widely practiced in prerevolutionary Eastern Europe—are two of the policies that serve these objectives.

I have deliberately characterized the source of unpredictability as *imperfect* observability, as opposed to *un*observability. The degree of imperfection obviously constitutes a continuum. Societies with strong democratic traditions exhibit less imperfection than ones with nonexistent or fragile democratic freedoms. This is because there is less preference falsification in the former group, at least with respect to the political system itself. Accordingly, one can track the course of antigovernment or antiregime sentiment more confidently for Norway, Switzerland, or France than for Pakistan, Brazil, or Ghana. This is why developments in Pakistan are more likely to catch the world off guard than are developments in Norway; by implication, Norway's political future can be predicted with greater confidence than can that of Pakistan. Most countries of the world lie closer to Pakistan than to Norway as regards the significance of preference falsification in sustaining their political regimes.

This emphasis on unpredictability should not be considered offensive to the scientific spirit: accepting the limits of what we can expect from science is not an admission of defeat. On the contrary, establishing these limits of knowledge is itself a contribution to the pool of useful knowledge. It is also a necessary step toward charting a realistic scientific agenda. "To act as if we possessed scientific knowledge enabling us to transcend [the absolute obstacles to the prediction of specific events]," wrote Friedrich Hayek in his Nobel Memorial Lecture, "may itself become a serious obstacle to the advance of the human intellect."[96]

[96] Hayek, "The Pretence of Knowledge" (1974), *American Economic Review* 79 (December 1989), 6.

The prediction of unpredictability is not to be confused with the un-falsifiability of the underlying theory. The theory developed in this essay is fully falsifiable. It implies that political revolutions will continue to surprise us, so a string of successful predictions would render it suspect. Simply put, it can be falsified by developing some theory of revolution that forecasts accurately. In principle, if not in practice, the presented theory can also be falsified by showing that preference falsification was not a factor in unanticipated revolutions of the past.

LEGITIMATION FROM THE TOP TO CIVIL SOCIETY
Politico-Cultural Change in Eastern Europe

By GIUSEPPE DI PALMA*

Power . . . is the priority of output over intake, the ability to talk
instead of listen. In a sense, it is the ability to afford not to learn.
                                                        —Karl Deutsch
                                                 The Nerves of Government

The Power of the Powerless
                                                        —Václav Havel

W HY did communism collapse in Eastern Europe, and what was
the role of East European societies in the collapse? This essay
addresses these two questions and in seeking answers focuses on the
unique way in which communist regimes obstinately sought to construe
their legitimacy as "legitimacy from the top." Eastern Europe suffered a
collective crisis of faith, precipitated by the physical and ideological desertion of the Soviet Union. The paper argues that a civil society of sorts
survived in Eastern Europe, not just as a conventional clandestine adversary but as a visible cultural and existential counterimage of communism's unique hegemonic project. This fact must be accorded its due in
any assessment of the capacity of East European civil society to rebound
during (and after) the transitions.

Lucian Pye, in his 1989 presidential address to the American Political
Science Association, described the gathering crisis of communism as follows:

> These are astonishing events, but behind them are historic forces at work
> today causing acute crises for all types of authoritarian regimes. . . . Dic-
> tatorial rule has failed to deliver on its promises of purposeful efficiency in
> all the regions of the world.[1]

Pye's analysis is assuredly attractive in its sweep. It revives neglected
modernization theory. It suggests that the demise of contemporary dictatorships, first in the West and now in the East, is propelled by the

---

* This is a revised version of a longer paper prepared for the conference "La rifondazione
dei partiti politici nell'Europa orientale," Società italiana di scienza politica, Ferrara, Italy,
October 1990.
[1] Pye, "Political Science and the Crisis of Authoritarianism," *American Political Science
Review* 84 (March 1990), 3–19, at 5.

imperatives of larger, often global socioeconomic transformations. These imperatives demand convergence toward Western pluralist models.

I intend to argue by contrast that such convergence is rarely what dictatorial regimes aim for or indeed achieve, even if they recognize their own socioeconomic obsolescence.[2] In particular, despite visible obsolescence, the crisis of East European communism was not one of reasonable convergence but one of obdurate and insulating divergence. For all that it shed of its erstwhile totalitarian layers, and indeed for all the scholarly reinterpretation of the nature of communist regimes, mature communism remained to the last hostage to a baseless theory of history according to which convergence would occur on communism's own grounds or not at all. This theory of history—not popular approval—constituted the permanent core of communist claims to legitimacy. But once even the Soviet hegemon could no longer deny the devastating costs of enforced obsolescence, communism could no longer escape a crisis of faith. No longer could communist power "afford not to learn."[3]

As communism lost faith, social resistance to its dogmatic and historically baseless claims turned the transitions in Eastern Europe into true revolutions of citizenship,[4] underscored by an extraordinary mobilization of civic identities and expectations. The level of modernization achieved by East European societies under communism is insufficient to account for these phenomena. Mobilization went well beyond what has usually been the case in the recent demise of often more modern Western dictatorships. One reason for the difference is that Western dictatorships, unlike their communist counterparts, rarely intended to elevate their denial of citizenship to a principle. Therefore, the reappropriation of citizenship by the East Europeans is an exquisitely *political* act. And since the emergence of a critical public sphere had been historically thwarted in Eastern Europe, well before the imposition of communism, one may well ask whether this political act has a world-historical significance of its own.[5]

---

[2] Pye himself points out in his address (fn. 1) that all crises of authoritarianism are marked by a clash between the Western culture of modernization and national political cultures. Who will win "(and hence the outcome of any particular crisis of authoritarianism) will depend on the character of the [national] political culture" (p. 12). On why the demonstration effects of modernization are unlikely to produce convergence, see Reinhard Bendix, *Force, Fate and Freedom* (Berkeley: University of California Press, 1984), 108–22.

[3] Karl Deutsch, *The Nerves of Government* (New York: Free Press, 1966), 111.

[4] Veljco Vujacic, "The Dual Revolution of Citizenship and Nationhood in Eastern Europe" (Unpublished manuscript, Berkeley, May 1990).

[5] This is so not despite but precisely because of the fact that for once the revolutions "proclaim no world-historical innovations. The truths which they seek to vindicate are distinctly old-fashioned, as are their aspirations." Cited in Martin Krygier, "Marxism and the

Some disclaimers are in order at the outset. Despite the assertive style, this is an exploratory essay, a proposal for a research agenda. First, evidence supporting the contention that East European communisms aimed at legitimating themselves from above as well as evidence that a loss of faith caused their collapse cannot be accommodated within the constraints imposed by a journal article. It is also, and unapologetically, an essay about commonalities—which in no way denies the important differences between countries, both in their communist and precommunist background and in the contingencies associated with the demise of communism. Indeed, the differences are especially salient in distinguishing between East-Central and properly East European countries, let alone between all of them on the one hand and the Soviet Union on the other, and in projecting individual futures. But there are nevertheless firm commonalities that are decisive for grasping what is unique in the crisis of East European communism, as compared for instance with the crises of dictatorships in Southern Europe and Latin America.[6] Common to communisms were the physical and ideological bonds that tied the satellites to the Soviet hegemon: hence their prolonged inability to shake loose an artfully enforced and increasingly obsolescent set of beliefs and behaviors; hence their precipitous loss of faith once Soviet blessing and buttressing were removed, irrespective of how much they had traveled on reforms. Adam Przeworski speaks of a domino effect: the removal of the Soviet dam unleashed waters that overran one regime after the other.[7]

THEORIES OF COMMUNIST CHANGE

Totalitarianism defines most appropriately the essence of communist rule as practiced under Stalin in both the Soviet Union and Eastern Europe. The term is less successful at capturing communist realities under the Khrushchevian experiment or during the long period of Brezhnevite normalization. Nonetheless, discarding the label does not necessarily enhance our ability to explain the demise of communism in Eastern Europe (let alone in the Soviet Union). At any rate, other labels (post-totalitarianism, post-totalitarian authoritarianism, failed totalitarianism, postrev-

---

Rule of Law: Reflections after the Collapse of Communism" (Paper presented at the annual meeting of the Law and Society Association, May–June 1990, no place indicated), 4.

[6] For a more extensive treatment of the comparison, see Giuseppe Di Palma, "Democratic Transitions: Puzzles and Surprises from West to East" (Paper prepared for the Conference of Europeanists, Washington, D.C., March 1990).

[7] Przeworski, "The 'East' Becomes the 'South'? The 'Autumn of the People' and the Future of Eastern Europe," *PS* 24 (March 1991), 20–24, at 21.

olutionary totalitarianism, welfare authoritarianism, neo-traditionalism), which were adopted beginning in the 1960s to capture the dynamics of post-Stalinist communist change, have been of very limited use in forecasting communist collapse and its special dynamics.

Before the demise of communism made the front pages around the world, few if any of the revisionist students of communism were betting on it. True, they seemed nonplussed when Jeane Kirkpatrick announced that Western-style authoritarianism could be reformed and even removed but that communist totalitarianism could not.[8] But then Kirkpatrick was a noisy and politically tainted interloper—which may account for her overlooking the developments in communist studies and for the disdain with which her pronouncement was greeted. Aspersions notwithstanding, in 1984 Samuel Huntington could still write, in a scholarly research on the global prospects of democracy, that "the likelihood of democratic development in Eastern Europe is virtually nil."[9] Also in 1984 Juan Linz, not an interloper but a highly regarded student of dictatorship and democracy, wrote à propos of the distinction between totalitarian and authoritarian dictatorships that "the essential criterion is that of the transformability or irreversibility of the regime."[10]

What, then, remains problematic in theories of communist change? Did they illuminate change correctly? If they did, was change of such a nature as to throw full light on the final demise?

Revisionist interpretations of change under communist rule are of two broad types. The first type is the offspring of modernization or convergence theory, which locates the mainspring of change in the dynamics of material progress and industrialism the world over. The global potential of modernization, which strives for a convergence toward Western pluralist models, is most recently summarized in Lucian Pye's presidential address:

[8] Kirkpatrick, "Dictatorships and Double Standards," *Commentary*, November 1979, pp. 34–46.
[9] Huntington, "Will More Countries Become Democratic?" *Political Science Quarterly* 99 (Summer 1984), 193–218, at 217.
[10] Linz, "Epilogue," in Guy Hermet, ed., *Totalitarismes* (Paris: Economica, 1984), 244; translation provided by Giuseppe Di Palma. Jacques Rupnik documented in the same volume how even as the concept of totalitarianism was being banned from Western Sovietology in the 1970s and 1980s, scholars in East-Central Europe were dissecting the new mechanisms of communist domination and bracing themselves for a protracted resistance. The new chinks that these scholars detected in the communist armor seemed to promise nothing more than a difficult and prolonged cohabitation between regimes obdurately seeking justification for their suffocating domination and civil societies obstinately surfacing to breathe. See Rupnik, "Le totalitarisme vue de l'Est," in Hermet, 43–71; his treatment of the topic appears in English in Rupnik, *The Other Europe: The Rise and Fall of Communism in East-Central Europe* (New York: Schocken, 1989), chap. 9.

The key factors were all identified as critical variables by the early modernization and political development theorists. Where we went wrong in the 1950s and 1960s was in grossly underestimating the magnitude these factors would acquire in the decades ahead and the extent to which they would become part of closely knit international systems. Modernization theory predicted that such developments as economic growth, the spread of science and technology, the acceleration and spread of communications and the establishment of educational systems would all contribute to political change. We cannot here document all the ways these factors have brought about the current crisis of authoritarianism, but we can note briefly the extent to which we failed initially to appreciate the orders of magnitude they would reach.[11]

Yet well before Pye uttered these words, Sovietologists had given plenty of attention to the imperatives of modernization. To some students, early communism—with its emphasis on terror, doctrine, and coerced mobilization—appeared extraneous to modernization, or at any rate an impediment to it.[12] To others, those same qualities served to accelerate modernization out of backwardness.[13] No matter: in the eyes of both, the needs of modernization (or *further* modernization) would finally prevail under mature communism. Thus, presumably, there came a qualitative change after Stalin: away from counterproductive (that is, no longer necessary) chiliasm and toward a more predictable, responsible, and differentiated modernizing order that gave technocrats and rational agents their due.

Are the imperatives of modernization sufficient to account for the demise of communism, however? And in precisely what way? What actually impresses in the present demise is not the resoluteness of the imperative—despite the objective costs of denying it—but its opposite: its inability to alter substantially "real living" socialisms.[14] Thus, relative and absolute stagnation and deprivation, not the unfettering of development, are very much behind the demise of communism.

In this regard, the second type of interpretation—incisively labeled

[11] Pye (fn. 1), 7.
[12] Richard Lowenthal, "Beyond Totalitarianism," in Irving Howe, ed., *1984 Revisited* (New York: Harper and Row, 1983), 209–67; Robert C. Tucker, *The Marxian Revolutionary Idea* (Princeton: Princeton University Press, 1970).
[13] Cyril A. Black, *The Dynamics of Modernization: A Study in Comparative History* (New York: Harper and Row, 1966).
[14] About the clash between the culture of modernization and communist political culture, Pye (fn. 1) writes:

This clash has produced a particularly acute crisis of faith in the Marxist-Leninist systems precisely because their ideology long informed the faithful that there could be no such contradiction for them. They were promised that through their identification with "scientific Marxism" they had been given a political identity that was universalistic and at the forefront of human progress. (p. 11)

devolutionist by Andrew Janos—has an edge over modernization theories.[15] Inspired by Weber's theory of routinization, devolution argues that a conflict will inevitably develop between the chiliastic aspirations of the totalitarian movement and the status or functional concerns of those members of the movement who are charged with implementing its goals. The conflict may endure unresolved for a long time,[16] but regime bureaucrats and normalizers should eventually prevail. For without the security of tasks and roles, the chiliastic goals of the movement would turn the regime into chaos.

Theories of devolution are better than theories of modernization at uncovering the early roots of the present demise because—instead of focusing on the global dynamics of material progress—they focus on the political core of the communist system: a system of government less threatening and somewhat less obtrusive after Stalin but still infinitely more threatening and obtrusive than any other in the industrial world and therefore more crucial in suppressing, heeding, or originating impulses to change. And by emphasizing that normalization is driven by the status concerns of a nonaccountable administrative class, devolution theories explain why and how normalization differs from modernization. They offer a persuasive account of communism's slide toward a "neo-traditional" stagnation that is unresponsive to global imperatives.[17] Yet neo-traditionalism also signifies a tenured, privileged, and ubiquitous political class, not responsible for its actions and not bound by contract and performance. So how did an entrenched class such as the one that emerged in the Soviet Union and its satellites under Brezhnev move from a position of security to one of accelerated crisis? This is a question that devolution theories have not been able to answer fully.

It is time to look at communist change from the somewhat different angle of system legitimacy. There is a triple advantage to focusing on legitimacy (specifically, on how the claims on which legitimacy is based have been affected by communist normalization). First, that focus reveals how the belief in one's normative legitimacy, a central feature of communist regimes, tended to trap the regimes in a potentially dangerous

---

[15] Janos, *Politics and Paradigms: Changing Theories of Change in Social Science* (Stanford, Calif.: Stanford University Press, 1986), 106–19; idem, "Social Science, Communism, and the Dynamics of Political Change," in this issue of *World Politics*.

[16] Stalin's purges, Mao's cultural revolution, but also Khrushchev's ill-fated efforts to cajole the party into more "heroic" performance can be seen as ways in which revolutionary leaders fought against routinization and for commitment to exceptional goals.

[17] Kenneth Jowitt, "Soviet Neotraditionalism: The Political Corruption of a Leninist Regime," *Soviet Studies* 35 (July 1983), 275–97; Andrew Walder, *Communist Neo-traditionalism: Work and Authority in Chinese Industry* (Berkeley: University of California Press, 1986).

denial of increasingly demanding domestic and global realities.[18] Second, it offers insights into how, in reaction to communist denial of reality, the question of civil society has emerged as central in communist transitions, and why one should speak of revolutions of citizenship. In sum (third), a focus on legitimacy highlights the importance of political discourse in driving the practices of communist power, in contributing to their abject failure, and in shaping societal defenses against them.

LEGITIMATION FROM THE TOP

Let it be clear that the East European perspectives on legitimacy must be a confined variant of the perspective of the Soviet hegemon. The remarks that follow have therefore as much to do with the hegemon as with its satellites.

One may be tempted to dismiss all talk of communist legitimacy as bogus and unproductive. Indeed, a combination of long-standing normative and material factors has eroded popular support for communism, especially in Eastern Europe. Also, regimes, in particular repressive ones, can persevere for a long time without genuine support. But lack of popular support is not invariably indicative of lack of legitimacy. The conceptual equation holds true, at least in part,[19] when the sovereign people are the authority that verifies and bestows legitimacy, as in a democracy or a liberal constitutional system. When the people are sovereign, support constitutes the essential ingredient of legitimacy. This is so whatever the criteria for bestowing legitimacy. The right of some to rule is thereby conditioned by others.

Claims to legitimacy, however, may be authenticated by quite a different sovereign source: in early modern times, for example, they were authenticated by the rulers themselves.[20] The suggestion here is that this principle of self-legitimation, or of "legitimation from the top," as Maria Marcus calls it, also occurs in communist regimes.[21] And when the rulers believe that their right to rule needs no popular verification, two conse-

[18] Maria Marcus, "Overt and Covert Modes of Legitimation in East European Societies," in T. H. Rigby and Ferenc Fehér, eds., *Political Legitimation in Communist States* (New York: St. Martin's Press, 1982), 82–93; Václav Benda, "Parallel Polis or an Independent Society in Central and Eastern Europe: An Inquiry," *Social Research* 55 (Spring–Summer 1988), 214–22.

[19] Renate Mayntz, "Legitimacy and the Directive Capacity of the Political System," in Leo N. Lindberg et al., eds., *Stress and Contradiction in Modern Capitalism* (Lexington, Mass.: Lexington Books, 1975), 261–74.

[20] Weber's tripartite typology of normative claims to rule does not address the issue of who—the people or the rulers—confirms the claim. We thus tend to overlook this very basic distinction.

[21] Marcus (fn. 18), 82.

quences follow. (1) Those subjects who fail to recognize the rulers' right
to rule are not thereby impugning the rulers; rather, they are impugning
themselves. And (2) if a crisis of legitimacy eventually strikes—that is, if
the rulers lose confidence in their right to rule—it becomes very difficult
to stop the crisis. A "virtuous" regime can live without popular support;
it can hardly live when it no longer believes in its own virtue.[22] For at
that point it loses the courage to rule against popular sentiments, by secret and devious means, if that is what is necessary.

The centrality assigned by communist regimes to legitimation from
the top is more than simply distrusting and legally dispossessing civil
society; that has been common to authoritarian regimes in the West as
well. The need to believe in one's right to rule, however, has not been as
central to these regimes as it has been to communism. The emphasis on
legitimation from the top is uniquely axiomatic in the case of communist
regimes. Communism, I wrote in a paper comparing regime transitions
in the West and East,

> is not a temporary care-taking affair, a *régime d'exception* with a limited
> self-imposed mandate to place a disrupted or disrupting democratic house
> in order, as many authoritarian regimes like to present/disguise/justify
> themselves. Communism's original ambition is to offer a permanent social
> and political alternative, not just domestic but above all global, to liberal
> democracy.[23]

The ambition was not immediately fulfilled by either the Russian Revolution or the regional system of communist states that arose after World
War II. Rather, with the birth of that system, ambitions and goals remained prospective, and the question of justification became ever more
central. The actual practices and accomplishments of one and then a
number of *long-existing* communist states had to be measured against
those goals.

Compared with the more mundane and contingent tasks of Western
authoritarian regimes, aimed at most at "catching up" with advanced
countries not at subverting their international order,[24] the goals of international communism required a singular unity of purpose, as well as
unshakable coordination both within and between communist states.
Above all, they required (and were nurtured by) an ideology that could
interpret reality and indeed guide and reorder it in its own image: reinvent it, even, if facts proved stubborn. It was therefore not sufficient to
silence civil society and keep it at bay. Rather, as a source of otherwise

[22] Of course, some nondemocratic regimes can still live without either virtue or support.
[23] Di Palma (fn. 6), 8.
[24] Janos (fn. 15, 1986), 100–102.

alternative perspectives on reality—usually divisive and "egotistical"—society had to be recruited to the truth. Put otherwise, the very concept of civil society as a critical agent was not simply cumbersome but more precisely extraneous to the communist vision.

Thus, from the beginning four features mark communist legitimation from the top:

1. Legitimation of rule in the light of goals implies legitimation of communist bureaucracies—in the light of tasks that are often military-like in conception, not in the light of procedures. Tasks and "campaigns" (to conquer new heights or stamp out evils) replace legal frames as the language of the state. The very notion of law becomes coterminous with the notion, typical of early modern absolutism, of instrumental administrative measures.[25] Weber's notion that legitimation concerns command (*Herrschaft*) is quite relevant in this context.[26]

2. Not unlike the absolutist prince, Soviet-like bureaucracies (the Party in particular) lay claim to command because their tasks are guided by a superior truth. They claim a monopoly on political discourse. Thus, their truth cannot be falsified by reality, their commands are always correct, and their tasks can never fail by their own shortcomings. Strictly speaking, then, poor results do not reflect on the goals. Karl Deutsch defined power as "the priority of output over intake, the ability to talk instead of listen[,] . . . the ability to afford not to learn."[27] Communist power was like that. It declared cognitive infallibility.

3. Authentication of the truth does not need the people. On the contrary, the truth enjoins the people to learn and disseminate it, to bear witness to it. Passivity, let alone resistance, will not do. Mihajlo Mihajlov speaks in this regard of "active unfreedom" in which the individual "is forced actively to support his slavery"[28] by participating in communist mobilization. This perspective explains Walter Ulbricht's emotional reproach of the East German workers after the Berlin revolt of 1953: by rebelling, the working class had proved itself undeserving of the Party's confidence.[29]

4. When legitimation comes from the top, the decisive operative relationship is not that between rulers and people, but that between rulers and Weber's administrative staff—in communist parlance, the *cadres*.[30] After all, the primary test concerns the passage from the given goals to the tasks that must be devised and carried out. When chiliasm becomes embodied in the state, cohesion among power holders, rooted in unimpeachable doctrine, becomes essential for endurance. Western authoritarian states may

[25] Krygier (fn. 5).
[26] T. H. Rigby, "Introduction: Political Legitimacy, Weber, and Communist Mono-organisational Systems," in Rigby and Fehér (fn. 18), 14.
[27] Deutsch (fn. 3), 111.
[28] Mihajlov, Letter to the Editor, *Commentary*, February 1986, p. 4.
[29] Brecht retorted in an unpublished dirge that the Communist Party might just as well dissolve the people and elect itself a new one; cited in Timothy Garton Ash, "East Germany: The Solution," *New York Review of Books*, April 26, 1990, p. 14.
[30] Rigby (fn. 26), 15.

base their tenure on alliances of convenience among potentially fissiparous institutions and social formations. Communism may not.

These four features constitute a sort of genetic code of communism's self-identity. Through the years, communism has adapted. It has undergone devolution and philistinization. Still, that original identity founded on the orthodoxy of communism's genetic superiority has been hard to shake. Paradoxically, this blind tenacity is an important factor in communism's move from cognitive self-assurance to cognitive defeat.[31]

The communist mandate to rule has had to face three challenges. The first is old: it came from inside the system of rule, which proved not as cohesive as millennial goals require. The second is more recent and came from society, which has shown itself not as subordinate as demanded. The third and last challenge is enduring, mounting, and global: the enemy of the promised global order proved unwilling to be defeated after all. Each challenge reflects different facets of a reality that did not oblige communist pretensions, and each conspired to undermine communist self-identity. But only the last one, by converging with the other two, has proved decisive. Until that convergence, and through its period of normalization, communism has remained stubborn in its denial of reality.

COMMUNIST NORMALIZATION

Trotsky, Stalin, Hitler, Mao, and Pol Pot each understood the dangers that postrevolutionary normalization poses to totalitarian goals. Each supplied an antidote: Trotsky preached global revolution; Stalin instituted massive purges;[32] Hitler prepared and executed a war of aggression; Mao called for a cultural revolution; Pol Pot systematically exterminated his own people. Be it clear that the pressure for normalization came not from a resilient civil society whose voice had to be accommodated nor from the modernizing challenge of global antagonists. To be sure, post-Stalinist normalization occurred in a global context marked by two novelties. The first was nuclear war—not the type of war fit to revive sagging revolutionary fervor. The second was the accelerating technological and economic superiority of the West. Both compelled communism to give a new military-ideological emphasis to "catching up" motives. However, it would be incorrect to see the international context as the most significant factor in setting the parameters and deter-

[31] Vujacic (fn. 4).
[32] The "patriotic war" against Nazism was also an antidote. Interestingly, however, the use of the war to legitimize Stalinist rule introduced new elements of legitimation from the bottom.

mining the manifestations of normalization. Rather, the determining factors were the shifting power relations within the frozen logic of the totalitarian system.

Revolutionary cohesion between leaders and administrative cadres—the cornerstone of legitimation from the top—is difficult to achieve and maintain. Instead, conflict is nearly unavoidable between leaders committed to revolutionary purity and a Thermidorean staff increasingly preoccupied with mundane tasks. Normalization, as Weber describes it, is one likely outcome of this internecine conflict. And ironically, leaders and cadres tend to develop a less conflictive and more reciprocal relation precisely in times of normalization. But as with the transition from arbitrary dynastic absolutism to bureaucratic absolutism,[33] reciprocity entails the triumph of the cadres and their tenured institutional orthodoxy. It does not entail a convergence with Western, be it even authoritarian, models of development—and of legitimation.

Normalization did not entail the transformation of communist states into developmental dictatorships. For all their emphasis on catching up, and for all their efforts to loosen the Russian straitjacket and turn their attention to redressing their own domestic retardation,[34] East European regimes still thought in terms of overtaking and replacing the Western model. In turn, this reaffirmation of global and collective goals demanded an equal reaffirmation of the genetic superiority and distinctive identity of communism. And in the case of communist satellites, it demanded in addition a concerted effort to eradicate, deny, or falsify, as necessary, national histories and referents. Much of this was artful and specious and done in bad conscience. The same inalterable communist myths persisted—even after de-Stalinization and even as the myths took on a secular tinge.[35] Further, it was not the goal of peaceful international competition with the West that set the tone of the industrial economic agenda. Rather, it was military investment and nuclear preparedness, plus a pattern of dependent cooperation between satellites and hegemon geared to Great Power military-economic concerns.

Normalization meant an end to Stalinist terror and greater predict-

[33] Hans Rosenberg, *Bureaucracy, Aristocracy and Autocracy* (Cambridge: Harvard University Press, 1958).
[34] Di Palma (fn. 6), 9.
[35] Khrushchev reasserted continuity by treating Stalin's crimes as products of the cult of personality. The leadership and cadres that replaced Khrushchev reasserted it by trying to erase the memories of those crimes and soft-pedaling de-Stalinization. According to Agnes Heller, this was necessary to give the Party a new self-legitimation by virtue of its continuity with tradition. See Heller, "Phases of Legitimation in Soviet-type Societies," in Rigby and Fehér (fn. 18), 57–58.

ability in the behavior of communist apparats,[36] but it did not mean the relativization of the Communist Party.[37] This would have been impossible without seriously scaling down communism's global objectives (which occurred only in the second part of the 1980s) and concomitantly the command economy geared to meeting those objectives. On the contrary, normalization marked the final triumph of the Party over the arbitrariness of salvationist leaders and thus the absolutization[38] of its routinized Thermidorean rule. Further, the Party sought no new legal-rational justification of its rule. The law was still conceived in instrumental terms.[39] And the legitimation of the Party was not dependent on its performance (of which in any event it remained the judge); rather, legitimation still came from the myth—perhaps philistinized, yet arrogantly asserted—of an inherent cognitive superiority. Even those in the political class who may have begun to nurture doubts (as some recurrently did in Eastern Europe) were nevertheless impelled, by external pressures but also through mechanisms of denial, to uphold the official myth.[40] Tenure, unaccountability, privilege, and reciprocity between leaders and cadres were thus the emerging features of the new *nomenklaturas*.[41] Brezhnev's call for trust in and protection of the cadres best captures the political essence of normalization.

Normalization, as seen by the citizens, did not entail liberalization, let alone democratization. Liberalization would require formal changes in institutions and procedures of a type to reopen the question of popular sovereignty: who legitimizes whom? It would require measures to reassert the rule of law, to allow a degree of electoral contestation and institutional competition for office, to strengthen representative institutions, to expand civil liberties, to make bureaucracies more open and accountable.[42] Liberalization usually creates halfway houses: bland dictatorships that liberalize to endure yet leave their sources of legitimation very much in question. But communist normalization was never intended to qualify

[36] Milan Simecka, *Le rétablissement de l'ordre* (Paris: Maspero, 1979).

[37] Aleksander Smolar, "Le monde soviétique: transformation ou décadence?" in Hermet (fn. 10), 162–65.

[38] Kenneth Jowitt, "Gorbachev: Bolshevik or Menshevik?" in Stephen White et al., eds., *Developments in Soviet Politics* (Durham, N.C.: Duke University Press, 1990).

[39] Krygier (fn. 5).

[40] By comparison, the issue of self-identity and therefore the trauma of defection are not as strongly felt among authoritarian regimes in the West. The difference has consequences for the way communist and Western dictatorships deal with their crises. See Di Palma, *To Craft Democracies: An Essay on Democratic Transitions* (Berkeley: University of California Press, 1990), chaps. 8, 9.

[41] Jowitt (fn. 17).

[42] Valerie Bunce, "The Transition from State Socialism to Liberal Democracy" (Unpublished manuscript, Northwestern University, October 1988).

legitimation and sovereignty. It was designed to give a new and more solid foundation to Communist parties, which Stalinism's charismatic élan had kept off balance. If normalization demanded a new and more stable relationship with the citizens, it demanded reciprocity (or what Fehér calls *paternalism*), not liberalization.[43]

The limits of paternalism, as Fehér describes them, are clear. In exchange for a halt to the nightmares of the past and for a more predictable and tolerable life, the citizen had to proffer political obedience. In the eyes of communist regimes, then, protection was bought at the price of civil and political rights.[44] Without liberalization, without the most basic rule of law, citizens were granted no more than the opportunity to petition for preferment. They were "promoted" to the status of wards of an all-powerful, presumably benevolent overseer who remained the ultimate judge of his own motives and discretionary actions. Further, because a ward is a minor, the state tended to determine the narrow range of life choices—in work, consumption, and amenities—to which people were entitled.

For all its self-confidence, however, normalization brought with it problems, stresses in the new armor of communist legitimation. Both paternalism and catching up with the West introduced a subsidiary criterion of legitimation: the promise of material performance, that is, of demonstrable change. To be sure, communist *nomenklaturas* continued publicly to claim cognitive infallibility. But the more general abandonment of salvationist language and the adoption of more mundane middle-range goals opened the way for more articulate citizens to verify whether those goals had been met. That those goals were nowhere achieved soon became plain enough.

Indeed, normalization overlapped decisively with the exhaustion of one propulsive phase of communist military-economic development: a phase of successful, intensive, and narrowly conceived "assembly line" industrialization. Subsequent economic advancement demanded more complex technological know-how and the voluntary cooperation of more

[43] Ferenc Fehér, "Paternalism as a Mode of Legitimation in Soviet-type Societies," in Rigby and Fehér (fn. 18), 64–81.

[44] In connection with this exchange, as well as to clarify the concept of civil society, Grzegorz Ekiert introduces a useful distinction between "domestic" and "political" society. Domestic society "represents the domain of purposeful action restricted to the private sphere and organized in terms of material needs and self-interests." (See Ekiert, "Democratization Processes in East Central Europe: A Theoretical Reconsideration," *British Journal of Political Science* 21 [July 1991], 285–314, at 300.) It is the domain that is offered protection under communist normalization. Political society refers to a critical and politically relevant public sphere. It is the domain to be sacrificed in the exchange. But the distinction is heuristic. I will argue later on that, despite regime expectations, the survival of domestic society may have beneficial implications for civil society proper (political society, if you wish).

highly educated professionals. Yet achieving this level of cooperation proved elusive, given communist unwillingness to undertake more daring, even politically threatening reforms beyond normalization. Thus, precisely as the public was becoming more critical, it became more difficult to justify, let alone deny, mounting failure. Gianfranco Poggi effectively captures the emerging difficulty of communist states to mold popular sentiments:

> While [the Soviet-type state] is committed to economic success, it is doomed to economic failure, at any rate insofar as its economic performance is measured against that of advanced capitalist economies. . . . The seriousness of the contradiction becomes apparent once one reflects that the above clause "insofar as" does not provide a let-out. For three reasons the Soviet state cannot but compare itself to the leading capitalist economies: because of the fateful connection between industrial-technological capacity and military preparedness; because a society projecting itself (as Soviet society does) as the model for universal social development must at the very least hold its own in terms of economic performance; and because for too long now the Soviet state has sold itself to its citizenry by promising to catch up with and overtake the standard of living of advanced capitalist countries. (The ambiguity of the expression "for too long" is intentional, for it points up a further contradiction. I mean by it both that the promise has been made for too long *to be believed* by those to whom it is made; and that it has been made for too long *to be surrendered* by those who make it.)[45]

None of this means that communist normalization after Stalin faced any immediate threat from the people. The antagonism between the two principles of legitimation—one from the top and elitist, the other based on material performance and therefore open to popular scrutiny—was simply dealt with by repressing dissent in the name of the first, preemptive principle. This applies to the Eastern satellites no less than to the Soviet Union. True, the claims of the former to legitimacy from the top were on shakier grounds: first, communism had been imposed largely from outside; second, appeals to auxiliary, country-specific sources of legitimation, based on nationalism or on local achievements and traditions, were either mostly sham or difficult to smuggle past Soviet doctrine of limited sovereignty. Still, as long as Soviet tutelage remained a fact, Eastern regimes continued to cling bleakly to the fiction of communist legitimation and, shielded by supervised fiction, to respond to dissent with resented repression.

[45] Gianfranco Poggi, *The State: Its Nature, Development and Prospects* (Stanford, Calif.: Stanford University Press, 1990), 168–69.

Given these features of communist normalization and legitimation, how did civil society fare?

CIVIL SOCIETY UNDER COMMUNISM

Civil society has turned out to be the surprising protagonist of the East European transitions—surprising for two reasons.[46] First, recent transitions from Western dictatorships show civil society most often taking a secondary role in the process of democratization, which has originated instead within the dictatorship itself. Second, since the notion of a civil society is fundamentally antagonistic to communist doctrine, communism, unlike Western authoritarianism, should supposedly leave no space for civil society.

Yet already for many years East European social scientists, most of them dissidents, have paid much attention to the fate of civil society during the period of normalization. They distinguish between the stated aims of totalitarianism and totalitarian achievements; that is, totalitarianism as an ideal type should not be confused with its various real-life approximations. Nor is totalitarianism, a strictly political construct, capable of predicting how *social* processes will react to *political* practices— that is more of an empirical matter.[47]

Many East European analysts[48] argue that communism's claim to a monopoly of public discourse, with cognitive remotion of increasingly degraded realities, has been one of its main weapons against civil society; but it is also the spark that ignited both societal resistance and then cathartic rebounding when the crisis of communism exploded. Emerging civil society under communism is thus similar to emerging civil society under absolutism: it is an antagonistic response with the potential to reshape power relations. Under democracy, civil society is an integral part of the system of rule. Under communism, the legal-political prerequisites for such a symbiosis are absent by definition. Similarly to absolutism, the impetus for civil society to emerge is a reaction to the *arcana imperii* of the rulers.

Economic independence (the independence of a bourgeois society) is not strictly necessary for resistance, except as viewed from a narrow

---

[46] See a more extensive treatment in Di Palma (fn. 6), 17–19.

[47] Vujacic (fn. 4), 24–25.

[48] Many of these analysts are discussed in Vujacic (fn. 4); I am much indebted to his insights in this section. On political discourse, cognitive monopoly, logocracy, and similar expressions of communist appropriation of the area within which public opinion normally operates, see several of the contributions in Hermet (fn. 10), as well as those in the double issue of *Social Research* 55 (Spring–Summer 1988).

Marxist perspective, and it was not necessary to the intellectual critics of absolutism.[49] This section argues, finally, that an exclusively domestic perspective cannot fully account either for the survival of East European societies under communism or for the nature of their civic demands and aspirations. The role of Western Europe as a *reference society*—to use Reinhard Bendix's terminology—is essential in this regard, more so even than in the instances of intellectual mobilization against dictatorships that grew on Western soil.

THE WEAKNESSES OF CIVIL SOCIETY

Because the objective of this section is to understand intellectual mobilization against communism, special attention must be paid to the way East Europeans perceived their predicament under communism. I have mentioned two weaknesses of civil society during normalization: the Party's cognitive monopoly of public discourse and the people's cooperation with the system of paternalism. These are weaknesses perceived by East Europeans themselves.

Every dictatorship tries to control the information that its society receives in regard to itself and to politics, present and past. Every dictatorship tries to emasculate society, so that it cannot operate as an independent source of such information. Most contemporary dictatorships do it out of situational convenience, usually by appeal to exceptional circumstances. Some also invoke the normative need for a more orderly balance between state and society. Only communism (like Nazism and Fascism in the past) claims outright cognitive monopoly as the trustee of a superior truth.

Communist truth acquired a secular edge, however, as communism moved from Stalinism to normalization, from salvationism to a socioscientific race with the West, and from massive extermination to select gulags and psychiatric wards. Nonetheless, precisely the shift from the "heat" of exterminations and purges/autos-da-fé to the "cool" of psychiatric testing suggests an attempt to codify cognitive control, not a wish to discard it. Similarly, changes in the types of victims suggest increasing outward compliance under normalization. During Stalinism the victims

---

[49] If economic independence were necessary, civil society would be possible in most Western dictatorships but impossible in communist states. On normatively driven Marxist equivocations concerning the early modern capitalist origins of civil society, see Alvin W. Gouldner, *The Two Marxisms* (New York: Oxford University Press, 1982), 355–63. Andrew Arato suggests three potential agencies for the constitution of civil society: the capitalist logic of industrialization, the etatist logic of modernization, and a public sphere from below. He examines the third possibility in connection with Poland. See Arato, "Civil Society against the State: Poland 1980–81," *Telos* 47 (Spring 1981), 23–47.

were "objective" class or party enemies: kulaks, entire nationalities, deviant party cadres. After Stalinism they were "subjective" and scattered intellectual dissidents. Aleksandr Zinoviev goes so far as to argue that during normalization communism produced a "totalitarianism from the bottom," in which dissidence and gulag no longer serve any purpose.[50] The former is manipulable; the latter is in fact unnecessary.

Few East European social scientists were as extreme as Zinoviev in their judgments. But no dissident failed to see the stifling effects that communist appropriation of political discourse exercised on dissidence—even where, as in East-Central Europe, dissidence was stronger. The distinction between truth and lie is obliterated, and only rulers, as trustees of secular history (or divine will), know which is which. As Norberto Bobbio points out, in a democracy a political lie is always observably such.[51] Democracy is public, that is, visible, government. But an absolute ruler who holds a received truth has no obligation to make his actions public. They are automatically correct. Leszek Kolakowski speaks of communism as follows:

> If . . . there is absolutely no way anybody can establish what is "true" in the normal sense of the word, nothing remains but the generally imposed beliefs, which, of course, can be again cancelled the next day. There is no applicable criterion of truth except for what is proclaimed true at any given moment. And so, the lie really becomes truth, or at least, the distinction between true and false in their usual meaning has disappeared. This is the great cognitive triumph of totalitarianism: it cannot be accused of lying any longer since it has succeeded in abrogating the very idea of truth.[52]

In turn, semantic prevarication stifles dissent by creating what Jadwiga Staniszkis, writing about Poland, calls "semantic incompetence" among regime opponents.[53] One might reject the rulers' definition of reality yet still be incapacitated. Poggi's statement is suggestive of Brezhnevite normalization: very few if any could possibly believe in its reality any more. Nevertheless, the semantic prevarication—what dissidents came to call the institutionalized or existential lie—could still spread cognitive confusion and self-doubt.

This takes us to the second source of weakness in civil society, which, as Václav Havel has argued, stemmed from the plain fact of having to

[50] Zinoviev, *Le communisme comme réalité* (Paris: l'Age d'homme, 1981); idem, *Homo sovieticus* (Paris: Julliard, 1983).

[51] Bobbio, "Democrazia e governo invisibile," *Rivista italiana di scienza politica* 10 (August 1980), 181–203.

[52] Kolakowski, "Totalitarianism and the Virtue of the Lie," in Howe (fn. 12), 122–35.

[53] Staniszkis, *Poland's Self-Limiting Revolution* (Princeton: Princeton University Press, 1984).

live within the institutionalized lie: people were driven to act as the system expected. Thus by cooperating with the system, people confirmed it. But the "reward" for political obedience—the paternalism described by Fehér—carried a more precise debasing effect. Not only did it turn people into wards of the state but also,

> together with individual initiative, competition and efficiency are likewise eliminated from work in "real socialism." The result . . . is a system of general incompetence and with it another advantage of paternalism: the absence of frustration caused by lack of skills. . . . [S]uch an "escape from frustration" into a world of collective irresponsibility and incompetence is one of the main comforts of unfreedom.[54]

People seemed to become apathetic about collective aspirations. For one thing, they were forced to invest an inordinate amount of their time in the business of daily survival. A productive system that, having lost its original impetus, fosters incompetence, irresponsibility, and shoddy work also tolerates impoverished consumer markets in which goods and services are scarce and inferior. Therefore:

> in the continuous struggle to have access to that impoverished market, and more in general in the struggle to organize one's life around it, people in communist societies were literally being robbed of an essential life resource: time. Time which they could have devoted to less demeaning and more attractive personal or public concerns.[55]

Given these life constraints, could civil society during normalization do otherwise? Could there be a "second society," as Elemér Hankiss calls it, uncompromised by the regime and offering a clear alternative, both organizational and ideal, to communist society?[56] Could such a society define a sphere that regimes could not touch, contaminate, or constrain? On the basis of the evidence and argument advanced so far, the answer should be negative. Most of those who inhabited the second society also inhabited the first; what existed therefore was largely a hybrid, unfinished parallel society.[57] In some of its manifestations, this society, far from being antagonistic to the regime, was actually drawn into a relation

[54] Fehér (fn. 43), 76.

[55] Di Palma (fn. 6), 26. That select *nomenklaturas* had exclusive access to a better and more plentiful market negated communist egalitarianism where it ultimately matters most: on life chances. See Victor Magagna, "Consumers of Privilege: A Political Analysis of Class, Consumption and Socialism," *Polity* 21 (Spring–Summer 1989), 30–41.

[56] Hankiss, "The 'Second' Society: Is There an Alternative Social Model Emerging in Contemporary Hungary?" *Social Research* 55 (Spring–Summer 1988), 13–42. See also idem, *East European Alternatives: Are There Any?* (Budapest: Institute of Social Sciences, 1988); and idem, "In Search of a Paradigm," *Daedalus* 119 (Winter 1990), 183–214.

[57] Benda (fn. 18) speaks of a parallel polis. Theoretically, parallel courses, in Benda's perspective, can eventually meet.

of semiloyalty. This was the case of the so-called second economy, which late communist regimes, faced with the emerging dysfunctions of their social model, encouraged; the regimes benefited from its nepotism, bribery, and administrative markets. As to the other manifestations of the second society—those that pertain more directly to the spheres of culture, community, and politics—we have already seen how dissent was undermined by the cognitive arrogance of the system. Add to this the reality of a life of penury.

THE STRENGTHS OF CIVIL SOCIETY

Was the glass totally empty? According to Hankiss's criteria, one would have to conclude, for instance, that there was no genuine second society in prerevolutionary France. The equivalent of a second economy—the prospective bourgeois economy—was hopelessly mired in the wasteful political economy of French absolutism: partially mercantilistic, partially appropriated by venal placemen and officeholders. And yes, intellectual dissidents often spoke against divinely ordained rule and caste privileges—but from the salons of the nobility. Yet these ambiguities did not prevent intellectuals from mobilizing against the regime. They drew sustenance from two sources: domestic bankruptcy, both moral and material, and the example of more dynamic and more open foreign societies (England and its American colonies). Some of the same open-ended ambiguity surrounded civil society under communism.

Communist monopoly of public discourse weakened civil society. But, as indicated above, it was also the motive force around which intellectual dissent was mobilized: the complete negation of reality is something attainable only in the ideal. It requires the extreme forms of totalitarian terror, permanent and subordinate mobilization, and disintegration of community, to which exceptional revolutionary leaders have unfettered recourse during "heroic" times. When revolutionary times gave way to normalization, reality—a reality more radically at variance with official doctrine—was more difficult to hide. And that dissonance was uniquely objectionable. Thus, the reassertion of reality and the recovery of community imbued dissent from communism with a moral justification and an impetus beyond that of most other movements against dictatorship. For the discrepancy between communist doctrine and reality showed that the responsibility for the degradation of reality stemmed from communism's refusal to learn. Communism was not the expression of degraded societies but the other way around.

A contrast with Western capitalist authoritarianism is instructive. Oftentimes, opponents of Western authoritarianism perceived their regimes as reflections of society, manifestations of ingrained class injustices and inequalities, images of historical backwardness. Rather than perverting society, regimes revealed it. This explains some differences in the targets of dissent. In the case of authoritarian regimes, the targets were not only the regimes but also society itself, in its older, historically unjust, typically capitalist manifestations. Also targeted were the semiliberal, latently autocratic regimes, which preceded authoritarianism and were held responsible for its advent. Further, opponents often divided on how to deal with the past.

Since communism broke with the past, there were no such complex political targets to divide dissenters. Their object—simpler, more immediate, and a source of greater cohesiveness and moral endurance— was to reappropriate society, to recover community, to sever those bonds with communism that were *now* corrupting society. This explains why in Eastern Europe one speaks of dissent, whereas in the case of authoritarian regimes one more often speaks generically of opposition. It also explains why dissent in Eastern Europe often described itself as nonpolitical. And it explains the singularity of purpose with which, also in anticipation of a long cohabitation under normalization, dissent aimed at creating a parallel (as Václav Benda would call it) public sphere. There was no such determined effort, and perhaps no such need for it, in the case of opposition to Western authoritarianism. Finally, the object of reappropriating society explains why dissent in Eastern Europe refused to live in secret—which, as Adam Michnik puts it, would have conceded the denial of society so desired by communism.

The distinctiveness and moral drive of East European dissidence was inspired in part by the model of Western Europe, which had a twofold role in destabilizing its communist neighbors. Here too, matters are subtly but significantly different from the case of oppositions to Western authoritarianism. First, as a model of socioeconomic development and a partner in the NATO alliance, Western Europe represented a successful alternative order.[58] In this regard, the role of Western Europe was not to cajole and attract—as it had been with authoritarian Southern Europe. Rather, it was to confront communist leaders with the emptiness of their global pursuits. Second, to the dissidents of Eastern Europe, Western Europe represented the antithesis of entropic autocracy: it was the cradle of civil society, of citizenship, and of polities legitimized by a transparent public discourse. In *this* regard, then, the West has served to bring Eastern societies back into the fold, to sustain intellectual mobilization dur-

[58] Di Palma (fn. 6), 15–17.

ing the doldrums of normalization. Paradoxically, the role played by the West was enhanced by the fact that the advent of communism made a tabula rasa of the political past. Therefore, there was very little room for divisive reinterpretations of the prerevolutionary period to dull the spirit of dissidence. Also, whether workers or intellectuals, most dissidents had not been associated with that past.[59] Even if they had been, postwar Stalinism marked a watershed in their personal political histories. And if they themselves had been communists, conversion tended to give their dissidence a sharper edge.

It may still be argued that dissidence, for all its moral drive, could not prevail as a parallel society in the climate of social irresponsibility, professional incompetence, and personal apathy fostered by the system of paternalism.

But were apathy and irresponsibility all there was? Were they the only mechanisms of survival? Mira Marody's discussion of empirical research on "public" and "private" attitudes and values in Poland paints a more shaded picture.[60] Such attitudes as the need for security in life, unwillingness to make independent choices, resentment of differentials in life opportunities, acceptance of professional mediocrity—hence, the seeming defense of the status quo—were situationally induced. They were rational public responses to debased government expectations and social opportunities. To offset them, there existed a parallel private sphere of aspirations *and* behavior in which the opposite values dominated.

Other research on Poland, reported by Lena Kolarska-Bobinska, underlines the situational character of publicly held social values and thus the possibility that they would be discarded were the political situation to change radically.[61] Support for equality of benefits and job security, argues the author, did not reflect an ingrained preference for the communist social order but the operation of a protective mechanism. In a system where the criteria by which work is rewarded are hidden, capricious, tied to political status and privilege, and institutionally unrelated to professional worth or to recognizable economic parameters, individual demand for equal benefits may be understood as latent protest. Equality

---

[59] In some cases, as in Poland, preciously few intellectuals and professionals survived the Nazi occupation. See M. M. Kovacs and A. Orkeny, "Promoted Cadres and Professionals in Post-War Hungary," in R. Andorka and L. Bertalan, eds., *Economy and Society in Hungary* (Budapest: Hungarian Sociological Association, 1986), 139–53; A. Gella, *Development of Class Structure in Eastern Europe: Poland and Her Southern Neighbors* (Albany: State University of New York Press, 1989), 167–202. Both are cited in Ekiert (fn. 44), fn. 55.

[60] Marody, "Antinomies of Collective Subconsciousness," *Social Research* 55 (Spring–Summer 1988), 97–110.

[61] Kolarska-Bobinska, "Social Interests, Egalitarian Attitudes, and the Change of Economic Order," *Social Research* 55 (Spring–Summer 1988), 111–38.

of benefits was advocated because equality of opportunity was not an option. It therefore should come as no surprise that, when engaged in a second economy, people adhered to norms that were at variance with those of apathy, mediocrity, and dependency. It was a way of sharpening their skills at the "art of survival."

I have spoken before of individuals budgeting inordinate amounts of their private time to survive in an impoverished market. But, far from driving a wedge between them, the art of survival often brings them together. As Steven Sampson describes it: "In Eastern Europe, highly valued and needed resources are constantly in scarce supply, due either to economic mismanagement or political expediency. This makes informal channels and social networks absolutely *vital* for the day to day existence of virtually *all* Eastern Europeans."[62] The spillover of even this lowest and most mundane level of association should not be underestimated. Western authoritarianism is largely "class conscious"; its victims of material deprivation are usually the poorer sorts. But impoverished communist markets treated everybody—with the exception of a pampered and highly select *nomenklatura*—with equal shabbiness. Sampson's emphasis on the commonality of both plight and response is well taken. The most articulate strata of society, the main activators of spillover effects, were no less affected than everybody else.

As they pooled their ingenuity in the art of material survival, the informal but also socially homogeneous and more resourceful microgroups that emerged assumed other functions. They became a potential source for various forms of dissent—more or less latent, more or less political. To begin with, the withdrawal into a circle of family and friends should not be taken as evidence of an atomized society that left a social vacuum which inadvertently fulfilled communist wishes. Withdrawal, or better the ability to withdraw,

> is actually a conscious reaction of society in defense of its acquisitions. . . . It is a means of defense that allows the preservation of a given society's social culture, be it only in customs, conversation, mentality, personality and character traits, when that becomes impossible in public and institutional life.[63]

[62] Sampson, "The Informal Sector in Eastern Europe," *Telos* 66 (Winter 1985–86), 44–66, at 50. For an experiential account of survival through the second market, see Martin Krygier, "Poland: Life in an Abnormal Country," *National Interest* 18 (Winter 1989–90), 55–64.

[63] Kazimierz Vojcicki, "The Reconstruction of Society," *Telos* 47 (Spring 1981), 98–104, at 102–3. See also fn. 44. The ability to forge a private and alternative microcosm was greater in Eastern Europe, where communism had been imposed from the outside. Still, this is not to say that in the Soviet Union there were no motives for articulating resentment and no groups to articulate it. Speaking of day-to-day reality in the Soviet Union under Brezhnev, Kenneth Jowitt writes that "for those members of Soviet society who were more educated,

Microgroups were also the natural habitat of horizontal[64] and oblique[65] voice. The phenomenon refers to the development of semantically coded critical communication, especially among those articulate strata that are more sensitive to the indignities of the system. To the category of coded communication belong political jokes, innuendo, emphases and mannerisms of language, and choice of topics that encode one's own political preferences. Voices are horizontal because they offer an alternative to "vertical voice," that is, to the communication of petition and command that dictatorships prefer. They are oblique because they are coded. Coding, though, is more than just a way of hiding from the authorities. Particularly in Eastern Europe, the aspiration to reject the system's opacity, to be public and transparent, was powerful. Coding created an emotional and cognitive bond among opponents of the regime, who came to recognize that they were not alone.[66]

Thus we come to one expression of dissidence that was unique to communism: samizdat, the phenomenon of widely circulated clandestine publications.[67] Three of its features are noteworthy. First, the publications—typically, personal political and parapolitical testimonials—were authored, reproduced, and circulated through self-generated, improvised networks, in which the authors and the disseminators at each step were often single individuals. Second, this meant that in certain cases, though the publications were illegal and alternative, they were not strictly clandestine. Full clandestinity would have defeated the testimonial function. Third, the individual nature of samizdat also meant that organizational infrastructures to sustain publication were, strictly speaking, not necessary. Instead, where infrastructures did not already exist, the production of samizdat was a unique additional factor that brought people together.

In sum, there was more to sustain opposition to communism than oblique voice and collective ingenuity in the art of personal survival. Per-

---

urban, skilled, *but above all* more individuated, articulate, and ethical this reality was embarrassing, alienating, and offensive; the source of increasing resentment, anger, and potentially of political rage." See Jowitt (fn. 17), 276.

[64] Albert O. Hirschman, *Exit, Voice, and Loyalty* (Cambridge: Harvard University Press, 1970).

[65] Guillermo O'Donnell, "On the Fruitful Convergence of Hirschman's *Exit, Voice, and Loyalty* and *Shifting Involvements:* Reflections from the Recent Argentinean Experience," in Alejandro Foxley et al., eds., *Development, Democracy and the Art of Trespassing: Essays in Honor of Albert O. Hirschman* (Notre Dame, Ind.: Notre Dame University Press, 1986), 249–68.

[66] Ibid., 261.

[67] For an extensive treatment linking samizdat with the issue of civil society, see H. Gordon Skilling, *Samizdat and an Independent Society in Central and Eastern Europe* (Columbus: Ohio University Press, 1989).

haps fostered by the experience of samizdat, illegal and alternative organizations also grew. To what avail? To some. Perhaps their main strength in the long run—a feature revealed after the fact—was precisely that their intent was not at all to conspire in the way that underground parties and movements conspire against more labile, authoritarian regimes. Rather, they sought to build, slowly and by the power of example, a parallel society. Participation in alternative organizations therefore had immediate advantages. Members and supporters developed modes of contestation that were less conspiratorial and power seeking and that were instead more appropriate to alternative, at times single-issue, movements in pluralist societies. Examples include challenging the official counterparts of unofficial organizations; collecting information on, reporting, and denouncing government activities and misdeeds; demanding redress of grievances; holding the authorities accountable; proposing alternative policies; negotiating with the authorities, if it came to that.[68] In turn, this unselfish mode of contestation, contrasting as it did with the reclusive and offensive opacity of *nomenklaturas*, gave organized dissent a popular credibility not dissimilar from that enjoyed by the more heroic examples of individual dissent.

A Short Balance Sheet

The above discussion should attune us to the ability of civil society in communist Eastern Europe to make inventive use of necessarily unusual, exceptional, and extralegal opportunities. By the same token, it invites some amendments to the role of factors that typically nourish civil society.

First, it may be factually correct that communism did not allow either the type of independent economic activities that capitalism encourages or the type of limited pluralism, rooted in the traditional socioeconomic and institutional structure of a country, that Western authoritarian regimes tolerate. But the thrust of the argument here has been that intellectual mobilization against communism did not need such nourishment. In fact, opposition to authoritarian systems that allow a limited pluralism lacks some of the drive and broad appeal that dissent from communism has enjoyed.

Second, it is also correct, indeed self-evident, that, for all its efforts to act as the critical conscience of communism, dissent lacked tested insti-

---

[68] For an extensive and insightful treatment of the latent functions of autonomous groups in Eastern Europe at both the micro- and macrolevel, see Christine Sadowski, "Autonomous Groups as Agents of Change in Communist and Post-communist Eastern Europe" (Unpublished manuscript, Stanford, Calif., July 1990).

tutional channels for official access to government. But the insight is beside the point. Had there been reliable access, there would have been no dictatorship. In other words, the criterion of formal access and other pluralist criteria for testing the emergence of a fully influential and autonomous civil society can only be applied after autocracy is over. Under autocracy, civil society, deprived of a formal structure of opportunities, seeks a place for itself by necessarily self-generated, unconventional means. Eighteenth-century public opinion under French and other absolutist regimes did not enjoy public channels of access to government, let alone active political citizenship. Nor did it ask for active participation. It asked, when it did, for transparency, legality, and an end to the politico-economic and cultural predominance of a sprawling and parasitic estate-like officialdom.[69] Such demands were already making inroads within absolutism before the French Revolution and without the aid of legal or official channels. They were making inroads because they helped expose a debased reality that absolutism could no longer wish away.

Something similar was happening in Poland and Hungary before the communist collapse. The single-mindedness with which dissidence openly fought the system of paternalism—thus managing to grow, in Poland, into a majority movement—is one factor in the decision of the regimes to liberalize and finally to open a dialogue. By pointing out failures, dissidence began to spread doubts within the system itself.

COMMUNIST CRISIS AND SOCIETAL REBOUNDING

Nothing said here implies that domestic resistance is sufficient to explain the sudden fall of communism. It is nonetheless a fact that East European societies rebounded with astonishing rapidity and vitality at the moment when communist normalization came to an end and communist regimes lost their will to rule—also with astonishing rapidity. To understand more fully that rebounding, its causes, and what this may portend for the future of civil society in the area, it is useful here to recapitulate the nature of the communist crisis.[70]

COMMUNIST CRISIS

The events in Eastern Europe are not the final act in a natural process of self-guided transformation that follows the global imperatives of mod-

---

[69] Gianfranco Poggi, *The Development of the Modern State* (Stanford, Calif.: Stanford University Press, 1978), 77–85.

[70] A longer treatment of the arguments in this section is found in Di Palma (fn. 6).

ernization. The crisis has not been one of converging growth, whereby communism sheds its totalitarian-salvationist carapace to join an integrated global economy dominated by capitalism. Nor is the crisis similar to that of Franco's dictatorship, which had become obsolete with respect to a society that had managed to modernize on its own. Instead, the crisis of communism has resulted from its long-standing inability to shed that carapace fully. Moscow kept its Warsaw Pact/Comecon acolytes anchored to a secularized version of salvationism in which the old global goal of replacing the West was largely defined in military-industrial, rather than market-industrial, terms. But in a strategic global order dominated by nuclear arms and in a global exchange economy dominated by more complex knowledge and production technologies, the anchoring had devastating consequences for East European societies and regimes. It isolated, impoverished, and degraded societies that enjoyed no significant spillover from narrowly conceived industrial-military policies. It caught the regimes in Moscow's finally acknowledged material and normative debacle.

So the failure of those global goals that, in Poggi's words, could not be surrendered led communist leaders to lose faith in their "mandate from heaven"—to find themselves in an identity vacuum. Being in an identity vacuum may not be ruinous (nor indeed likely) for run-of-the-mill authoritarian regimes, which may survive or not by situational expedience; but it has proved to be ruinous in Eastern Europe. Party and bureaucratic integrity and primacy, the foundation of Brezhnevite normalization, had evaporated. *Nomenklaturas* who had been hiding stubbornly behind their axiomatic claims to cognitive superiority had no choice but to face their distorted perception of reality,[71] and as failures rapidly accumulated, cognitive arrogance turned into cognitive defeat.[72]

It is no surprise that the crisis of communism has been more serious and precipitous in Eastern Europe than in the Soviet Union, even where regimes have dragged their feet. That East European communism was largely an imported product meant that legitimacy from the top was more difficult to assert, whereas popular legitimation for domestic performance, in which East European communism invested more heavily,

---

[71] In the words of Kolakowski (fn. 52):

In the functionaries' minds the borderline between what is "correct" and what is "true," as we normally understand this, seems really to have become blurred; by repeating the same absurdities time and again, they began to believe or half-believe in them themselves. The massive and profound corruption of the language eventually produced people who were incapable of perceiving their own mendacity. (p. 129)

[72] Vujacic (fn. 4).

was still not forthcoming. For this reason East European regimes had clung desperately to the double fiction of international and domestic credibility and to the hegemonic guardianship of the Soviet Union, on which that credibility perversely hung. But once the Soviet hegemon voluntarily and formally abandoned its global goals, East European countries found themselves left to their own devices. Thus, their fiction stood unabashedly and authoritatively exposed. Having been chained together by the global goals (with Romania and Albania the exceptions), the East European regimes found themselves in an identity vacuum all the more glaring and debilitating. Indeed, such was the domino effect that even Romania and Albania could not escape it.

SOCIETY REBOUNDING

Set against this background of crisis, the dramatic surge in social mobilization that occurred in the fall and winter of 1989, well surpassing mobilization in other recent dictatorial demises, looks less surprising. There are four ways of accounting for the surge.

First, the surge reflected the depth of the communist crisis. Once communist regimes lost their will and confidence—that is, once they abdicated—the gates were open to the venting of popular resentment. The reverse dynamic is also true. To be sure, the surge in mobilization was not the sufficient or main cause of abdication: everything points to a crisis that took decisive shape at the core of the system. Nevertheless, when a loss of confidence occurred at the top, the ensuing popular mobilization tended to *confirm* communist regimes in their belief that they had lost the right to rule—and hence to repress.

Second, the surge benefited from uniquely powerful diffusion effects across countries. Contagion was essential in the case of Romania, where society rebelled against a dictator who had lost no confidence in his mandate to rule and repress. The same would happen later in Albania.

Still, what motivated single individuals to mobilize? The answers above beg a good part of the question. Third, mobilization reflected individual reactions to the experience of living under dictatorship, an experience that most people in all dictatorships share to some degree. Although the recent transitions both in the West and in the East suggest that we have tended to overestimate the repressive effectiveness of dictatorships,[73] living under one nonetheless remains a thwarting experi-

[73] Guillermo O'Donnell and Philippe Schmitter treat extensively the significance of the resurrection of civil society in recent Western transitions. See O'Donnell and Schmitter, *Transitions from Authoritarian Rule: Tentative Conclusions about Uncertain Democracies* (Bal-

ence. Mobilization, then, means rebounding in reaction to that experience; in psychological terms it is the personal recovery of public dignity and space.

Elsewhere,[74] I discuss at greater length a singular similarity between the way the psychology of rebounding has been interpreted by perceptive analysts of Western dictatorships[75] and the way it has been experienced by East European dissidents. In all dictatorships, outer compliance may be accompanied by a loss of self-esteem. Compliance can be exacted through ideological and organizational enforcement but also, in more compromising fashion, through co-optation and selective incentives (for example, the corrupting incentives offered in Eastern Europe by state paternalism). In sum, the resulting long cycle of individual retreat from the public[76] is not natural and voluntary but is, rather, artificial. Therefore, when a dictatorship meets its crisis, the rebounding is inevitable, magnified, and targeted against the dictatorship. As people bear witness against the regime—which they did most dramatically in the squares of Eastern Europe—most of them strive for catharsis: by rejecting the regime, they cleanse themselves. Thus, utilitarian free riding is not a factor. Instead, individual participation, previously banned, becomes the necessary step—its own reward, even—to recover one's public self.

But peculiar to Eastern Europe is a fourth and more valuable way of understanding the surge in mobilization. Simply put, the moral and intellectual experience of living under communism is particularly stultifying and offensive and therefore particularly conducive to rebounding. Poggi captures the reasons best: by retreating to a secularized version of salvationism, communism opened itself to factual scrutiny. On the principle that the higher they climb, the harder they fall, the lie by which communism had lived was magnified, for communism's profession that it created a totally new socialist citizen-producer involved a lie incomparably bigger and more pretentious than any by which other postwar dictatorships have lived.

Further, the lie touched every aspect of the lives of its victims. I have described the debasing features of daily life under communist normalization—its effects on work, on consumption, on personal time, on life chances and choices. I have also argued that the debasement of life was

---

timore: Johns Hopkins University Press, 1986). The vast literature on civil society in Eastern Europe under communism adds new evidence to the point of survival. But Linz's extensive work had already consistently stressed the fact that dictatorships are rarely of one piece in their treatment of civil society.

[74] Di Palma (fn. 6).
[75] O'Donnell (fn. 65).
[76] Hirschman (fn. 64).

not the historical product of some inherited societal retardation against which communism was called to fight; rather, it was the eminently political product of communism itself. As normalization elevated the primacy of communist cadres to an absolute principle,[77] it became clear that the corruption of everyday life originated in the corruption and parasitism of communist parties: their abandonment of impersonal discipline and combat tasks in favor of neo-traditional concerns about status.[78] Thus, people and regimes lived by the terms of a make-believe social contract: feigned socialist work in exchange for feigned socialist rewards. The mutual lie was therefore more resonant, personally more demeaning, more difficult for people to live down, more traumatic to remove— in sum, more resented. By the same token, that made it more likely to produce the liberating outburst that it did.

A Revolution of Citizenship

The crisis of communism and the rebounding of society, then, vindicated dissent and widened its popular appeal. For dissent did not retreat; instead, it kept intellectual mobilization alive, chose transparency over conspiracy, laid bare the deadening effects of communist normalization, and made the recovery of truth its banner. And because the recovery of truth is inextricably connected with the revival of a debating public sphere and with the transparency of government, the East European revolutions may be seen as revolution in its pristine meaning of "return": an effort by East European societies to appropriate-reappropriate distinctively Western ideas and principles from which they had been severed by communism (and at times by much that preceded communism). In also representing the recovery of national identities denied by communism's "organized forgetting," these revolutions of citizenship recall as well the wave of modernizing liberal national revolutions against kingly restoration of the mid-nineteenth century.[79]

Much of this, and much in the behavior of dissent under communism,

[77] Jowitt (fn. 38).
[78] Jowitt (fn. 17).
[79] Similarities with the French Revolution hold up much less well, however. The rejection of *corps intermédiaires*, the religion of general will, the creed of revolutionary rationality, and other aspects of the French revolutionary discourse amounted to the denial of the autonomous public sphere that had been emerging before the Revolution. In this, Jacobinism anticipated communism's cognitive monopoly. But revolutionary France and the Eastern Europe of recent months existed in radically different international environments. The Jacobins denied an autonomous public sphere, in part because revolutionary France lived in a continuous state of war in order to protect itself from the great powers of Europe. East European transitions are occurring in a more hospitable setting, one able to accommodate a postcommunist intellectual mobilization committed to civil society.

explains why the organized opposition that emerged when communism collapsed tended to take the form of broadly conceived and somewhat undifferentiated civic forums. The forums were something different from those temporary alliances of civilian parties and other opposition groups that have typically operated in preparation for and then during the crises of Western authoritarian regimes. The latter targeted the regimes to remove them from power. But once democracy has been inaugurated, the various forces resume their own independent quest for a share in democratic government, which leads to arguments over the best material policies and institutional arrangements—in sum, over the instrumentalities of democratic government. The East European forums were less time-bound, less instrumental, and broader in scope, their success, therefore, perhaps not measurable by electoral criteria. Culturally, they were metademocratic movements of collective identity. They aimed at defining postcommunism by an alternative (though nonetheless traditional) set of shared civic values and at consolidating a public sphere, a critical public opinion (that is, a civil society), as the core of a transparent democratic order. Is their ambition likely to exhaust itself in the near future?

Conclusions

This essay has a retrospective focus: to assess the relation between communist regimes and societies and thereby to understand the nature of communist demise as stemming not from global growth but from enforced and insular decay. I would like to offer, as well, a necessarily brief, largely methodological reflection on the future of civil society in Eastern Europe.[80]

There is by now an abundant literature, ranging from published volumes to unpublished conference papers, that takes a bleak view of that future. The all-too familiar reasons for this pessimistic outlook range from the historical weaknesses of civil society in Eastern Europe, to the monumental conundrum of moving from command to market economies, to the social costs of the operation, and to the revival of frozen mininationalisms. Albert Hirschman has recently commented on this pessimism: "It does not seem to have occurred to these people that if the events, which are the points of departure of their speculations, were so

[80] More extensive treatments are in the original version of this essay, prepared for the conference "La rifondazione dei partiti politici nell'Europa orientale," Società italiana di scienza politica, Ferrara, Italy, October 1990; and in Di Palma, "Why Democracy Can Work in Eastern Europe," *Journal of Democracy* 2 (Winter 1991), 21–31.

hard to predict, considerable caution is surely in order when it comes to appraising their impact."[81]

Rather than being stymied by the prevailing pessimism, we should ask ourselves whether we are theoretically equipped to accommodate the novelty of the events in Eastern Europe and to extrapolate from those events in ways that incorporate their novelty. Perhaps we are not, for two reasons. First, as social scientists impelled to make sense of unfinished cycles of events, we tend to reify theory, to see each event as the unmediated fulfillment of some broader socioscientific theory. Thus, by collapsing facts and models, our hurried efforts to place impending events in perspective paradoxically cause us to be driven by events even more. Second, we tend to seize upon, and therefore to reify, those theories especially that see progress as the fulfillment of steadily evolving sociocultural and cultural-structural preconditions; in the absence of fitting preconditions we tend therefore to attribute negative effects to rapid change. Also, by stressing structural preconditions, we underplay the role of choice.

But if we live by these theories (theories of democratic development, of backwardness, of late development), it becomes difficult to take the historically unexpected at face value. The paradigmatically inclined social scientist prefers to explain away historical turning points as the foreseeable result of a steady, convergent evolution amenable to paradigmatic thinking. Yet, as Hirschman argued years ago, "Large-scale social change typically occurs as the result of a unique constellation of highly disparate events and is therefore amenable to paradigmatic thinking only in a very special sense."[82] In particular, it seems to be difficult to make sense of swift change that is surprisingly positive: where markets emerge, democratic cultures take root, and civil societies rebound. Hirschman wrote as follows about Latin America and theories of underdevelopment:

> Since the theory teaches that *in the normal course of events* things will be increasingly unsatisfactory, it is an invitation not to watch out for possibly positive developments. On the contrary, those imbued with the gloomy vision will attempt to prove year after year that Latin America is going from bad to worse. . . . [H]opeful developments either will be not perceived or will be considered exceptional and purely temporary. In these

[81] Hirschman, "Good News Is Not Bad News," *New York Review of Books*, October 11, 1990, p. 20.
[82] Hirschman, "The Search for Paradigms as a Hindrance to Understanding," *World Politics* 22 (April 1970), 329–43, at 339.

circumstances they will not be taken advantage of as elements on which to build.[83]

My simple reflection is that, for all we know, we may be witness to one of those rare moments in history described by Hirschman—a moment when a new zeitgeist is being born, when people and governments become convinced that things must and can change. H. R. Trevor-Roper calls them the "lost moments of history."[84] Moreover, the breakthrough in pursuing a new civic culture—a culture that wishes to deny the historical prophecies that stem from regional retardation and fragmentation—has been made by dissident movements. Uncharacteristic of intellectual mobilization in backward countries, the East European movements made an anti-Leninist (hence, anti-Jacobin) choice, one that entrusts progress to the proper constitution of citizens' relations to one another[85] rather than to a guiding state.

We may therefore wish to pause before embracing normal social science expectations about the impermanent legacy of social movements that surface at exceptional times in exceptionally problematic social contexts.[86]

[83] Ibid., 337–38, emphasis added.

[84] Trevor-Roper, "The Lost Moments of History," *New York Review of Books*, October 27, 1988.

[85] See fn. 79. For an extensive treatment of these and similar points about the culture of postcommunism, see Jeffrey C. Goldfarb, *Beyond Glasnost: The Post-Totalitarian Mind* (Chicago: University of Chicago Press, 1989), chaps. 4–7.

[86] For an analysis of why prevailing theories of social movements and social mobilization left us unprepared for the wave of protest mobilization in Eastern Europe, see Sidney Tarrow, " 'Aiming at a Moving Target': Social Science and the Recent Rebellions in Eastern Europe," *PS* 24 (March 1991), 12–20. Tarrow suggests that cycles of protest produce a "master theme" that links the emerging social movements. "It will be interesting to see," he writes, "whether the new movements now forming in Eastern Europe build on extensions of the themes of 1989 or—as some have feared—return to 'primordial' sentiments" (p. 15).

SOCIAL SCIENCE, COMMUNISM, AND THE DYNAMICS OF POLITICAL CHANGE

By ANDREW C. JANOS*

D URING the past two years events in the communist societies of
Europe, Asia, and even Central America followed each other at a
dramatic pace. Although it may be somewhat premature, and ultimately
inaccurate, to speak of a "transition from socialism to capitalism," not to
mention the "end of history" and the beginning of a liberal millennium,
the restoration of multiparty systems in Eastern Europe, the floundering
perestroika of the Soviet Union, and the prodemocracy movement in
China and its violent repression all indicate that communist states have
reached a critical juncture in their history. The confluence of these events
raises a number of obvious questions about both the past and the future
and more generally about the dynamics of change in the communist societies of the world. For the student of comparative politics it also raises
questions about the record of the social sciences in the field of communist
studies and about their ability to satisfy these curiosities.

This article sets out to answer some of these questions. It first reex-
amines some of the propositions of classical theory as they apply to the
history of communism, then attempts to pull together different strands
of social thought into a single, more comprehensive analytic scheme. To
the extent that this enterprise is successful, the scheme will provide us
with an opportunity to make more meaningful comparisons than heretofore, to find a better fit between theory and historical fact and, within
the limitations of social theory, a way to anticipate future developments
more accurately.

THE BEGINNINGS: FROM TOTALITARIANISM TO DERADICALIZATION

The entry of the social sciences into the field of communist studies was
slow and hesitant. Prior to 1945 the subject of communist government

* Acknowledgments by the author are due to the Institute of International Studies of the
University of California, Berkeley, for financial support; to Carl G. Rosberg, the former
director of the institute, for encouraging the project; and to Lowell Dittmer, Giuseppe Di
Palma, Julie Erfani, Russel Faeges, Andrew Gould, Clement Henry, Jeffrey Kopstein, Jason
McDonald, Carol Timko, and Aaron Wildavsky for generous, if often critical, comments on
the several drafts of this paper.

was largely shunned by social scientists and allowed to remain almost exclusively within the domains of journalism and historiography.[1] It was only after World War II that social scientists, inspired by perceived similarities between Soviet communism and German national socialism, made their first attempt to formulate explanations that transcended the somewhat narrow empiricism of the early years. The result was the model, or more accurately models, of totalitarianism: the plural being justified by the fact that underneath the uniformly applied and very popular label, there were at least three variations on the central theme. The first, enshrined in Hannah Arendt's famous volume, explained totalitarianism as an existential response to the social and psychological damage inflicted upon the individual by modern industrialism.[2] The second, derived from Karl Wittfogel's study of "hydraulic" societies, related the phenomenon to the endemic scarcities of water and, by extension, of other necessities of life.[3] A third theory, then, saw totalitarianism as the manifestation of cultural configurations—the traditions of German and Russian absolutism coming alive in the age of industrialism.[4]

Diverse as these explanations were, they shared two common themes: a highly asymmetrical and absolutistic view of political power and an epistemology that provided insights into the origins, but not into the dynamics, of political change. This formula may have been credible and intellectually appealing for dealing with the terror and highly centralized institutional arrangements of Stalinism, but it was found to be increasingly inadequate for explaining the obvious instances of political change in the Soviet Union and Eastern Europe of the post-Stalin years. A few observers of the communist scene continued to cling to the view that these changes represented only temporary deviations from the earlier totalitarian norm; but others suggested new paradigms that henceforth would serve as the foundations for the new subdiscipline of comparative communism.

Perhaps the most influential of these paradigms was the one provided by the writings of Max Weber, to which students of communism were attracted for several reasons. One of these was Weber's theory of power, which at the highest level of abstraction presents a triangular relationship

[1] See Daniel Bell, "Ten Theories in Search of Reality: The Prediction of Soviet Behavior in the Social Sciences," *World Politics* 10 (April 1958), 327–65, reprinted in Bell, *The End of Ideology: On the Exhaustion of Political Ideas in the Fifties* (New York: Collier, 1961), 315–54.
[2] Arendt, *The Origins of Totalitarianism* (New York: Harcourt-Brace, 1951).
[3] Wittfogel, *Oriental Despotism: A Comparative Study of Total Power* (New Haven: Yale University Press, 1957).
[4] See, e.g., Reinhard Bendix, *Nation-building and Citizenship* (New York: John Wiley, 1964).

of subordination and superordination among "chiefs," their "administrative staff," and the rest of the polis, or "corporate group," so defined by virtue of its ability to regulate its membership.[5] The central figure in this relationship is the chief. This feature has been particularly appealing to students of communism, for unlike class and group theories of power, it does not downplay the role of individuals but recognizes them as actors in their own right with spheres of autonomy that follow from their position. At the same time, Weber's chiefs are not like Pareto's leaders or Nietzsche's heroes, whose unlimited powers over others derive from their presumed ability to assign meanings to social phenomena, thus shaping human expectations, wants, and needs, so to say, by brainwashing. Unlike these elite theorists whose ideas inform the various totalitarian models, Weber recognizes the autonomy of human needs: leaders can rule but only if they provide benefits, be they miracles or their subjects' daily bread. Whereas both class and elite theories of power emphasize (though in different ways) the fundamental asymmetry of the relationship between chiefs and subjects, Weber's theory of power rests on the notion of reciprocity. This notion inevitably leads away from the idea that political control can be total or absolute.

Weber's concept of an "administrative staff" also helps locate the party and its auxiliaries between the two polar extremes of pre-Weberian political theory: the staff is not a ruling class in the sense of the British aristocracy prior to the mid-nineteenth century; nor is it a herd of mindless servants or agents ready to execute every command of the chief. Rather, Weber's staff is a political class. This last designation, while not Weber's, appears to be appropriate. For like other classes, members of the staff have a set of common interests that derives from their common position in the division of labor. But unlike members of economic classes, such as the bourgeoisie or the aristocracy, they are also bound to obey the commands of the chief even if these run counter to their own material interests. Thus, to use the language of sociology, the staff is integrated both horizontally and vertically. Between interest and duty, between the two forms of integration, there will be inevitable tensions that are apt to provoke various forms of subterranean bickering and to threaten subversion of commands by feigned compliance—a modus operandi that T. H. Rigby aptly describes as "crypto-politics."[6]

[5] Weber, *Economy and Society: An Outline of Interpretive Sociology*, ed. Guenther Roth and Claus Wittich (Berkeley: University of California Press, 1978), 1:214–15; or Weber, *The Theory of Social and Economic Organization*, ed. Talcott Parsons (1947; reprint, New York: Free Press, 1964), 145–46.

[6] Rigby, "Crypto-Politics," *Survey* 50 (January 1964), 183–94. For more about politics in

Students of comparative communism were also attracted by Weber's interest in charismatic salvationism, or authority based on the promise of a perfect universe, as articulated by prophetic leaders.[7] The terminology used here refers to the religious origins of the concept, but for Weber the terms had both "this worldly and other worldly" connotations.[8] So expanded, the category seemed to be directly applicable to both the theory and the practice of Marxism-Leninism. Lenin, Stalin, Mao, and even some of the lesser heroes in the communist pantheon were, after all, celebrated as geniuses of the first order with extraordinary insights into the laws of history. And Marx's *Manifesto* and *German Ideology* foresaw the movement leading ultimately to a world without scarcity or conflict and even without the boredom of functional specialization. Raised on these tenets, and sharing the boundless optimism of the nineteenth century concerning the human mastery of the environment, Lenin, Trotsky, and others easily envisaged the withering away of the state[9] or the coming of a "red paradise" in which the average worker could easily reach the creative potential of a Marx, Michelangelo, or Aristotle.[10] Moreover, this Marxist-Leninist salvationism was reflected not only in rhetoric but also in the very logic that defined the structure of authority in communist systems. It was in the name of this charismatic salvationism that communist leaders emancipated themselves from moral and legal restraints and felt free to impose immense sacrifices on their populations and to exact not only compliance with the law but also devotion to leaders and the cause. The same salvationism permitted the regimes to reject conventional probabilistic notions of organizational shortcomings and to reconceptualize them as treason or as the result of the penetration of the movement by hostile outsiders. Thus, while the scope of the purges may have been the result of personality and historical circumstance, their style and logic was inherent in organizational principle and may even be anticipated by reading Weber.

organizations, see Reinhard Bendix, *Work and Authority in Industry* (Berkeley: University of California Press, 1974), xl–xlvi.

[7] More generally, Weber distinguishes between substantive and institutional-instrumental aspects of authority. The former refer to the material versus the "higher" interests of an actor (the prototype of which is interest in one's salvation), the latter to the familiar trio of charisma, tradition, and contract. Although Weber does not say so and in general is of little help in further elaborating the relationship, these two aspects of politics may be drawn into a single scheme. Certain types of legitimacy are well suited to articulating some purposes and not others. Charisma is most appropriate for articulating salvationist purposes.

[8] Weber (fn. 5, 1978), 1:xc, 212–13; or Weber (fn. 5, 1964), 120–23, 324–25.

[9] V. I. Lenin, "The State and Revolution," in Lenin, *Selected Works* (Moscow: Progress Publishers, 1970), 2:283–376.

[10] Leon Trotsky, quoted in "Kommunismus," in C. D. Kernig, ed., *Soujetsystem und demokratische Gesellschaft* (Soviet system and democratic society) (Freiburg: Herder, 1969), 3:746.

We should note here that this idea of communism as a chiliastic-salvationist movement is not far removed from earlier concepts of totalitarianism. Indeed, some writers well within the Weberian school have identified such salvationism as the essence of totalitarianism, thereby divorcing the concept from uniquely twentieth-century structures of industrialism and modernity.[11] What distinguishes Arendt and Weber is not so much their views of the subject matter as their explanations of the underlying dynamic. If Arendt saw totalitarianism as a fundamentally irrational, existential phenomenon, Weberian theory saw it as a matter of rational choice of persons who viewed the world through a particular cognitive prism. And where Arendt saw powerful psychological drives at work to reproduce the system, Weber taught his disciples lessons about its fragility and its losing battle against the ordinary and the routine. This being the case, Weberian ideas did not really replace the earlier models of totalitarianism. Instead, via the theory of routinization, they bridged the gap between the earlier model and the new realities of the post-Stalin years.

The point of departure for Weber's theory of routinization is what might be called the revolutionary dialectic: a conflict between the higher, salvationist aspirations of a movement and the mundane but stubbornly persistent material needs of its members. These needs manifest themselves in the

> material interests of the members of the administrative staff, the disciples, the party workers, or others in continuing [to serve] in such a way that both from an ideal and material point of view their own position is put on a stable everyday basis. This means, above all, making it possible to participate in normal family relationships or at least to enjoy a secure social position in place of the kind of discipleship which is cut off from ordinary worldly connections, notably in the family and in economic relationships.[12]

This of course implies an element of "opportunism" that so vexed communist leaders like Trotsky, Stalin, and Mao and that led Milovan Djilas to formulate his theses concerning the rise of a "new class" in communist societies and the aristocratization of the party elite.[13] But Weber's theory is more complex. Whereas disciples and party workers may act out of altruism for the "continuation and continual reactivation" of

---

[11] For this view of totalitarianism and revolutionary chiliasm, see Norman Cohn, *The Pursuit of the Millennium*, 2d ed. (New York: Harper, 1961), esp. 307–19; and Barrington Moore, Jr., "Totalitarian Elements in Pre-Industrial Societies," in Moore, *Political Power and Social Theory* (New York: Harper and Row, 1962), 30–89.

[12] Weber (fn. 5, 1978), 1:246.

[13] Djilas, *The New Class: An Analysis of the Communist System* (New York: Praeger, 1957).

the revolutionary community,[14] that very desire may require attention to some of the material needs of its members. Thus while the revolutionary movement, much like the charismatic sect, is initially held together by the promise of salvation, some of its members will still have to deal with such matters as the procurement of food, shelter, and other necessities. This in turn sets certain psychological forces in motion: those who devote themselves to providing mundane necessities have their attention diverted from the salvationist purpose, and they acquire, apparently by habituation, what Mao described many years after Weber as "role consciousness."[15] It is the rise of this consciousness that causes major cleavages in both communist and other revolutionary societies. On the one side of this cleavage stands the revolutionary leader, yearning for "revolutionary immortality"[16] and insulated from recalcitrant realities by his faith in the charismatic qualities of the movement. On the other side stand members of his staff, the line officers of the revolution, who are all too aware of the multitude of obstacles that stand between them and their image of a perfect world, yet who must attend to the whims of the leader. One can argue that this conceptualization anticipates Stalin's purges and Mao's cultural revolution, though there is nothing in it to suggest what many students of communism have assumed—that revolutionary leaders will always prevail by the logic of the system. Indeed, common sense would say that such conflicts between chiefs and staffs may well provoke successful palace revolutions or that regimes may simply lapse into chaos and become extinct early on in their existence.

If in the short run the outcome of conflicts between staff and leader is uncertain, in the long run the odds favor the devolution of salvationist regimes. This at least is Weber's hypothesis, and it is confirmed by the history of modern revolutions since the seventeenth century. Thus, the forces of change may be at work from the very inception of a revolutionary regime, but they become "conspicuously evident with the disappearance of the [original] charismatic leader."[17] At this point, the salvationist objectives of the regime, though still referred to on ritual occasions, are replaced by a world view that grows out of the staff's practical experiences. As a corollary, the new chief assumes a more businesslike style even while professing to act in the name of the founder hero. Perhaps

[14] Weber (fn. 5, 1978), 1:246.

[15] Mao Zedong, "On Dialectics," U.S.D.C. Joint Publication Research Service, February 20, 1974; idem, "On Krushchev's Phoney Communism," *Peking Review*, July 17, 1964, pp. 7–28.

[16] Robert J. Lifton, *Revolutionary Immortality: Mao Tse-tung and the Chinese Cultural Revolution* (New York: Random House, 1968).

[17] Weber (fn. 5, 1978), 1:246.

inspired by Trotsky's classical thesis,[18] many observers of communist systems construed these changes as "bureaucratization."[19] But in fact, more practical thinking about priorities, or the substitution of ritual for personal magnetism, is not tantamount to the acceptance of the strict formal rules and procedures that the term bureaucracy implies. Other routines may develop more slowly by accumulated precedent, leaving ample room for arbitrary behavior.[20] So while bureaucracy was the dominant term of reference in the 1960s, in the 1970s students of Soviet government redesignated their subject as an example not of bureaucracy but of paternalism, patrimonialism, or neo-traditionalism.[21]

These elements of Weber's theory have provided us with convenient shorthands for describing change in communist societies, especially in the post-Stalin period, and they do so in a manner that takes us beyond historically unique configurations of events. Indeed, these shorthands were so useful that they guided research on change in both communist and noncommunist societies, thereby bridging the gap between the otherwise separate Second and Third World studies.[22] But what about the capacity of Weber to explain the origins of communism? Here Weber is somewhat less helpful. As Talcott Parsons notes, he was more interested in the character and consequences of charismatic movements than in the conditions that favor their development.[23] Insofar as Weber concerns himself with these conditions, his remarks are ambiguous. In his words,

[18] Leon Trotsky, *The Revolution Betrayed* (New York: Pathfinder, 1970), esp. 86–114, 248–52.

[19] See especially Alfred Meyer, "The Comparative Study of Communist Political Systems," *Slavic Review* 26 (March 1967), 3–12. For a critical view and a comprehensive survey of this literature on "bureaucratism," see Jan Pakulski, "Bureaucracy and the Soviet System," *Studies in Comparative Communism* 19 (Spring 1986), 3–24, esp. 6–8.

[20] Weber (fn. 5, 1964), 363–66.

[21] Zygmunt Bauman, "The Party in the System-Management Phase: Change and Continuity," in Andrew C. Janos, ed., *Authoritarian Politics in Communist Europe* (Berkeley: Institute of International Studies, University of California, 1976), 81–108; Kenneth Jowitt, "Soviet Neo-Traditionalism: The Political Concept of a Leninist Regime," *Soviet Studies* 35 (July 1983), 275–97; Andrew Walder, *Communist Neo-Traditionalism: Work and Authority in Chinese Industry* (Berkeley: University of California Press, 1986).

[22] For communist studies, see Samuel P. Huntington, "Social and Institutional Dynamics of One Party Regimes," in Samuel P. Huntington and Clement H. Moore, eds., *Authoritarian Politics in Modern Society* (New York: Basic Books, 1971), 3–48; Robert C. Tucker, *The Marxian Revolutionary Idea* (New York: W. W. Norton, 1970), 172–214; Seweryn Bialer, *Stalin's Successors: Leadership, Stability and Change in the Soviet Union* (Cambridge: Cambridge University Press, 1980); Lowell Dittmer, *China's Continuous Revolution* (Berkeley: University of California Press, 1987). For the institutionalization of other postrevolutionary regimes, see John Waterbury, *The Egypt of Nasser and Sadat: The Political Economy of Two Regimes* (Princeton: Princeton University Press, 1983); and Raymond A. Hinnebusch, Jr., *Egyptian Politics under Sadat: The Post-populist Development of an Authoritarian-Modernizing State* (Cambridge: Cambridge University Press, 1985; rev. ed., Boulder, Colo.: Lynne Rienner, 1988).

[23] "Introduction" to Weber (fn. 5, 1964), 71.

"Charismatic rulership . . . always results from unusual, especially political and economic situations, or of extraordinary psychic, particularly religious states, or from both together."[24] "Unusual" and "extraordinary" being essentially subjective in nature, they do not readily provide the stuff from which good theory is made. To be sure, as Parsons suggests, the thrust of Weber's oeuvre points in the direction of cultural factors out of which emerge such explanatory variables as "relatively generalized and diffuse 'anomie' and insecurity" as well as "specifically structured sources of strain and frustration."[25] But if so, the problem becomes empirical. Whereas a number of followers of Weber and Durkheim, including Arendt and Norman Cohn,[26] attempt to relate the origins of totalitarianism and salvationism to cultural discontinuities, the existence of these discontinuities, especially in the case of Russia, has always been inferred from the very rudimentary commercialization of agrarian society or the beginnings of industrialism but never demonstrated conclusively. Indeed, the countless references to cultural continuity—to the "Russian" or "Orthodox" characteristics of Stalinism and of communism more generally—and the oft-reiterated proposition that Russian society had to be atomized by terror *after* the revolution seem to raise questions concerning the validity of this cultural hypothesis.

For different reasons, Weber's theories are also only moderately useful for anticipating the decline of communism and such recent developments as Gorbachev's reforms or the democratization of communist regimes. Weber, of course, writes about the "transformation of charisma in an anti-authoritarian direction" and still more extensively about the tensions that arise between bureaucratic and democratic principles, one based on freedom, the other on hierarchy.[27] But he fails to provide any clue as to the nature of the forces that push politics in one direction or another. To learn more about the probabilities of democratization and pluralization, therefore, social scientists have had to turn to other paradigms, most notably to the paradigms of modernization and industrialization, which had been an integral part of social thought even before the formulation of Weber's hypothesis on political change.

MODERNIZATION: TOWARD INDUSTRIALISM OR MILITANCY?

To many social scientists the terms industrialism and modernization are synonymous. To others who follow a well-established sociological tradi-

[24] Weber (fn. 5, 1978), 2:1121.
[25] Weber (fn. 5, 1964), 71.
[26] Cohn (fn. 11), 107–19.
[27] Weber (fn. 5, 1964), 386–92; Weber (fn. 5, 1978), 1:266–71 and 2:956–1002.

tion,[28] the terms acquire specific meanings in a causal relationship in which technologies of production (industrialism) are linked to political change through the intervening variables of culture, social structure, and scarce resources. It is in terms of these intervening variables that one can formulate specific theories of political "development" that form the backbone of the disciplines of political anthropology (culture studies), sociology, and economy.

The master concepts of these theories are rationalization, differentiation, and variations in the scarcity and abundance of material goods. As technological breakthroughs occur with respect to laborsaving devices and the uses of inanimate sources of energy—the quintessential elements of industrialism—people acquire a growing sense of choice and mastery vis-à-vis their physical and social environment; the division of labor becomes more specialized and the social structure more complex; and, finally, with the increasing use of inanimate implements and sources of energy, the volume of material resources available for distribution also increases. These changes in turn have an impact on the structure and scope of public authority: principles of divine right are replaced by the secular idea of popular sovereignty; structures of command and coordination have to be adjusted to the growing complexity of the "underlying" social structure; and the growing abundance of material goods diminishes social tensions, which permits ever greater numbers of people to participate in politics. So formulated, this three-tiered theory of industrialism predicts not just change but human progress as well. As such, it has been used to counter the voices of the doomsayers of modernization—Comte, Durkheim, Mannheim, and more recently Ortega and Arendt—who believed that the growing complexities of industrial life might eventually destroy individual freedoms and social autonomies.

Represented by the writings of Talcott Parsons and a host of other political sociologists and economists,[29] this optimistic view of modernization dominated American social science in the 1950s and in the 1960s entered the field of communist studies. According to this school of thought, prerevolutionary Russia, China, and Eastern Europe (as indeed Marxist-Leninist societies in the Third World) were underdeveloped areas, and communism nothing but a comprehensive design and an ideological mask for policies of development. In the words of Theodore von Laue, the Bolshevik revolution was in essence "a revolt against backwardness" that "established a new category, the revolution of underde-

---

[28] Bendix (fn. 4), 6–7.
[29] See Andrew C. Janos, *Politics and Paradigms: Changing Theories of Change in Social Science* (Stanford, Calif.: Stanford University Press, 1986), 31–64.

veloped countries. . . . Underneath the travail of revolution and counter-revolution . . . terror and counter terror, [this] deeper necessity took its course. Not always clearly expressed . . . it aimed at the conversion of the Russian state and society to modern industrialism."[30]

Much in the same vein, the concept of industrialization was used to explain changes in the structure of established communist governments. Political economists led the way, arguing that terror, propaganda, and personalized leadership were instruments for mobilizing the manpower and resources of an economically backward society and hypothesizing that the post-Stalin changes in effect reflected the success of these policies of mobilization. According to John Kautsky, as the task of primitive accumulation and development is accomplished, "a progressively decreasing proportion of the population needs to be subjected to terror and heavy handed regimentation."[31] Or, in the words of Isaac Deutscher, it was the "phenomenal growth of Russian real income between 1930–1950" that made the "primitive magic" and "elaborate mythology" of Stalinism socially useless and counterproductive.[32] Political sociologists likewise focused attention on the success of industrialization. They argued that the growing complexity of Soviet society had already compelled, or would eventually compel, changes in the centralized pattern of party rule and ideological conformity.[33] Some see the proposition vindicated by the rise of Gorbachev and by the current trend toward the pluralization of politics in the Soviet orbit.[34] Others, focusing on the psychocultural consequences of industrialization, suggest that the factory system itself served as a breeding ground for empathy, fellow feeling, broadening horizons, and a commitment to a "reasonably lawful world under human control"[35]—qualities that appeared to be present, in communist societies as well, although with "some ambiguity, and at times fraught with considerable tension."[36] All these arguments carried to their

[30] Von Laue, *Why Lenin? Why Stalin?* (New York: Lippincott, 1971), 3, 208.

[31] Kautsky, *The Political Consequences of Modernization* (New York: John Wiley, 1972), 196.

[32] Deutscher, *Russia: What Next?* (London: Hamish Hamilton, 1953), 123–25.

[33] See, e.g., Leo Labedz, "Ideology: The Fourth Stage," *Problems of Communism* 7 (November–December 1959), 1–10; and Richard Lowenthal, "The Ruling Party in a Mature Society," in Mark G. Field, ed., *The Social Consequences of Modernization in Communist Societies* (Baltimore: Johns Hopkins University Press, 1974), 81–120. For a review of the entire literature, see T. Anthony Jones, "Modernization Theory and Socialist Development," in Field (pp. 19–49).

[34] See Moshe Lewin, *The Gorbachev Phenomenon: A Historical Interpretation* (Berkeley: University of California Press, 1988), esp. 146; Lucian W. Pye, "Political Science and the Crisis of Authoritarianism," *American Political Science Review* 84 (March 1990), 3–19.

[35] Alex Inkeles and David Smith, *Becoming Modern: Individual Change in Six Developing Countries* (Cambridge: Harvard University Press, 1976), 17.

[36] Alex Inkeles, "The Modernization of Man in Socialist and Non-Socialist Countries," in Field (fn. 33), 53–54.

logical conclusion provide building blocks for a theory of convergence, which holds that in the long run, as a result of industrialization, communist countries are likely to develop political institutions similar to those of the highly advanced Western societies.

In the 1960s these theories of convergence enjoyed considerable popularity among students of comparative communism. There remained though some vexing problems for scholarship, the most conspicuous being the weakness of the link between the goal of industrialism and the ideology of early Bolshevism. To be sure, Lenin wrote on the subject, most notably on the industrialization of Russia.[37] He was also concerned with the phenomenon of uneven development, one of the catch phrases associated with his name. But Lenin and his associates explored the subject mainly to satisfy their curiosity about the origins of a revolutionary situation; they were not out to develop a blueprint for a future revolutionary government. His major work on the Bolshevik future, *The State and Revolution*, speaks of the abolition of administrative and coercive organs, rather than of the installation of factories; it is the prime example of a chiliastic prophecy of a world in harmony. Certainly, the years of the NEP created a flurry of argument about the market, as well as about public and private ownership. But the issues of development and industrialization did not become central to the Bolshevik agenda before the great debates of 1926–27.

This lack of "fit" between theory and history gave rise to a significant revisionist movement among students of communism, who attempted to resolve the dilemma by integrating the modernization hypothesis with elements of Weberian theory. Barrington Moore, Jr., was an early pioneer of such a synthesis. His first major work on Soviet politics laid the foundations for a new argument by pointing to conflicting strands in the politics of communist regimes.[38] One of these strands derived from the Marxist idea of building an egalitarian social order, the other from the imperatives of survival in a hostile environment, which pulled the egalitarian movement in the direction of industrialism. The theory that arises from Moore's writings was elaborated further by Zbigniew Brzezinski,[39] Chalmers A. Johnson,[40] Richard Lowenthal,[41] and Robert Tucker.[42]

[37] Lenin, *The Development of Capitalism in Russia* (Moscow: Progress Publishers, 1964).
[38] Moore, *Soviet Politics: The Dilemma of Power* (Cambridge: Harvard University Press, 1950).
[39] Brzezinski, *Ideology and Power in Soviet Politics* (New York: Praeger, 1964).
[40] Johnson, "Change in Communist Nations," in Johnson, ed., *Change in Communist Systems* (Stanford, Calif.: Stanford University Press, 1970), 1–33.
[41] Lowenthal, "Development vs. Utopia in Communist Policy," in Johnson (fn. 40), 33–117.
[42] Tucker (fn. 22).

Their theories, like Moore's, have a distinctly dialectical quality: in making revolution, the Bolsheviks pursued chiliastic-salvationist goals, but in order to survive, indeed to realize their goals, they were forced to adopt a series of policies that subverted the tenets of the "ideology" (Brzezinski), "goal culture" (Johnson), and "utopia" (Lowenthal) and by requiring organization and discipline, set in motion the inexorable forces of "de-radicalization" (Tucker) in Leninist political regimes. Though not as optimistic as the "strict" developmentalists and convergence theorists, these writers of the revolutionary dialectic believed that history favored modernity over ideology.

Another notable attempt to wed the substantive issue of modernization to Weberian thinking about authority systems emerges from the work of Cyril Black,[43] Samuel Huntington,[44] and Kenneth Jowitt.[45] These three writers see communism not as a movement for modernization or for the building of a utopian order; rather, they see it as part of a worldwide drive to create viable political communities in response to the functional requisites of survival in an inhospitable environment. But whether the goal is "political modernization" (Black), "political development" (Huntington), or "nation-building" (Jowitt), it still requires the building of a modern economy and value system, for without them nation-states cannot operate in the contemporary world. Weber's notion of charisma then serves to link together economic and political—the intermediate and the ultimate—ends with a unique organizational and ideological device that justifies the ruthlessness required in "breaking through" (Jowitt) the structures of traditional society. Above all, the function of charisma and of the salvationist ideology is to encourage methods of military combat, not only in pursuing revolutionary struggle but also in performing the more mundane, though equally necessary, tasks of resource mobilization and economic development. In contrast to other revisionists, the members of this school eschew the dialectics of Weber's theory in favor of a more linear theory of stages (or, in Huntington's case, sequences) in which charisma is routinized as a matter of choice or functional necessity. Though initially quite optimistic about the prospects of this strategy, at least one member of the school realized that such

[43] Black, *The Dynamics of Modernization: A Study in Comparative History* (New York: Harper and Row, 1966).
[44] Huntington, *Political Order in Changing Societies* (New Haven: Yale University Press, 1968).
[45] See especially Jowitt, *Revolutionary Breakthroughs and National Development: The Case of Romania, 1945–66* (Berkeley: University of California Press, 1971); and idem, *The Leninist Response to National Dependency*, Research Monograph no. 37 (Berkeley: Institute of International Studies, University of California, 1978).

breakthroughs would not always materialize and that the movement could regress and be corrupted into some form of "neo-traditionalism."[46]

All of these developmental schemes hark back in some way to nineteenth-century evolutionary theory, perhaps most directly to Herbert Spencer's once-celebrated and influential writings about "industrial society" and modern industrialism.[47] Overall, Spencer saw societies in terms of organic analogies: they faced and responded to challenges emanating from their internal and external environment. In Spencer's view, a society responded to these challenges principally and most generally by means of technological innovation, which in turn led to differentiation and growing complexity. But this response may be embedded in different organizational purposes and principles. It may indeed take place in the context of "industrialism" in that some societies—or their elites, if we want to shake off the theoretical encumbrances of Spencer's functionalism—respond to the challenges of the environment by fostering "internal activities," above all, by the "growth of agriculture, manufacture and commerce,"[48] so as to be able to satisfy the material needs of their citizens. However, in contemplating the range of possible responses to the challenges of the environment, Spencer was keenly aware that industrialism was only one option for organizing society and that throughout history people have frequently availed themselves of another option—militancy—in the pursuit of their welfare and objectives. According to Spencer, this second principle of organization orients actors not toward the peaceful development of their productive capacity but toward such "external activities" as plunder and conquest, to which we may add, in the Weberian vein, religious or political crusades designed to reshape the international environment. Although Spencer refers to this principle of organization as "military society," he has in mind more than a society dominated by the military. Rather, he thinks in terms of one that is organized to fulfill the functional requisites of a garrison state and that is ruled by political classes, whether civilian or military, whose self-justification derives from the "external orientation" of a militant ideology.[49] To be sure, in modern times such external activities, much like their

---

[46] Jowitt (fn. 21), 275–97.
[47] Spencer, *On Social Evolution*, ed. J. D. Y. Peel (Chicago: University of Chicago Press, 1972), 41.
[48] Ibid., 152.
[49] As a functionalist, Spencer is more concerned with society than with elites. Yet it is important to bear in mind that such orientations may sometimes reflect the interest—material or ideal—of only the elites, who may treat their own society as the means and not as the end of their policies. The modern world is full of such examples, from Hitler to Saddam Hussein, including many communist elites. Thus, what may appear to be "imperial altruism" to the functionalist will in reality only conceal the supreme selfishness of an elite.

internal counterparts, require an industrial base. But in these military societies, Spencer writes, the "industrial part of society continues to be essentially a permanent commissariat, existing solely to supply the needs of governmental-military structures, and having left over for itself enough merely for bare maintenance. Hence the political regulation of its activities."[50] In writing this, Spencer was aware that in any concrete case the structure of society may include different mixtures of militancy and industrialism, but he was also aware that the two principles were in fundamental conflict. The principles of militancy were apt to subvert the potential benevolence of a trading nation, whereas principles of industrialism were likely to hamper activities of an "external" and military nature.

The idea that the Soviet Union and other communist societies had military and expansionist characteristics has not been totally absent from historical and sociological analysis. For one thing, a number of historians have emphasized the external orientation and activities of Soviet politics.[51] For another, a number of social scientists have noted the militaristic features of communist regimes. In this vein Oscar Lange observed the existence of parallels between the socialist economies of Eastern Europe and the war economy of imperial Germany,[52] while William Odom,[53] Karl Spielmann,[54] and Victor Zaslavsky[55] called attention to the "militarization" of Soviet life and to the important role of the military-industrial complex in communist societies. More recently, there have also been occasional references to a "barracks economy" (kazarmennaya ekonomiia) or "barracks society" (kazarmennoe obshchestvo) in the East European and the Soviet press.[56] But whatever the merits of these works and references, neither separately nor together do they amount to a full-fledged theoret-

[50] Spencer (fn. 47), 154.

[51] Among them, Hugh Seton-Watson, The Imperialist Revolutionaries (Stanford, Calif.: Hoover Institution Press, 1978); Adam Ulam, Expansionism and Coexistence: Soviet Foreign Policy, 1917–73, 2d ed. (New York: Praeger, 1974); Richard Pipes, Survival Is Not Enough (New York: Simon and Schuster, 1984); and "Z" [Martin Malia], "To the Stalin Mausoleum," Daedalus 119 (Winter 1990), 295–344.

[52] Lange, The Political Economy of Socialism (The Hague: Van Keulen, 1967), 18; or idem, Papers in Economics and Society (New York: Pergamon, 1970), 102–3.

[53] Odom, "The 'Militarization' of Soviet Society," Problems of Communism 25 (September–October 1976), 34–51.

[54] Spielmann, "Defense Industrialists in the USSR," Problems of Communism 25 (September–October 1976), 52–69.

[55] See especially Zaslavsky, "Soviet Transition to a Market Economy: State Dependent Workers, Populism and Nationalism," in Stanislaw Gomulka and Cyril Lin, eds., Limits to the Transformation of Soviet-type Systems (New York: Oxford University Press, 1991).

[56] I thank my colleagues Gregory Grossman and George Breslauer for calling my attention to these. For a reference to these references, see Stephen Kotkin, "Perestroika in the Soviet Rustbelt," Harriman Institute Forum 4 (February 1991), 1–16, at 5.

ical alternative to the popular hypothesis of the industrial society. On the whole, the Spencerian ideas of a military society and garrison state have remained alien to the mainstream of Western social science of recent decades. To some observers this may be a reflection of the politics of academe—its wishful thinking about the ultimately benevolent nature of Soviet society or its desire to be unduly fair to regimes that for a brief period had been maligned as totalitarian. In this respect, critics will recall Reinhold Niebuhr's characterization of communists as the "misguided children of the light" (in contradistinction to fascists, who were simply the "children of darkness").[57] But then social scientists also had trouble with fascism, conceptualizing it varyingly as an instrument of modernization,[58] as an alternative road to industrialism,[59] as a reaction to modernization,[60] or as an aberration on the road toward a more rational modern world.[61] This being the case, the bias seems to have been less political than epistemological, and rooted in some of the "pernicious postulates"[62] of neoclassical sociology, according to which both causes and effects of social change are to be sought within the structures of autonomous and self-sustaining social systems.

And yet, nothing would seem to be more obvious than the external orientation and activities of communist states. To begin with, much of the Russian Marxist discourse and the entire debate between Mensheviks and Bolsheviks centered on whether the forthcoming revolution would have a Russian or a global character. The Mensheviks argued in terms of the orthodox epistemology of a theory of stages—socialism in a less developed country meant less chance for freedom; the Bolsheviks were early pioneers of a world system paradigm, arguing that the Russian Revolution was meaningful only as a part of the process of global revolution that would result in an international system without markets and states. This point, too well known to be belabored here, is echoed in the works of Trotsky, Lenin and Stalin, and Bukharin.[63] The Bolsheviks

[57] Niebuhr, The Children of Light and the Children of Darkness: A Vindication of Democracy and a Critique of Its Traditional Defense (New York: Scribner's, 1944).

[58] A. James Gregor, Italian Fascism and Developmental Dictatorship (Princeton: Princeton University Press, 1974).

[59] Barrington Moore, Jr., The Social Origins of Dictatorship and Democracy (Boston: Beacon Press, 1966), 433–52.

[60] Kautsky (fn. 31), 208–17.

[61] Talcott Parsons, "Some Sociological Aspects of Fascist Movements," in Parsons, Essays in Sociological Theory (Glencoe, Ill.: Free Press, 1954), 124–41.

[62] Charles Tilly, Big Structures, Large Processes, Huge Comparisons (New York: Russell Sage Foundation, 1984), 11–12.

[63] Lenin, "Imperialism as the Highest Stage of Capitalism," in Lenin, Selected Works (Moscow: Progress Publishers, 1976), 1: 667–768; Trotsky, The Permanent Revolution: Results and Prospects, trans. J. G. Wright and B. Pierce (New York: Merit, 1969), esp. 31, 133; I. V. Stalin, "The Foundations of Leninism" (1924), in Bruce Franklin, ed., The Essential Stalin: Major

subsequently demonstrated that this was not empty rhetoric or mobilizational propaganda, by founding the Comintern to coordinate external activities and to foment revolutions across the European continent.

In his rise to the top, Stalin both changed and consolidated the external orientation of the Leninist system. On the one hand, he abandoned the earlier insurrectionist tactics of the Comintern and eventually liquidated the leaders of the organization. On the other hand, he strove to build an externally powerful Soviet state that could carry the torch of world revolution further forward—to be sure, an endeavor masked by the slogan of building socialism in one country. But it is clear from Stalin's own pronouncements on international might and right and on the replacement of the capitalist encirclement of socialism with the socialist encirclement of capitalism[64] that the domestic tranformation of the Soviet Union was not an end in itself but rather was part of a larger international design. This was acknowledged even by Trotsky, Stalin's archenemy, and by then a relentless critic of the Soviet Thermidor, when writing about the two-faced character of the Soviet regime: reactionary toward the Russian masses but progressive in waging the international class struggle against the global bourgeoisie.[65] Isaac Deutscher, one of Trotsky's disciples, was even more emphatic about the external orientation of Stalinism: yes, Stalin was creating new institutions in Russia, but these were not in the service of socialism in one country; they were, rather, in the service of a new worldwide civilization that would supersede the existing capitalist world system.[66] Once again, this external orientation did not remain empty rhetoric. While ever cautious tactically, Stalin acted upon the principle by annexing territories to the Soviet Union in 1939, by laying down the foundations of the Soviet bloc between 1945 and 1948, and, less successfully, by initiating or sanctioning the Korean War in 1950.

This thesis concerning the continued external orientation of communism seems to be contradicted by the Stalinist drive to industrialize Rus-

---

Theoretical Writings, 1905–1952 (New York: Doubleday, 1972), esp. 90–98. For Bukharin's views on the struggle between the "world city and the world countryside," with an emphasis on the future role of the peasantry in the world revolution, see Stephen E. Cohen, *Bukharin and the Bolshevik Revolution: A Political Biography, 1888–1938* (New York: Random House, 1973), 168.

[64] See Stalin, "Report to the Seventeenth Congress" (1934) and "Report to the Eighteenth Congress" (1939), in Stalin (fn. 63), 281, 387.

[65] Perry Anderson, "The Trotskyist Interpretation of Stalin," in Tariq Ali, ed., *The Stalinist Legacy: Its Impact on Twentieth-Century World Politics* (Middlesex, England: Penguin Books, 1984), 120.

[66] Deutscher, "Socialism in One Country," in Ali (fn. 65), 104. On the same theme, see Ken Jowitt, "Moscow Centre," in *Eastern European Politics and Societies* 1 (Fall 1987), 296–348.

sia, which subsequently became a centerpiece of modernization literature in the field of communist studies. True, this drive was a key ambition and accomplishment of Stalinism, aimed at building a new system of production in the country. But the character of the process and its accomplishments were distinctly different from what they were in the Western historical experience: not only was the process driven by the state, but it was also designed to benefit the state. This is to say that Stalinist industrialization contributed little to popular welfare. Indeed, the very opposite was the case: millions were sacrificed to enforce mobilization campaigns and famines. Nor did this drive bring about "self-sustaining" (that is, noncoercive) growth or international economic competitiveness, the hallmarks of Western economic development. Stalin created a perfect example of Spencer's model of militancy—a powerful military state in which the "industrial part of society" remained a "mere commissariat existing solely to supply the needs of governmental-military structures of an externally powerful state."[67] The term *garrison state* is therefore not an inappropriate description of the Stalinist political system. It is worth noting that this designation was recently resuscitated not only by detractors but also by one of the erstwhile champions of Stalinism.[68]

The relevance of the garrison state model becomes still more obvious in the context of the broader sociocultural aspects of Soviet Marxism or state socialism. Today, of course, the very terms are seen by many as oxymorons, and it has become fashionable to assert that Stalinism had little to do with genuine Marxism or socialism. Yet Stalin's thinking was deeply steeped in the ideas of nineteenth-century Marxism, except that as a practical matter these ideas were carefully filtered through the functional requisites of maintaining a powerful and effective state. Some elements of Marxist orthodoxy passed etatist muster and were retained for formulating public policy. Thus, Stalin unhesitatingly carried out the Marxist mandate to abolish private property, because this "socialization" of the means of production was really etatization leading to a form of ownership that gave the state direct access to society's manpower and resources. Similarly, and much like Bismarck, who had little love for socialism, Stalin embraced some of the welfare aspects of classical socialism—improvements in public health and education and even some access to high culture—because these old socialist objectives converged with the interests of the state in assembling a literate and physically fit cohort of recruits for army and industry. At the same time, the Stalinist

---

[67] Spencer (fn. 47), 154.

[68] See interview with Edward Ochab in Teresa Toranska, *"Them": Stalin's Polish Puppets*, trans. A. Kolakowska (New York: Harper and Row, 1988), 37.

state, again much like its Prussian counterpart, had no use for feminism, sexual license, or challenges to the traditional family, so these elements of classical Marxism were dropped from the socialist agenda in the 1930s, together with the idea of strict egalitarianism in both army and industry. Indeed, such egalitarianism was contemptuously dismissed as *uravnilovka* (a game of equalizing) and replaced by the symbols and realities of hierarchy and discipline. The restoration of military ranks, braids, and decorations was only one conspicuous case in point. The result was a web of social relationships more reminiscent of historic Austria, Prussia, or the Byzantine world than of the class structure associated with the modern industrial societies of the West.

The post-Stalin period witnessed the decline of charismatic salvationism but not the end of militancy and externally oriented public policy. The period may have seen "the withering away of the concept of utopia and utopianism in the thought and practices of the political elite,"[69] but the conviction that there was a "historical trend toward the inevitable victory of socialism over capitalism" survived.[70] During the Khrushchev years this conviction was articulated publicly in a new doctrine that combined talk of "peaceful coexistence" with bluster about "burying" capitalism. The Brezhnev years were those of détente, and the rhetoric became less shrill. Nonetheless, it was accompanied by an unprecedented effort to build up the military strength of the Soviet Union; the rate of growth of the military sector was maintained at a steady 4 percent per annum[71] until it reached, by recent calculations, between one-fourth and one-fifth of the Soviet national product.[72] Just as significantly, the buildup and the policy of détente were linked to the support of national liberation movements in the Third World, an effort that required the massive mobilization of the resources of the Soviet state.

In view of Gorbachev's habit of dismissing the Brezhnev years as a period of stagnation, it is important to reiterate Bialer's view that in their own terms these Soviet policies represented a major success.[73] It was during these years that the Soviet Union emerged as a full-fledged global power by acquiring nuclear parity with the U.S., reaching and maintaining conventional military superiority in Europe, and developing a naval capability to project its military might to faraway corners of the world. But despite these military and political advances, the Soviet Union re-

---

[69] Seweryn Bialer, *The Soviet Paradox* (New York: Alfred A. Knopf, 1986), 54.
[70] Ibid., 191.
[71] Ibid., 46.
[72] John Eckhaus, "How Life in the USSR Compares with the U.S." *San Francisco Chronicle*, June 18, 1990, p. A6.
[73] Bialer (fn. 69), 46.

mained an economically backward country with a relatively low per capita GNP and with a still lower level of per capita consumption.[74] Bialer describes this as the "Soviet paradox."[75] But like all paradoxes, this one is only apparent; in reality it reflects the logic of a military society that pursues external objectives at the expense of the welfare of its citizens.

Not surprisingly, therefore, the vulnerabilities of Soviet society have been those of militancy and not of industrialism. And what are these? To begin with, we are dealing here with a "barracks economy" to which the metaphor of growth has only limited applicability, for the bulk of investment capital is used for economically unproductive purposes. Indeed, for each quantity of surplus that increases military power, the civilian sector becomes weaker, or at least does not become stronger. There are, then, definite limits to the extent that a garrison state can increase its power by drawing on the manpower and resources of its domestic base. Historically, leaders of such states resorted to a three-step grand strategy to overcome these limits, a strategy that reflected the logic of their ends, means, and potential vulnerabilities. First, they engaged in a burst of mobilization to gain temporary strategic advantage over their adversaries; then they executed a coup de main against an area within the heartland of the rival domain; finally, they consolidated their gains by replenishing their resources, by paying off their populations, and by preparing for the next round of confrontation. In essence, this was the strategy followed by Germany in the first half of this century. Neither one of the two world wars broke out accidentally: Germany initiated them at a time when its military had acquired a strategic edge that its leaders felt would slip away if war were further delayed. The same conventional strategy of militancy was followed by Stalin in 1939–40 and again in 1944–49. In both instances the Soviet state acquired more advanced economies and manpower to provide resources for the reconstruction of its military machine. In so doing, the Soviet leadership was already preparing for the next stage; the Berlin blockade, the creation of an East German state, and the inclusion of the French and Italian parties in the Cominform are then easy to construe as preparations for a European coup de main.

[74] Eckhaus (fn. 72) puts Soviet per capita GNP at 34.3 percent of U.S. figures and per capita consumption at 28.2 percent of the latter. Other sources see Soviet income as either stagnant or declining in relation to the economies of the U.S. or the European Defense Community. Earlier estimates put these figures at 42 percent and 37 percent, respectively. See Herbert Block, *The Planetary Product,* Special Report no. 58 (Washington, D.C.: U.S. Department of State, 1979), 6–12; and Paul Marer, *Dollar GNP's of the USSR and Eastern Europe* (Baltimore: Johns Hopkins University Press, 1985).

[75] Bialer (fn. 69), 191.

This strategic concept took on a different coloration with the dawning of the nuclear age—the risks of militancy were infinitely higher than those faced by the leaders of Germany and Japan when they launched World War II. Slowly, therefore, Stalin and certainly his successors assimilated the idea of mutually assured destruction and steered their strategy away from the objective of a coup de main. True, there were some probings of Western resolve in Cuba and Berlin, but in the interim the Cominform with its Franco-Italian orientation was dissolved. A Euro-centered global strategy gave way to the doctrine of peaceful coexistence, in which the control of nuclear weapons combined with the promise of aggressive support for wars of "national liberation" in the Third World. But this policy had its own dialectic: it was successful in establishing a number of revolutionary governments, but these impoverished countries yielded no economic assets, only liabilities. If in the short run these liabilities could be covered from unexpected energy windfalls and Western loans to the satellite governments, in the long run they were the source of endemic shortages.

However obvious these dilemmas may appear in retrospect, they were not well articulated in Soviet policy debate. Major decisions were postponed by an aging and ailing leadership whose hesitation also reflected the inability of the political class to come to terms with a harsh reality. Even Gorbachev seems to have arrived on the scene with a mandate to make the old system work rather than to take extremely bold and risky initiatives, and there is every reason to believe him (and Shevardnadze) that he became fully aware of the magnitude of the dilemma only after becoming first secretary. Certainly, his first measures in office were corrective if not palliative, a throwback to the "incrementalism" of earlier days. But then he proceeded quickly, moving from the ridiculous to the sublime, from the rationing of vodka to a "new thinking" that "subordinated foreign policy to domestic reform"[76] for the first time in Soviet history. With that, Gorbachev abandoned the political notion of an international class struggle for the ideas of economic competition and competitiveness.[77] Translated into Spencer's language, this was nothing less than a genuine shift from the principles of militancy to true industrialism.

Further examination of Gorbachev's new thinking reveals two closely

---

[76] Vendulka Kubalkova and Albert Anderson Cruickshank, *Thinking New about Soviet "New Thinking"* (Berkeley: Institute of International Studies, University of California, 1989), 3.

[77] Ibid. See also Jack Snyder, "The Gorbachev Revolution: The Waning of Soviet Expansionism?" *International Security* 12 (Winter 1987–88), 93–131.

related aspects. One is the famous perestroika, the restructuring of the economy to make it internationally competitive. The other is the creation of a "common European home" stretching from the Urals to the Atlantic. Though taken by some as a piece of propaganda, this slogan is in fact rooted in the very logic of perestroika: the Soviet economy cannot successfully adjust to the international market without some measure of cooperation from the most advanced states. In this respect history is repeating itself. The idea harks back not only to the dreams of nineteenth-century "Westernizers" but also to the prerevolutionary Bolsheviks who had hoped to solve the problem of "primitive accumulation" by establishing a single continentwide socialist economy. Then as now the advanced countries were expected to share their wealth out of a deeper impulse of fellow feeling.

While this design of perestroika cum Europe stands up to the test of logic, its elements have their own dialectic. First, perestroika required glasnost, the free flow of information that is a prerequisite for successful adjustment to the international market. But such an open stream of economic information can easily spill over into politics, to permit the massive mobilization of popular sentiment, perhaps even against perestroika itself. Meanwhile, the "common home" strategy also had its price: to win the acceptance of the West, the Soviet Union had to abandon Eastern Europe, as well as its long-standing support for wars of liberation. In some quarters this had the smell of treason, the sacrifice of high principle for rank economic benefit. The policy thus may have had its enthusiasts in the streets of Germany and Britain but certainly not among Soviet conservatives or among radicals of the global periphery. Perhaps still more significantly, cooperation with the West required that the Soviet Union put a Western democratic veneer on its institutions, to win the approval of the club of bourgeois nations of the Continent. This democracy, rudimentary though it is, threatens not only the stability of the government but the very integrity of the state by giving rise and legitimacy to the centrifugal forces that Gorbachev is currently trying to tame.

It has been argued here that the Soviet Union was a military society under Stalin, remained a military society under Stalin's successors, and is currently in the throes of devolution from Spencerian militancy to competitive industrialism. But what about the rest of the communist world? To begin with Eastern Europe: its countries were closely integrated with the Soviet Union into a single large imperial unit within which little diversity was tolerated; yet within only a few years of Stalin's death, the member states of the bloc began to drift in different directions. Whereas the literature customarily distinguishes between the "soft" and the "hard" regimes, it makes sense from the vantage point of this essay to speak of "domesticists" and "internationalists," because these terms roughly correspond to the Spencerian categories of militancy and industrialism. The domesticists comprised four countries—Yugoslavia, Hungary, Poland, and Romania—whose elites more or less conspicuously disengaged themselves from the external designs of Soviet geopolitics and tried to create new identities for themselves as "developers" who focused on the economic welfare of their own peoples. The first three of these countries experimented with new property relations, simulated markets, and softer political controls to permit the more efficient flow of information to their production units. By contrast, the fourth country, Romania, set out to apply the classical Stalinist framework of military mobilization to obtain such non-Stalinist objectives, the building of a prosperous, internationally competitive, and "multilaterally developed" industrial economy. Neither model worked, though. Reflecting the logic of political rationality, even the reforms of the "liberal" economies could not surmount some of the structural constraints of garrison economies, bureaucratic meddling, centralized indicators, and regulated prices. As Janos Kornai recently observed, these policies faltered not because managers in the social sector were corrupt or incompetent but because they were forced to operate in an institutional context and culture that had not prepared them—because it could not prepare them—to behave like economically rational entrepreneurs.[78] This economic failure ultimately destroyed not only popular confidence in the regimes but the self-confidence of the political classes of these countries as well.

Unlike the domesticists, four East European countries—Bulgaria, Czechoslovakia, East Germany, and Albania—remained good internationalists to the very end. One of them, Albania, went its own quirky revolutionary way. Whether by choice or necessity, the elites of the other three remained part of the bloc, eager promoters of the grand design of Soviet geopolitics. They lent credence to their tough anti-imperialist rhetoric with their large military budgets and their active support for revolutionary movements of the Third World. Their ultimate failure was brought about not by economic crisis but by the grand transformation of Soviet politics that left them bereft of their very raison d'être.

Being a huge country, the Chinese People's Republic could strike out on its own and fashion its own institutions. China's leaders accepted the Leninist logic of militancy but applied it to the conditions of the 1950s, that is, to the conditions of the nuclear age, the technology of which

[78] See the review of Kornai, *The Road to a Free Economy*, in *Socialist Economies in Transition* 1 (June 1990), 3.

China acquired early. In Mao's own thinking these weapons could in the short term serve as an umbrella; in the long term, even as an instrument of the world revolution. This at least is the conclusion one can draw from his statement of 1957, that in a nuclear war socialism would suffer only demographic losses, easily replenished, while capitalism would lose its very last war.[79] Strategic principles were revised, and Mao returned to the concept of a worldwide guerrilla war, à la Bukharin, in which the global countryside would surround and destroy the global metropole.[80] But throughout these years the concept of a nuclear umbrella obviated the need for "mainline" mobilizational strategies that so much characterized Soviet society during the previous decades. If in the 1930s military might demanded the building and maintenance of vast armies of tanks, airplanes, and artillery that required broad-based industrialization in depth, the era of nuclear arms required only narrow sectoral and functionally specific infrastructural development. Whatever the validity of this reasoning, it permitted Mao and other Third World revolutionaries to indulge in their own "populist" priorities and to pursue more egalitarian and consensual politics. These policies may have raised revolutionary morale, but they did not promote economic efficiency: China, Vietnam, Cuba, Cambodia, North Korea, and Nicaragua could all boast victories on the battlefield, all of them against larger and better equipped enemies. Yet their respective labor forces could not perform such simple production tasks as the harvesting of rice and sugar cane. The communist regimes of this century will be remembered then for their military prowess and not for their successes in social engineering.

It is not entirely clear to the outside observer whether China's post-Mao reforms were motivated by these failures of social engineering or by the weakness of China's army in a conventional encounter with its Vietnamese communist neighbor. Like their Soviet counterparts, China's leaders understood that effective markets require a free flow of goods, people, and information. And like the Soviets, they, too, saw their own version of glasnost spill over into the political sphere as a demand for political participation. Like many in the Soviet Union, the majority of the Chinese political class perceived these demands not only as a threat to the markets but also as a threat to the existence of the state. Herein lie the similarities. But lacking an economically prosperous "home" to which they could return, Deng and Li were far less restrained than their Soviet counterparts had been. They drowned the movement in blood,

[79] See Stuart Schram, *The Political Thought of Mao Tse-tung,* rev. ed. (New York: Praeger, 1974), 128.
[80] Ibid., 128–32.

ironically in hopes of creating a "softer" authoritarian regime that could balance freedom and efficiency in the interest of development. There is some precedent for the success of such a strategy in the Soviet suppression of the Hungarian uprising of 1956, though the long-term success of the strategy remains questionable.

INDUSTRIALISM: FROM SOCIETY TO WORLD SYSTEM

Does the above discussion of revolutionary militancy imply that the concept of industrialism is irrelevant to the study of seventy years of communism in the Soviet Union, and to forty-some years of the same in China and Eastern Europe? The answer is negative. On the contrary one can argue quite convincingly that technological innovation, including its impact on beliefs, structures, and social goods, represents the only logical point of departure for the study of both communism and the dynamics of political change across the wider landscape of the modern world. But this requires dropping some of the postulates of the classical paradigm that saw societies as analytically self-contained units and that depicted social processes like industrialization as repeating themselves from society to society "plucked from all space and time."[81] Instead, some recent contributions to world systems theories suggest, first, an examination of the modernizing experience of the innovative "core" societies as a whole and then an examination of the impact of this experience on the societies themselves, as well as on social, economic, and political outcomes in the global peripheries and semiperipheries. The finding will be that economic processes are interdependent and that while the progress of one sector may become the source of a beneficial "spread" effect, it can also cause a more deleterious backwash, creating stagnation and decay, even as it reproduces and magnifies existing patterns of international income inequality.

Marxist scholars were the original proponents of this concept. They argued that this backwash was the result of exploitation: one version of the theory considers this exploitation a matter of coercion, pure and simple; another version derives from the controversial Marxist theories of surplus value and unequal exchange. These theories hold that when economies at different levels of sophistication trade with each other, surplus value is transferred from the less to the more developed economy.[82]

[81] Robert A. Nisbet, *Social Change and History* (London: Oxford University Press, 1969), 303.

[82] See, e.g., James D. Cockcroft, André Gunder Frank, and Dale L. Johnson, *Dependence and Underdevelopment* (Garden City, N.Y.: Doubleday, 1972); or see Immanuel Wallerstein, *The Modern World System* (New York: Academic Press, 1974).

In some versions of the theory, these exchanges presume a strict division of labor and distribution of power among three sectors of the world economy—the core, the periphery, and the semiperiphery.[83]

Especially popular in the context of Third World studies, these theories of surplus transfer also entered the field of comparative communism and have stirred a lively debate as to whether Soviet-type economies should be regarded as underdeveloped, developed, or developing. Theorists of the world economy generally argued that the more recent economic stagnation of communist societies was largely the result of their reentry into the capitalist world market, and that in this market communist societies occupied a semiperipheral position as both exploited and exploiters. Victims of the capitalist core, they were also victimizers of the still weaker peripheral economies.[84]

Another, perhaps less controversial explanation of the backwash is presented by what may be referred to as neo-liberal theory.[85] Like classical liberal thinkers, these theorists regard markets as the realm of rational choice in the pursuit of private gain. But unlike Smith and other classical liberals, they do not see these private choices producing equilibrium or adding up to public benefit. When a computer scientist leaves New Delhi for California, his private gain will translate into public loss for his country and thereby contribute to the disequilibrium that already prevails in the world economy. The same can be said about the flight of peripheral capital in search of a better ratio between risk and return. These flows of capital and talent are endemic and are believed to result in the development of still more underdevelopment on the global peripheries.

While never very popular among students of communist societies, the phenomenon is of considerable relevance to communist political behavior. In general, less developed countries confronting such potential for drain must choose between two unpalatable alternatives: either they allow the wages for skilled labor to rise to world market levels, thus contributing to domestic income inequality, or they prevent the free move-

[83] Wallerstein (fn. 82), esp. 15, 60–63.

[84] For this argument, see Timothy W. Luke and Carl Boggs, "Soviet Subimperialism and the Crisis of Bureaucratic Centralism," *Studies in Comparative Communism* 15 (Spring–Summer 1982), 95–124; and Timothy W. Luke, "On the Nature of Soviet Society," *Telos* 63 (Spring 1985), 178–87. For a vigorous counterargument, see Victor Zaslavsky, "Soviet Society and World System Analysis," *Telos* 62 (Winter 1984), 155–68; and Andrew Arato, "Between Reductionism and Relativism: Soviet Society as a World System," *Telos* 63 (Spring 1985), 178–87.

[85] Gunnar Myrdal, *Rich Lands and Poor* (New York: Harper, 1958), esp. 28–38; Albert Hirschman, *The Strategy of Economic Development* (New Haven: Yale University Press, 1962), 183–98.

ment of labor to the high-wage areas of the world economy. Communist governments tended to adopt the latter strategy. The iron and bamboo curtains, the Berlin Wall, and the recurrent attempts by these governments to put price tags on emigrants are explained at least in part by these countries' peripheral position in the world economy.

A third set of explanations grows out of modernization theory itself. Whether or not the core may develop at the expense of the periphery, the success of the process itself may have an additional relativizing and deleterious impact on the outsiders. First, technological breakthroughs have historically changed human consciousness by creating an awareness of choice. Born out of particular social configurations, this new consciousness knows no physical boundaries and will be diffused globally at a faster rate than the diffusion of production technologies. Together with the spread of new images of consumption, the spread of new expectations creates a sense of relative deprivation[86] and accounts for what neoclassical writers perceived as the "reversal of historical sequences"[87] or the chronic "gap" between "mobilization" and "development."[88] As a corollary, the successful industrialization of the core societies, with their complex institutions and military capabilities, creates a more complex international system in which the less advanced societies must upgrade their own administrative, military, and political institutions if they want to interact effectively with the leading societies of the world. This makes further demands on scarce resources and impedes savings for investment.

While these hypotheses were first developed in the context of Third World studies, the concepts underlying them are relevant to communist history as well. First, the paradigm offers a new perspective on the origins of communism. Looking through the prism of the world system, one would still be inclined to locate these origins in modern industrialism, much as do the works of Hannah Arendt or Adam Ulam.[89] However, this term will no longer refer to the industrialization of Russia (or China); it will refer instead to the industrial revolutions of England, Western Europe, and the U.S., with all their adverse consequences for the countries of the periphery. If Russia and China were troubled lands before their respective communist revolutions, it was not because their societies were changing too rapidly. Rather, it was because the industri-

---

[86] See Ted R. Gurr, *Why Men Rebel* (Princeton: Princeton University Press, 1972), esp. 92–122; and Nicholas Xenos, *Scarcity and Modernity* (New York: Basic Books, 1989).
[87] See Lucian W. Pye, *Aspects of Political Development* (Boston: Little, Brown, 1966), esp. 188–200.
[88] See Huntington (fn. 44), 54–56.
[89] See Arendt (fn. 2); and Adam B. Ulam, *The Unfinished Revolution: Marxism and Communism in the Modern World,* 2d rev. ed. (Boulder, Colo.: Westview Press, 1979).

alization of the core countries had created a new international system that put immense pressures upon them to mobilize their resources. Further, it fostered widespread aspirations that the economic and social systems could not possibly fulfill. If the peasants suffered absolute deprivation under the burden of taxation for purposes of state building, the workers suffered from a deep sense of relative deprivation as their rising wages continued to lag far behind those of the workers of the advanced societies. The radical intelligentsia that arose toward the end of the nineteenth century was a political class that sought to establish its own status and identity by organizing these popular frustrations into coherent political programs.

The concept of a world system also takes us a step closer to understanding the roots of Bolshevik utopianism and charismatic salvationism. Durkheim, Arendt, and, more ambiguously, Weber related these phenomena to discontinuities in the cultural systems of particular societies, which, as noted, raised the problem of empirical referents. The new paradigm offers a way out of this dilemma by focusing not on the crisis of Russian or Chinese culture but on the crisis of the broader, liberal world culture, or zeitgeist, of the nineteenth century. A key element of this culture was the belief, widely held, institutionalized, and enforced, that the virtues of hard work, "self-command," and sacrifice would enable the societies of the periphery to catch up with the nations of the core—a belief that was shattered by the invisible forces of the market by the beginning of this century.[90] Marxist salvationism was a response both to this anomie and to the cognitive vacuum created by the failure of the developmental promises of liberalism.

To move one step further, this globalized version of modernization theory permits of a fuller appreciation of the pressures that had to be borne by the economies of the Soviet Union and other communist countries. While the systems by their very nature and objectives manufactured shortages, these shortages were aggravated by their position in the international economy. The Soviet Union, much like Germany in the first half of the century, was not just a military challenger of the status quo but was also a challenger coming from a position of relative economic inferiority. Yet such a military-political challenge requires a parity or superiority in real expenditures. By all available evidence, in the Soviet case at least, these expenditures were indeed appropriated, but from a society in which per capita GNP was only a fraction of the American

[90] For an excellent discussion of this crisis, see Robert W. Tucker, *The Inequality of Nations* (New York: Basic Books, 1977), 21–24.

figure.[91] Worse still from the Soviet point of view, given its own position in the world economy as a leading producer and potential borrower, the United States was in a position to raise levels of spending and thus to accelerate the pace of the arms race. When this happened after 1979, the Soviet leaders were not only squeezed, but they also faced Hitler's make-or-break dilemma of 1938, whether to use their temporary advantage then or to change their overall geopolitical concept.

Related to this are the social and political consequences of relativized scarcity and deprivation generated by the international demonstration effect of the more advanced Western societies. In the interwar period the Soviets neutralized this demonstration effect by building physical barriers and by banning travel to and from the Soviet Union. After 1945 China and Eastern Europe followed that example: their iron and bamboo curtains were designed to keep people in as well as to keep ideas out. Still more drastically, after World War II millions of Soviet soldiers and prisoners who had been exposed to the substantially higher living standards of Central Europe were consigned to concentration and reeducation camps. The logic of this brutal policy became evident during the Brezhnev years, when some of the existing barriers were taken down, and people and images from the West and from certain Third World countries began to penetrate the various curtains. Once this happened, the communist political classes responded like the political classes of other backward countries: they began to use their official powers to expropriate, whether by legal or corrupt means, goods from the rest of the population. Thus, like most other peripheral states, the communist states began to act as instruments of income equalization—but not so much among the different strata of the citizenry as between the communist political class and the elites of the advanced industrial societies. The populations meanwhile suffered a twofold effect of relative deprivation: one by comparison between their own living standard and that of their counterparts in the West, the other by comparison between themselves and the elites of their ostensibly egalitarian societies. Directly or indirectly then, the international demonstration effect was the single most important destabilizer of communist states. The sense of relative deprivation and cries of corruption went together to delegitimate communist regimes.

Finally, the perspective of the larger modern world system should permit us to adjudicate the debate on whether communist societies ought to be treated as developed, developing, or underdeveloped. On the one

[91] See Eckhaus (fn. 72); Block (fn. 74); and Marer (fn. 74).

hand, adherents of the convergence school rightly point out that over the past forty to seventy years communist societies have become more complex and differentiated (even though one should still examine more closely the orders and kinds of complexity encountered in military societies). On the other hand, one can also agree with those observers who point out that over the same period communist societies underwent a quantum change, whether measured by domestic product or by indicators of health, education, and welfare. But while this record may be impressive in its own terms, or in comparison with a Third World society, it was relativized by the experience of the West, the only yardstick by which the citizens of communist societies measured material progress. The case of China is as illustrative here as are the cases of Czechoslovakia, Bulgaria, and East Germany.[92] Soviet-type societies are characterized by complexity cum scarcity, a combination that sets them apart from both First and Third World countries and especially from the historical experience of Western Europe and the United States. In the latter, the growth of complexity and material abundance went hand in hand and together were responsible for the rise of liberal democracy and political pluralism. This historical contrast has on the whole been ignored in the sociological treatment of the countries of the Soviet bloc, yet it is precisely this contrast that vitiates the seemingly powerful logic of convergence theory. For while the logic of complexity may well be the logic of decentralization, this logic is challenged by the hard realities of relative and absolute scarcities that the leaders of these societies had to contend with. Gorbachevism may well have stemmed from the realization that a more complex society cannot be effectively managed from a single center of economic and political authority. But this logic alone does not predict democracy or successful pluralism.

CONCLUSIONS

The triple agenda of this essay was to identify competing theories of political change, to examine their relevance to communist studies, and to pull these theories into a single, more comprehensive intellectual scheme. The most relevant constructs identified were Weber's theories of routinization and salvationism, Spencer's models of militancy and industrialism, and finally, the notion of a "modern world system," originally identified with Marxist scholarship but easily accommodated within other schools of thought as well. For while one may not want to accept the

[92] For this problem of relativization and the "power of corruption," see Chinese officials Shen Beijang and Wang Daohan in the *San Francisco Chronicle*, June 1, 1989, p. A24.

proposition that the "core" of the world system had arisen by sucking away the lifeblood of the peripheries, it is hard to refute the argument that the historical fact of economic development in the global metropole has created a plethora of adverse, confining, and debilitating conditions that peripheral actors are trying to overcome or escape. Spencer's grand dichotomy enters the picture because it provides two alternative routes, or ideal models, for the escape from these conditions. Meanwhile, Weber's idea of salvationism is relevant as a particular way of conceptualizing the art of the possible and as a response to crises of consciousness at critical historical junctures. Change under communism has accordingly been a two-track affair: first, the rationalization of salvationism, second, the tranformation of militancy into some form of industrialism. Although both of these processes have an internal logic, it would be a gross mistake to ignore the influence of external conditions upon actual outcomes.

Pursuing these themes one by one the article attempted to develop a better view of the past and show how certain pieces of the communist puzzle may fit this more comprehensive scheme. It also tried to show how communism fits into a larger family of political movements and regimes. The question that remains is how this broader paradigm can help us to map out the future of communism and, more generally, of revolutionary militancy in the modern world.

Clearly, in the last few years a number of communist regimes simply melted away. In others communist elites claim to have abandoned the path of revolutionary militancy in favor of developmental strategies, in some cases combined with the quest for democracy. In some cases at least doubts will linger concerning the sincerity of this choice. But even where it seems certain that such a choice has in fact been made, outcomes will be beset by contraditions, as policymakers confront "confining conditions" that only few nations have been able to overcome on their own in modern history. The most successful cases on record are those of European and Far Eastern nations in the aftermath of World War II. They seem to suggest that success is most likely when development is undertaken in the context of a larger cooperative design sponsored by the more advanced nations of the world. This is a perception that Gorbachev, Yeltsin, and so many East European leaders subscribe to by conjuring up images of a common market or, more loftily, of a common home shared with the richer nations, as preferable to images of autochthonous development. Indeed, just as this article was being prepared for press, one Soviet leader was in Tokyo, the other in Strasbourg, painting bleak pictures of the Soviet future and pleading for economic generosity and political sympathy. The impulse to respond to such dire warnings may not be absent; in fact it may be quite strong. But questions remain as to the capacity of Westerners to absorb such sacrifice and, in the last analysis, as to how large that common edifice can be. The sheer volume of demand for resources is staggering and may vastly exceed available supply in funds, opportunities, and technical expertise. While some of the lesser nations of Europe may find admittance into a common home, the major nations of the former communist world may simply be too big to salvage and for solutions other than their own. Under these circumstances in many of these countries democracy may well remain a dream, or mere facade, and regression into militancy a perennial temptation. The political classes of big nations in particular may be tempted to believe that it is easier to adjust the world market than to adjust themselves to its rules.

For a while, especially during the heady winter months of 1989–90, the view was widely held that Leninism, together with other revolutionary movements, had exhausted itself and that the future belonged to liberal elites with rational designs of economic markets and political pluralism. This argument rested on fragile foundations, however, and overlooked some of the harsh realities of our modern world. Most significantly, it overlooked the fact that the global inequalities that had produced Leninism in Russia are more salient now than then and are being reproduced at a much faster rate than in the early modern age. Thus, even if old cleavages between East and West were closed and the conflicts of the cold war era contained, other cleavages, most notably between North and South, are likely to deepen further, with billions remaining on the wrong side of the economic fence. Thus while Leninism as we have known it for decades may not replicate itself in exact detail, other forms of revolutionary militancy are likely to arise and have mass appeal. Curiously, just as we were spinning our dreams about the "end of history," a revolutionary war was in the making, to display within a few months all the features that we associate with the behavior of Spencer's military societies and states: the marshaling of resources for investment in the military sector; an expedition of plunder tied to higher geopolitical purposes; a challenge to the structure of the existing world system, together with a revolutionary challenge to basic norms of international conduct that, while of "core" origin, have been universalized in the past century. The major peril now is that such movements of righteous militancy may have access to vastly more destructive technologies than heretofore and that with their highly instrumental view of their own society, they may be willing to take risks that will make the Leninist regimes of the past appear as models of moderation and responsibility.

To prevent this from happening must be the first priority of international cooperation in what has rhetoricallly been designated as a "new" order of the world. Should such cooperation fail, not only those who occupy the few niches of global privilege, but the entire human race, will find themselves in jeopardy.

POLITICAL DYNAMICS OF THE POST-COMMUNIST TRANSITION
A Comparative Perspective

THERE is an understandable tendency among observers of recent transformations in the communist world to be impressed by the uniqueness of the entire phenomenon. While earlier attempts at limited reform of communist polities and economies are numerous, the dismantling and disintegration of communist structures witnessed in the 1980s have never before been successfully attempted and achieved on such a scale. Although there remain important differences in the degree to which communist institutions have been displaced in various countries, the scope and depth of change have, on the whole, been sufficient for many to now speak of a "post-communist" era or even "the end of history."[1]

However unique these developments have been on one level, the transition from communism may, nevertheless, be usefully viewed as a subcategory of a more generic phenomenon of transition from authoritarian rule. In recent decades, efforts to liberalize and democratize authoritarian regimes in Latin America and Southern Europe have been quite numerous and have achieved varying degrees of success. Students of communist and post-communist regimes can learn a great deal from those cases and from the efforts that have been made to generalize about the transition process and the dilemmas and choices to which it gives rise.[2]

In this paper, the focus will be on the still uncertain process of transition currently under way in the USSR. The goal is to bring a comparative perspective to bear in order both to provide new insight into the dynamics of the disintegration of the communist order and to consider

* The author would like to thank Mark Ruhl for his helpful comments on an earlier draft of this paper.

[1] Francis Fukuyama, "The End of History?" *National Interest* 16 (Summer 1989), 3–18.

[2] Students of the USSR and other communist regimes in transition have not made much use of these cases or of the literature on postauthoritarian transitions that they have spawned. Noteworthy exceptions are Thomas F. Remington, "Regime Transition in Communist Systems," *Soviet Economy* 6 (April–June 1990), 160–90; and George W. Breslauer, "Evaluating Gorbachev as Leader," *Soviet Economy* 5 (October–December 1989), 299–340.

the prospects for successful Soviet democratization. In the process, a case will be made for a more comparative approach to the issue of post-communist transitions in general. Before moving to substantive issues, however, a brief digression on the issue of comparability is necessary.

THE QUESTION OF COMPARABILITY

The debate over the importance of the unique versus the universal in history is certainly not new, and it is not the intention here to reiterate the old and ultimately unresolvable arguments made in that regard. Instead, what follows is addressed to those who accept that there are elements of both the unique and the universal present in every situation, who believe that comparison can, in principle, illuminate common patterns of behavior across disparate political cultures, but who may question whether—in comparing transitions from communist authoritarianism to transitions from non-communist authoritarianism—one is really looking at the generically same phenomenon. As political scientist Giovanni Sartori has noted, the higher one climbs the "ladder of abstraction" (i.e., the more extensive the class of phenomena one labels with the same conceptual apparatus), the greater the risk of "conceptual stretching" in which the extension or denotation of a concept is expanded by "obfuscating the connotation."[3] Comparing the Soviet case and other instances of post-communist transformation with transitions from non-communist authoritarian regimes raises this problem of conceptual stretching on three different levels.

In the first place, there may be significant differences in the goal of the regime transition. Although "democratization" is a common theme in cases of transition in Latin America, Southern Europe, and the communist world alike, the meaning of that term can vary tremendously. Numerous Western observers have argued that the goal of the transition initiated by Gorbachev in the USSR was never democracy in the Western sense but merely a less "totalitarian" and, perhaps, more enlightened form of authoritarian rule.[4] Assuming that to be the case, one might view the transition under way in the USSR as a transition *to* rather than *from*

[3] Giovanni Sartori, "Concept Misformation in Political Science," *American Political Science Review* 64 (December 1970), 1040–41.

[4] See, for example, Seweryn Bialer, "Gorbachev's Program of Change: Sources, Significance, Prospects," in Seweryn Bialer and Michael Mandelbaum, eds., *Gorbachev's Russia and America's Foreign Policy* (Boulder, Colo.: Westview, 1988), 256–58, 299. Also see Jerry Hough, *Russia and the West: Gorbachev and the Politics of Reform* (New York: Simon and Schuster, 1988), 209–12.

the kind of authoritarian rule that other nations in Europe and the Third World have been trying to transcend.

Comparison of such diverse efforts would thus appear to be quite problematic were it not for the fact that the goals of the transition, as articulated by those factions of the old regime responsible for the initiation of change, may ultimately prove to be of little consequence. As will be discussed in more detail later, most efforts to transform authoritarian regimes take on a life and dynamic of their own that quickly sweep away the most carefully laid plans of the architects of reform. Goals change as once-cautious reformers become more daring and come to accept changes that far exceed those initially intended.

A second problem in comparing such events is related to differences in the process of regime transition. Is it useful, for example, to compare the Soviet transition initiated by civilian reformers within the ruling elite to the Portuguese case in which a military coup overturned the old regime and allowed the issue of democracy a place on the political agenda? In raising that question, however, it follows that one must also ask whether the process of transition in the USSR can be compared to that of Romania or Hungary, where the specifics of the post-communist transition process have differed both from one another and from those of the USSR. Similarly, can the Portuguese situation be usefully compared to that of Spain, which, in many respects, resembles the Soviet case more than that of its Iberian neighbor? As one observer has summarized the Spanish reform process:

> It was a question of reformist elements, associated with the incumbent dictatorship, initiating processes of political change from within the established regime. Equally, it was a question of reformists seizing and, for some time, maintaining the initiative in the face of opposition from both their own backward-looking colleagues and from the dictatorship's opponents who were dedicated to a complete break with the old order.[5]

That characterization of the Spanish situation should sound more familiar to students of the Gorbachev era than to observers of the Portuguese case.

Since there appears to be as much variability in the transition process on each side of the communist/non-communist divide as there is across it, the issue of the comparability of transitions from communism to transitions from other forms of authoritarian rule seems, in this respect, to be beside the point. Instead, the concern should be to delimit a universe

---

[5] Kenneth Medhurst, "Spain's Evolutionary Pathway from Dictatorship to Democracy," in Geoffrey Pridham, ed., *The New Mediterranean Democracies: Regime Transition in Spain, Greece and Portugal* (London: Frank Cass, 1984), 30.

of potential cases for comparison by identifying characteristics of the transition process common to each. In this paper, the interest is with efforts at nonrevolutionary transitions from authoritarian rule in which elements of the old regime play an important role in the initiation and/ or direction of political change. This definition is not meant to exclude the probability of societal pressures for reform or the possibility that reforms initiated from above can eventually be overtaken by revolution from below. Rather, the focus here is simply on those forms and periods of transition in which reformist segments of the old order have a part to play and which are, by definition, distinct from periods of systemic stability, on the one hand, and mass revolutionary movements, on the other.

Thus defined, all of the cases noted above (the Soviet, Romanian, Hungarian, Spanish, and Portuguese) could, despite their differences, be included, as can many others from the Third World and Europe. To use Sartori's terms once again, the "extension" of the concept of postauthoritarian transitions has been achieved not by obfuscating the connotation of the concept but by limiting it. That is, we have enlarged the class of things to which this concept refers by reducing some of its attributes while, at the same time, making sure to be reasonably precise about those common attributes that remain.[6]

The final problem of comparability to be addressed—and perhaps the place where the perception of conceptual stretching is potentially the greatest—is related to the nature of the authoritarianism being transformed. Proponents of the "totalitarian" model in communist studies have always at least implicitly argued that totalitarianism was different not only from democracy but from old-fashioned authoritarianism as well.[7] In essence, the latter distinction was rooted in the perceived ambition and success of totalitarian regimes in regard to the extension of state power and initiative. Whereas traditional authoritarianism built walls to demarcate the boundaries beyond which civil society could not tread, totalitarian regimes aimed to crush the preexisting civil society altogether.

As an ideal type, totalitarianism certainly differs from forms of authoritarian rule common in much of the non-communist world. As an empirical concept, totalitarianism also retains utility as a distinct variation on the authoritarian theme. Nevertheless, the distinction should not

[6] Sartori (fn. 3), 1041–42.

[7] For the classic exposition of the concept of totalitarianism, see Carl J. Friedrich and Zbigniew Brzezinski, *Totalitarian Dictatorship and Autocracy* (Cambridge: Harvard University Press, 1956). For the most well known recent effort to distinguish authoritarian from totalitarian regimes, see Jeane Kirkpatrick, "Dictatorships and Double Standards," *Commentary*, November 1979, pp. 34–45.

be exaggerated. Communist regimes have not only failed to achieve the total control envisioned by the totalitarian model but, especially in the post-Stalin era, have also scaled back those ambitions.[8] Even in the economy where the conceptual distinction between authoritarian and totalitarian regimes is sharp, the reality is much more muddled. It has been estimated that in the USSR of the late 1970s the proportion of income per capita derived from the private sector (legal and illegal) ranged from roughly 20 percent in the eastern RSFSR to more than 60 percent in Armenia.[9] At the same time, state economic ownership and control is hardly unique to self-proclaimed communist regimes.

Even where important empirical differences between communist totalitarianism and other forms of authoritarian rule remain, they should not be viewed as a barrier to comparison. While the concern over conceptual stretching is legitimate and must be kept in mind, "conceptual constriction" that ultimately reduces all phenomena to exclusive sets of single, unique entities should be of equal concern. Successful use of comparative political analysis requires the coexistence of both commonality and diversity in the cases to be examined. In fact, there is a case to be made for maximizing diversity insofar as claims to the universality of common patterns of political behavior are thereby strengthened.[10] Then again, to the extent that the patterns of political behavior differ, the distinctions in the cases examined may provide clues toward an explanation. In the discussion to follow, sensitivity to and explanation of points of both convergence and divergence in the politics of regime transition across the communist/non-communist divide is the goal.

THE DYNAMICS OF DISINTEGRATION

Transitions from authoritarian regimes actually involve two analytically distinct but empirically interrelated phenomena. On the one hand, there is the process of breaking down the preexisting structures of authoritarian rule. On the other hand, there is the task of creating new structures to take their place. In pursuing the transition, the stated goal of many reformers is to provide for a more democratic process of government,

[8] For a more detailed critique of the concept of totalitarianism, see Amos Perlmutter, *Modern Authoritarianism* (New Haven: Yale University Press, 1981), 62–75.

[9] Gregory Grossman, "Roots of Gorbachev's Problems: Private Income and Outlay in the Late 1970s," in U.S. Congress, Joint Economic Committee, *Gorbachev's Economic Plans* (November 23, 1987), 213–29.

[10] Frederick W. Frey, "Cross-Cultural Survey Research in Political Science," in Robert T. Holt and John E. Turner, eds., *The Methodology of Comparative Research* (New York: Free Press, 1970), 200.

but successful dismantlement of the old order does not guarantee a democratic outcome. The former is a necessary but not a sufficient condition
of the latter. The February 1917 revolution in Russia ended tsarist rule
but failed to establish the foundations for an effectively functioning democracy. Similarly, by the end of 1990 Gorbachev's reforms had stripped
the Communist Party of much of its power, yet the prospects for democracy seemed as remote as ever.[11] In accordance with this analytic distinction between the destructive and constructive components of regime
transition, the disintegration of Soviet communism will be examined first
and will be followed by an analysis of the dilemmas of democratization.

THE INITIAL DECOMPRESSION

It was under the banner of glasnost that the reformist spirit of the Gorbachev era was first introduced. In its original and most narrow sense,
"glasnost" referred to a policy aimed at increasing access to information,
thereby reducing the veil of censorship and secrecy that had long smoth-
ered Soviet society. In short time, however, the "glasnost era" came to
represent a larger package of liberalizing reforms that included greater
protection of individuals from the coercive power of the state, expanded
freedom of political expression and association, easing of some restrictions on travel and emigration, and a new tolerance toward religious
activity.

While glasnost did involve a significant increase in the flow of information and liberty, it was Gorbachev who maintained his hand on the
control valve. Consequently, as numerous Western and Soviet observers
have noted, glasnost shared little in common with the Western idea of
"freedom of information" and even less with Western notions of democratic, constitutional government. As if to underline those distinctions,
some observers have emphasized the Russian heredity of Gorbachev's
policy. One author began an article on the subject by promising to place
glasnost "in a broader context by tracing the origins of glasnost' to 19th-
century Russia."[12] Another observer has stated simply, "Glasnost' has
Russian national roots."[13]

Without denying the existence of Russian precedents in this regard,

---

[11] The conservative reaction of late 1990 and early 1991 appears less the result of a resur-
gent Communist Party than a military-KGB-Gorbachev alliance. See summary of Alexander
Rahr's presentation to the Kennan Institute for Advanced Russian Studies by Peggy Mc-
Inerny, "Democratic Opposition at the Crossroads" (Meeting Report 8:7, Washington, D.C.).

[12] Natalie Gross, "Glasnost': Roots and Practice," *Problems of Communism* 36 (November–
December 1987), 69.

[13] Victor Yasmann, "Can Glasnost' Be Reversed?" *Radio Liberty Report on the USSR* 3
(February 1, 1991), 28.

the fact remains that glasnost is not a uniquely Russian phenomenon. In a recent study of more than a dozen cases of transition from authoritarian rule in Latin America and Southern Europe, it was found that in every case the transition began with a period of glasnost-like liberalization.[14] This liberalization, often referred to in discussions of the Latin world as *decompressao* (decompression) or *apertura* (opening), typically involves the institution, restoration, or strengthening of the civil rights and liberties of individuals and groups. Guarantees of protection from arbitrary state power are introduced, the rights of free expression and association are strengthened, and access to information is increased.

For opponents of authoritarian rule, the decompression is typically viewed with some ambivalence. While a clear and welcome departure from past practices, liberalization is clearly not democratization. At a minimum, democracy involves both the provision of means to pursue the representation of diverse interests in government and the institutionalization of mechanisms to hold rulers accountable to the public will— including mechanisms that allow for the peaceful removal of governments from power. Furthermore, democracy precludes the possibility of altering outcomes after the fact. As Adam Przeworski has noted, everyone in a democracy, including rulers, must live with the fact that the outcome of political competition is uncertain and unalterable except through another round of equally uncertain democratic political struggle.[15] In a regime of "liberalized authoritarianism," in contrast, not only does the power apparatus remain intact but it retains "its capacity to control outcomes ex post."[16] Thus, the liberalization enjoyed always feels somewhat tenuous and insecure. It is granted and controlled from above and is potentially subject to revocation at any time.

Invariably, this liberalization process begins with a split within the ruling regime between reformers (soft-liners) and conservatives (hard-liners). Of course, even during more routine periods of authoritarian rule, divisions within the elite over issues of power and policy tend to be a constant. In periods of significant liberalization, however, not only are

[14] Guillermo O'Donnell and Philippe C. Schmitter, *Transitions from Authoritarian Rule: Tentative Conclusions about Uncertain Democracies* (Baltimore: Johns Hopkins University Press, 1986), 10. The influence of the O'Donnell and Schmitter volume permeates much of the analysis contained in this paper even though only the most direct references will be footnoted as such. (Note that the reference here is the fourth volume in a series on transitions from authoritarian rule. The four were published both separately and in a combined edition. All the page references to the four volumes in this paper are from the combined edition.)
[15] Adam Przeworski, "Democracy as a Contingent Outcome of Conflicts," in Jon Elster and Rune Slagstad, eds., *Constitutionalism and Democracy* (Cambridge: Cambridge University Press, 1988), 61–62.
[16] Ibid., 61.

such divisions deeper but they lead some members of the regime to seek support outside the ruling elite.[17] In December 1976, just five months after assuming office, Prime Minister Suarez of Spain held a referendum to garner public support for his constitutional reforms.[18] In the USSR, Andrei Sakharov's return from banishment in Gorky in December 1986 and the cultural thaw that was, in effect, the first wave of glasnost were both clear efforts by Gorbachev to appeal for support to the country's intelligentsia. As time went on, Gorbachev's appeals for outside support would become even more direct. During the course of a February 1989 visit to the Ukraine, he appealed to his public supporters to help fight enemies of reform in the following terms: "You keep up the pressure. We'll press from the top, and you keep pressing from the bottom. Only in that way can perestroika succeed."[19] While common in democracies, such calls for support outside the regime constitute a radical change in the practice of authoritarian politics. While modern authoritarianism is distinguished by its efforts to mobilize the entire society behind the regime and its cause,[20] efforts to enlist outsiders as weapons of internal factional battles are generally taboo. In the Soviet case, the Leninist tradition of "democratic centralism," with its emphasis on demonstrating a united front vis-à-vis the larger society, is a very explicit statement of this principle.

Reformers within a liberalizing authoritarian regime often vary in their views of how far the process of reform should progress. While some might be satisfied with a liberalized authoritarianism, others might envision further movement in the direction of democratization. However, in comparison with regime hard-liners (who reject all but the most cosmetic changes) and opponents of the regime (who want a complete and immediate break with the past), reformers in the regime, by definition, occupy the position of the political center. While this centrist position carries with it the risk of alienating both hard-liners and regime opponents alike, at least in the early stages of the liberalization process the advantages of occupying the political center seem to outweigh the risks.

On the one hand, the reformers are initially in a strong position in relation to more radical opponents outside the regime. Emerging from the repression and persecution of authoritarian rule, the opposition is

[17] Adam Przeworski, "Some Problems in the Study of the Transition to Democracy," in Guillermo O'Donnell, Philippe C. Schmitter, and Laurence Whitehead, eds., *Transitions from Authoritarian Rule: Comparative Perspectives* (Baltimore: Johns Hopkins University Press, 1986), 56.
[18] Medhurst (fn. 5), 37.
[19] *New York Times*, February 21, 1989, p. A3.
[20] On this point, see Perlmutter (fn. 8), esp. chap. 1.

likely to be weak and disorganized. Perhaps even more important is the fear of political regression. Reflecting on the Latin American and Southern European cases, O'Donnell and Schmitter note:

> Their [the soft-liners'] ace in the hole is the threat that if the opposition refuses to play according to the rules they propose initially—usually a modest liberalization confined to individual rights and a restricted democratization with tight limits on participants and a narrow agenda of permissible policy issues—they will simply cancel the game and return to the authoritarian status quo ante. This tends to weaken and divide the proponents of further democratization. Some believe the threat and, preferring to avoid the worse outcome, agree to play the soft-liners' game.[21]

In the USSR, this logic provides part of the explanation for the failure of the radical Inter-Regional Group of Deputies in the Congress of People's Deputies to transform itself into an organized political party. According to one Western analyst who has worked with the group, there was a fear among some of its members of a return to "extreme discipline and an iron hand."[22] Although he never abandoned his principles, it is this logic that may have led Andrei Sakharov to give Gorbachev's policies his qualified support and to work for greater change within the reformed political institutions of the Gorbachev era. Similarly, in Lithuania, where the independence movement developed most rapidly, a parliamentary declaration of independence did not take place until March 1990, by which time Soviet toleration of the distintegration of its East European empire had raised questions as to how far Gorbachev would go to preserve his internal empire.

In the early stages of liberalization, the position of reformers vis-à-vis regime hard-liners also tends, for a time, to become increasingly strong. In the first place, the initial restraint and disorganization of the opposition lends support to reformers' claims to have the situation under control.[23] While conservatives, like Ligachev in the USSR, continue to harbor doubts, and though they may persist in their attacks on the reform process, they tend to remain on the defensive. That Ligachev's criticisms of the direction of change rarely attacked Gorbachev directly and almost always included pro forma endorsements of the general idea of glasnost and perestroika were good indications of the weakness of his position.

A second important weakness of conservatives stems, ironically, from the fact that the authoritarian structures, norms, and psychology of the old regime often make it surprisingly easy for reformers in positions of

[21] O'Donnell and Schmitter (fn. 14), 24.
[22] McInerny (fn. 11).
[23] O'Donnell and Schmitter (fn. 14), 26.

power to dismantle that regime from within. Despite the presence of large numbers of conservative opponents of reform, a resolution promoting the democratization of the USSR passed unanimously at the nineteenth conference of the CPSU in June 1988, with only two abstentions.[24] A few months later the Supreme Soviet voted overwhelmingly to approve new laws on elections and constitutional reform that, in effect, denied to many of those who had voted their status, power, and perquisites.[25] Similarly, in 1976 the members of the Francoist rubber-stamp legislature, the Cortes, voted 425 to 15 for political reforms in what one observer called an act of "collective suicide."[26]

Aside from these political dynamics, the strength of reformers within the regime is also a function both of the context of the larger environment and of the political and leadership skills of key reform leaders. The existence of serious unresolved political, social, and economic crises is what leads to splits inside the authoritarian regime in the first place, thereby setting off the political dynamic discussed above. At the same time, political skills are necessary if reformist leaders are to take advantage of the opportunities at least temporarily available. Thus, Gorbachev was able to go further in his reforms than had Khrushchev, both because the problems facing the USSR in the 1980s were much more severe than those of the 1950s and because of Gorbachev's superior skills in playing the strong hand that the political center initially holds in such circumstances. It is this interaction of structural, political, and individual factors that explains the puzzle of Gorbachev's rapid consolidation of political authority in the mid-1980s.

COLLAPSE OF THE POLITICAL CENTER

Just as surely as reformers in the regime are favored with certain political advantages in the early stages of the transition process, so too, in turn, do those advantages eventually begin to wither. The political center, once such an asset, can rapidly become a liability and can bring down reformist leaders who fail to adjust. The cause of this shift can best be understood through a consideration of the relationship between legitimacy and stability. As Przeworski has emphasized, while legitimacy may be a sufficient condition of regime stability, it is not a necessary condition.[27] The inability of the Communist Party to demonstrate public support in the

[24] *Pravda*, July 2, 1988, p. 12.
[25] TASS, December 1, 1988. Reported in "Constitutional Amendments Approved," Foreign Broadcast Information Service, *Daily Report: Soviet Union* (December 1, 1988).
[26] Paul Preston, *The Triumph of Democracy in Spain* (London and New York: Methuen, 1986), 101.
[27] Przeworski (fn. 17), 51.

new political milieu of the Gorbachev era certainly raises doubts as to the legitimacy of communist rule; yet, prior to Gorbachev, the political stability of the communist regime was not in question.[28] Similarly, relatively quick mobilization of support for democratic change in Portugal, Spain, and Brazil in the 1970s suggests a lack of legitimacy of authoritarian rule in those countries as well, yet, in these as in the USSR, change had to be initiated from within the regime itself. In none of those cases did there exist significant prior threats to authoritarian rule from outside the regime.

The explanation for the political stability of unpopular regimes is that stability is often less a function of legitimacy than of the perceived lack of availability of preferable alternatives.[29] Put somewhat differently, legitimacy itself may be less an *absolute* than a *relative* concept conditioned by the array of feasible alternatives present. Unpopular regimes can maintain their domination of society through repression that makes the cost of opposition very high, thus making the possibility of significant change seem remote. Compared with a return to harsh Stalinist rule, which for most Soviet citizens must have been seen as the only possible alternative, Brezhnev's comparatively mild dictatorship might even have gained some relative legitimacy. With the onset of liberalization, however, not only do the costs and risks of opposition begin to fall but alternatives to the status quo ante that once seemed impossible now appear to be within the realm of possibility. As a result, one often encounters the paradox of rising absolute legitimacy coupled with a decline in relative legitimacy and increasing instability. This comes about because increases in absolute regime legitimacy derived from the process of reform are outmatched by a sense of the expansion of the possible.

Failing fully to appreciate the dynamic at work here, reformers often overestimate both the support and the goodwill that limited liberalization has bought them as well as their ability to keep the process of change they unleashed under their control. According to O'Donnell and Schmitter, this was true of "the Argentine military in 1973, the Brazilian generals in 1974, the Portuguese MFA in 1975, the Uruguayan junta in 1980, [and] the Turkish military in 1983."[30] Gorbachev was, perhaps, more sensitive and realistic in this regard than most in his position. He was, for example, openly critical of those on his team who, by mid-1989, had

[28] For an alternative view of communist legitimacy that was written before the Gorbachev era, see Seweryn Bialer, *Stalin's Successors* (Cambridge: Cambridge University Press, 1980), chap. 9.
[29] Przeworski (fn. 17), 52.
[30] O'Donnell and Schmitter (fn. 14), 58.

begun to express surprise and alarm at the instability reform had produced. In his concluding remarks to a July 1989 conference in the CPSU Central Committee, Gorbachev asked in a rhetorical fashion: "Is it really necessary to panic when revolutionary processes become a reality? It is we who brought them about with our policy. Didn't we understand that when all this was being discussed?"[31] Likewise, his unwillingness to stand for direct election to the presidency of the USSR was another indication of a realistic estimate of the strengths and liabilities of his position.

Still, to understand the forces at work is not necessarily to control them. Maintaining control through the threat of reversing the reform process becomes less believable over time, insofar as the political fate of those who initiated liberalization becomes increasingly tied to its continuation. Indeed, the reformers' threat to reverse the process has been characterized as little more than a bluff from the outset.[32] Once called on that bluff, reformers' leverage with the opposition is reduced, and they often find themselves accepting changes that were once anathema to them. In Spain, Prime Minister Suarez was to find himself in a battle with the opposition over control of the transition and was forced to make a number of concessions, including legalization of the Spanish Communist Party.[33] Likewise, in Brazil, the Geisel government found that its plans for a closely controlled process of liberalization in the 1970s were under constant pressure from an opposition emboldened to push for quicker and more sweeping changes.[34] In a variation on the same theme, the radical leaders of the 1974 Portuguese coup were to play midwife to the birth of a liberal democratic order that they had not originally envisioned.[35]

In Gorbachev's case, it would certainly be an exaggeration to suggest that he had lost all control over events or that his reform strategy had degenerated into a completely ad hoc response to crisis. Equally exaggerated, however, are assertions that developments in the USSR have all gone according to Gorbachev's grand design.[36] At the end of 1989, Gorbachev was still resisting calls to eliminate the constitutional guarantee

---

[31] *Pravda*, July 21, 1989, p. 1.

[32] O'Donnell and Schmitter (fn. 14), 24.

[33] Preston (fn. 26), 95; Medhurst (fn. 5), 34.

[34] Thomas E. Skidmore, "Brazil's Slow Road to Democratization: 1974–1985," in Alfred Stepan, ed., *Democratizing Brazil: Problems of Transition and Consolidation* (New York: Oxford University Press, 1989), 10–19.

[35] Thomas C. Bruneau, "Continuity and Change in Portuguese Politics: Ten Years after the Revolution of 25 April 1974," in Pridham (fn. 5), 73.

[36] Jerry Hough comes closest to this position among Western analysts. See "Gorbachev's Endgame," *World Policy Journal* 7 (Fall 1990), 639–72.

of the leading role of the Communist Party and to create a multiparty political system.[37] Continued pressures for reform, however, were soon to force a dramatic reversal. In March 1990 the Congress of People's Deputies, with Gorbachev's consent, formally abolished article 6 of the Soviet constitution, which guaranteed the CPSU's monopoly on power, and this began to clear the way for the emergence of other parties.

Just when it seems that the pressures for change from below are irresistible, however, previously moribund hard-liners within the regime typically appear to be granted a new lease on life. By late 1980 and early 1981 many observers of Brazilian politics began to speak of the irreversibility of the liberalization process, only to have this optimism destroyed by subsequent reports of military terror against the opposition.[38] In Spain, the growing optimism of the opposition led directly to ever more defiant and determined cooperation between military and civilian critics of change.[39] Likewise, in the USSR, the conservative resurgence of 1990–91 followed closely on the heels of the challenge to the one-party monopoly, the discussion of a five-hundred-day plan to marketize the economy, and the rapidly developing challenges to the very existence of the multinational union. The timing here is not fortuitous. Given the concessions made by regime soft-liners, conservatives are less convinced than ever of the ability or will of soft-liners to rein in an increasingly assertive civil society. Feeling that their conservatism has been vindicated by events, they are reenergized in their struggle against reform.

The upshot of this entire process is a society increasingly polarized, and, in such a context, the centrist position of the reformist leadership becomes increasingly untenable.[40] Briefly seen by conservatives as insurance against popular rebellion and by radicals as the main obstacle to a conservative coup, the reformist center quickly becomes the object of scorn and distrust from both sides. The Gorbachev government in the USSR, the Suarez government in Spain, and the Geisel government in Brazil each came to face this dual challenge to its authority.[41] Indeed, critics on both ends of the political spectrum, feeling equally betrayed by

---

[37] See *Pravda*, November 26, 1989, pp. 1–3.

[38] Luciano Martins, "The 'Liberalization' of Authoritarian Rule in Brazil," in Guillermo O'Donnell, Philippe Schmitter, and Laurence Whitehead, eds., *Transitions from Authoritarian Rule: Latin America* (Baltimore: Johns Hopkins University Press, 1986), 86.

[39] Preston (fn. 26), 96.

[40] Dankwart A. Rustow notes that the hallmark of the preparatory phase of the transition to democracy is "polarization rather than pluralism." See Rustow, "Transitions to Democracy: Toward a Dynamic Model," *Comparative Politics* 2 (April 1970), 354.

[41] On the Spanish case, see Preston (fn. 26), 96. On the Brazilian case, see Martins (fn. 38), 84.

regime soft-liners, typically come to spend more time and energy attacking those reformers than they do each other.

At such points in time, the entire process of reform might be said to reach a crossroads. It often appears that the only possible outcomes are the reversal of the liberalization process (with or without the support of regime reformers) or further descent into chaos and, perhaps, civil war. For supporters of democracy, these are often times of pessimism. The reemergence of conservative forces and the polarization of society do seem to bode poorly for democracy. Observers of the Soviet situation in early 1991 certainly had cause to adopt this mood of pessimism.

However, the political dynamics at work here do not always guarantee the failure of the democratization process. The chaos, polarization, conflict, and tension that characterize this period of the transition can sometimes be seen, in retrospect, to have been the birth pangs of a more democratic order. As Dankwart Rustow argued in his seminal 1970 article on democratic transitions, "What infant democracy requires is not a lukewarm struggle but a hot family feud."[42] Indeed, many nations in Latin America and Southern Europe have managed to maneuver through these powerful political currents toward relatively democratic outcomes.

It is not the intention in this paper to make any firm predictions as to whether the USSR can ride those currents to a similarly positive conclusion. Instead, in the pages that follow, the intention is to go back to the literature on regime transition outside the communist world, to examine the factors that make a successful transition to democracy more or less likely, and to apply the lessons learned to the Soviet case in a manner that emphasizes less the certainty of future trends than one that analyzes what has already transpired and examines the possibilities thereby spawned.

DILEMMAS OF DEMOCRATIZATION

In the literature on transitions to democracy, some analysts emphasize variables of context while others stress those of process. Included among the former variables are the level of economic development, the character of the national political culture, the degree of national integration, and the nature of the country's class structure. These factors are usually discussed in the course of considering the "preconditions" or "determi-

[42] Rustow (fn. 40), 355.

nants" of democracy.[43] In contrast, those who stress process adopt a less structuralist approach, preferring, instead, to focus on the "making" of the democratic transition and the choices and strategies adopted by key actors.[44] Still others have argued the need to draw upon and integrate the lessons of both approaches.[45] It is this latter advice that guides the present effort to understand the issue of Soviet democratization.

THE DEMOCRATIZATION PROCESS

The first tentative steps from a process of liberalization to one of democratization were taken by the Gorbachev regime in mid-1988. At the CPSU conference held in June of that year, a resolution entitled "On the Democratization of Soviet Society and Reform of the Political System" was adopted.[46] A few months later, two laws designed to spell out and implement the political changes embodied in the spirit of that resolution, the "Law on Elections of USSR People's Deputies" and the "Law on Amendments and Additions to the USSR Constitution," were approved by the Supreme Soviet.[47] Taken together, the two laws provided, at both the all-union and local levels, for multiple candidate elections to legislative bodies whose powers and authority were significantly increased. At the all-union level, for example, there would be popular election of a new Congress of People's Deputies that would, in turn, select from among its membership a new streamlined Supreme Soviet of 542 members. Most significantly, the new Supreme Soviet would meet in regularly scheduled spring and fall sessions each of three to four months' duration. In effect, the USSR seemed to be at least hesitantly groping its way toward a system in which the articulation and representation of diverse interests were legitimized and which institutionalized some means of promoting the responsiveness of political leaders.

Of course, as both Soviet and Western observers noted at the time, this new version of Soviet democracy was an imperfect one at best. As designed and implemented by the Gorbachev leadership, the reforms contained a number of elements intended to circumscribe electoral outcomes and to protect the interests of the traditional Soviet elite. Most important in this respect were the refusal to legalize the creation of competing po-

---

[43] A predominant (although not exclusive) emphasis on the structural preconditions of democracy can be found in Larry Diamond, Juan J. Linz, and Seymour Martin Lipset, *Democracy in Developing Countries*, 4 vols. (Boulder, Colo.: Lynne Rienner, 1989).

[44] The volume by O'Donnell and Schmitter (fn. 14) is the best example.

[45] See Terry Lynn Karl, "Dilemmas of Democratization in Latin America," *Comparative Politics* 23 (October 1990), 1–21.

[46] For the text of the resolution, see *Pravda*, July 5, 1988, p. 2.

[47] For the text of the two laws, see *Pravda*, December 4, 1988, pp. 1–3.

litical parties; the broad and often vaguely defined powers granted to electoral commissions to oversee the nomination, registration, and election of candidates;[48] and the reservation of one-third of the seats in the Congress of People's Deputies for election by such pro-regime social organizations as the Communist Party, the trade unions, and the Komsomol.[49] Furthermore, the simultaneous expansion of the powers of the newly redesigned Soviet presidency led some, including the writer of these lines, to argue that the main purpose of the political reforms was to increase Mikhail Gorbachev's power and independence of action.[50]

Despite these limitations, an examination of paths to democracy in other parts of the world suggests that regime insistence on maintaining decidedly undemocratic elements in the early stages of the postauthoritarian transition does not necessarily render democratization either a fraud or a failure. On the contrary, the historical record suggests that those initial limits on democracy are often a necessary part of the road to a successful and stable democratic system. In an examination of attempted transitions from authoritarian rule in Latin America, Terry Lynn Karl found that political democracies have tended most successfully to emerge from transitions from above in which "traditional rulers remain in control, even if pressured from below, and successfully use strategies of compromise or force—or some mix of the two—to retain at least part of their power."[51] By way of contrast, she notes that in Latin America "no stable political democracy has resulted from regime transitions in which mass actors have gained control, even momentarily, over traditional ruling classes."[52]

The explanation for this pattern is related to the need to assure members of the old elite that their vital interests will not be threatened, thus decreasing the chances that they will attempt to subvert the process of reform. Hence, democratization requires some initial institutional compromises, often taking the form of explicitly negotiated pacts, which contain one or more of such obviously undemocratic components as restric-

---

[48] The authority of the electoral commissions was spelled out in the "Law on Elections" and in an article in *Pravda*, January 24, 1989, p. 2.

[49] The specific allocation of seats in the Congress for each social organization was not written into law but is to be determined in each election by the Central Electoral Commission. The CPSU and the trade unions were the largest recipients the first time around with one hundred deputies each. The smallest recipients were allocated one deputy each and included organizations such as the All-Union Music Society and the All-Union Society for the Struggle for Sobriety. The complete list was published in *Izvestiia*, December 28, 1988, p. 1.

[50] Russell Bova, "Power, Efficiency, and Democratization: The Faces of Soviet Political Reform" (Unpublished paper presented at the Mid-Atlantic Slavic Conference, Carlisle, Pa., April 1, 1989).

[51] Karl (fn. 45), 8–9.

[52] Ibid., 8.

tions on participation, a limited policy agenda, or limited contestation.[53] In an earlier period, undemocratic compromises of this sort were a crucial aspect of democratization in Western Europe and North America as well. Property requirements attached to the franchise, indirect elections, the protection of less democratic Upper Houses were just a few of the means utilized to protect certain strata and interests from the "excesses" of democracy.[54] In reflecting on the early history of existing Western democracies, Robert Dahl has noted that the transition to democracy (or polyarchy, to use his term) has tended to be most successful when the transition was taken slowly, initially limiting political contestation to a small stratum of the population.[55] Viewed in the light of this historical pattern, the much-maligned undemocratic elements of Gorbachev's political reforms take on a very different hue as a crucial component of a potentially historic compromise on the path of democratization.

Admittedly, the problem of finding and maintaining a workable compromise acceptable to the old ruling stratum remains inherently more difficult in the transition from communist rule than in other cases. In capitalist economies, former rulers and bureaucrats can often retreat from positions of political power to the world of wealth and property. In communist systems, however, wealth and property are directly tied to one's political position.[56] Thus, the communist *nomenklatura* potentially has more to lose and less to fall back upon than elites in other authoritarian systems undergoing transition. Except for the unlikely possibility that some way will be found to institutionalize the privileges of this class in a post-communist era, resistance to democratic compromise will often be intense.[57]

While this situation makes successful institutional compromise and pact making more difficult, it is not impossible. While many party and state officials in the USSR have been reluctant to subject their privileges and status to the uncertainties of even a restricted democratic process, others supported Gorbachev's democratization program. Even more important to emphasize is that it is less the civilian bureaucrats than those who control the instruments of state violence whose attitudes are most

[53] For examples of each, see ibid., 11–12. Breslauer (fn. 2), 323–24, also applies this logic to the Soviet case.

[54] See Przeworski (fn. 15), 68–69.

[55] Robert Dahl, *Polyarchy: Participation and Opposition* (New Haven: Yale University Press, 1971), chap. 3.

[56] Przeworski (fn. 15), 74–75.

[57] For an interesting pre-Gorbachev era discussion of the institutionalization of elite privileges, see Alexander Yanov, *Detente after Brezhnev* (Berkeley: Institute of International Studies, 1977), 1–16. Note also the attempts of party and state officials to lay claim to state property in the course of the transition currently under way in Eastern Europe.

vital. It is the willingness of the military establishment to tolerate liberalization and democratization that has typically been crucial to the fate of postauthoritarian transitions around the world.

In this regard, Soviet democratization efforts actually enjoy certain advantages in comparison with Latin American attempts. In the latter case, military establishments often bear direct responsibility for the repression and policies of the authoritarian regime.[58] In many cases the military *was*, in fact, the old regime, having forcibly taken political power directly into its own hands. Despite the close relationship in the USSR between the military establishment and the CPSU, the former has generally avoided direct participation in the political process. One can more easily envision, therefore, a process of pact making in which the vital interests of the military as an institution are protected from the feelings of popular retribution so common in Latin America. Indeed, the most recent evidence of military discontent with Soviet reform notwithstanding, military tolerance of the reform process in the USSR through at least the first five years of reform—despite steadily growing political and economic chaos—was noteworthy.

What then has gone wrong? If Gorbachev's cautious and compromising approach to democratization was appropriate in light of historical experience and if there was at least a temporary willingness of key sectors of the Soviet elite to engage in the process of institutional compromise, why then, in early 1991, did the democratization process appear in jeopardy?

One part of the answer to this question is found in the fact that conservative forces were not positioned to participate very successfully in a democratic polity. The results of the March 1989 elections, the first semifree elections since 1917, must have given many party officials a jolt. Overwhelming electoral victories for key reform leaders such as Sakharov and Yeltsin and the stunning defeat of virtually the entire Leningrad party/state apparatus were certainly bad omens in this regard.[59] Still, the combination of the formal election rules and the informal pressures Communist Party officials could bring to bear did allow for significant representation of conservative and centrist forces in the Congress of People's Deputies and Supreme Soviet. While not quite the rubber-stamp legislatures of old, each of these newly elected bodies has, in fact,

[58] For a discussion of this point in the Latin American and Southern European contexts, see O'Donnell and Schmitter (fn. 14), 28–29.

[59] For a summary of the March 1989 election results, see Dawn Mann and Julia Wishnevsky, "Composition of Congress of People's Deputies," *Radio Liberty Report on the USSR* 1 (May 5, 1989), 1–6.

proven itself sufficiently malleable in Gorbachev's hands. As a result, it took yet another round of elections a year later, this time to elect deputies to republic-level soviets, for the writing on the wall to become crystal clear. In many of the republics, the formal and informal mechanisms for manipulating the electoral outcome were of little effect in preventing either the poor showing of establishment candidates or the strong performance of pro-independence forces.[60]

The great paradox here is that the prospects of democratization would, over the long haul, have been improved had conservative forces fared better.[61] As it was, the electoral results eroded any conservative confidence that the continuing ban on opposition parties, the reservation of legislative seats for loyal social organizations, and the other institutionalized limits on democratic "excesses" could successfully protect their vital interests or, perhaps most importantly, the integrity of the union. Some even began to call for an electoral change that would emphasize voting based less on territorial districts than on production units, on the assumption that such a change would produce outcomes more favorable to conservative candidates.[62] Although that proposal was not adopted, it reflected a declining tolerance for the centrist compromise that Gorbachev has tried to forge.

While the problem confronting conservative forces has been that of a large head (the party/state machine) with a relatively small body of popular support, the problem facing the democratic opposition has been that of a large body without a head. Unlike the Polish case, where Solidarity and Lech Walesa provided Jaruzelski with a partner in pact making, Gorbachev had no one to bargain with in making such a pact. In fact, his democratization program was not a pact at all but rather a set of reforms imposed by him unilaterally. In doing this Gorbachev simultaneously acted as representative of the old regime and of the reformist elements. While some have characterized his role as that of both Pope and Luther, the more contemporary analogy would be to see Gorbachev as both Jaruzelski and Walesa.

The problem posed by this situation is that the reforms never received the legitimation that pact making can provide. The democratic opposition never signed on to those reforms as such, and there was no commonly recognized opposition organization with the leadership to provide

[60] For a summary and analysis of these results, see Commission on Security and Cooperation in Europe, *Elections in the Baltic States and Soviet Republics* (Washington, D.C., December 1990).

[61] For an elaboration of this logic in a non-Soviet context, see Przeworski (fn. 15), 71–74.

[62] See, for example, the interview with Mikhail Popov, one of the initiators of the proposal, in *Moscow News* 34 (August 27–September 3, 1989), 12.

guarantees to the Gorbachev regime that the boundaries of the compromise would be respected. There is, in fact, some speculation that Gorbachev was looking to reach some such agreement with opposition forces in early 1990. In June there was a report of a secret meeting between representatives of the democratic opposition and two top Gorbachev advisers who were looking to cut a deal.[63] Gorbachev's role and intentions in that regard remain unclear; but, even assuming the very best of intentions, it is not clear who—if anyone—could bargain for and make concessions in the name of the opposition. The only conceivable possibility in this regard was Boris Yeltsin. However, his stormy, almost operatic relationship with Gorbachev (combined with the fact that, as leader of the Russian Republic, Yeltsin headed what is, in effect, a rival government) made cooperation between the two extremely difficult at that point in time. As a result, whatever inclinations Gorbachev may or may not have once had, he probably decided by the end of 1990 that an escape from the collapsing political center in the direction of the opposition would be a jump into a political abyss, while an escape in the other direction into the arms of conservative forces left some hope, however slim, that his centrist policies might eventually be salvaged.

By the spring and early summer of 1991, however, a resurrected emphasis on radical economic reform and a shaky yet hopeful truce in the war of words between Gorbachev and Yeltsin were but two manifestations of a radical reversal of the political current. This shift in direction may be a tactical move on Gorbachev's part, designed to re-create a viable political center. By zigzagging from right to left his hope may be to continue, on average, along the moderately reformist political course that he has long advocated but that lacks much of a base of support in the polarized politics of the era. More optimistically, the January resistance and bloodshed in Vilnius, the bold yet disciplined March demonstration in Moscow in defiance of Kremlin orders, and the impressive June electoral victory of Boris Yeltsin may, in demonstrating the growing confidence of the democratic opposition, have collectively provided both an indication of the high costs of further repression and, at the same time, a new opportunity to deal with an opposition whose organization and leadership have become more impressive over time. As of mid-summer 1991, it remained unclear whether it was the former short-term shift in tactics or the latter longer-term shift in strategy that was at the root of Gorbachev's renewed courtship of radical reformers.

[63] Elizabeth Teague, "Gorbachev Advisors Meet Secretly with Opposition Leaders," *Radio Liberty Report on the USSR* 2 (June 22, 1990), 1–2.

THE QUESTION OF PRECONDITIONS

While the analysis to this point has focused on issues of political process and dynamics, it would be inappropriate to conclude without considering whether the problems and obstacles most recently encountered along the path of Soviet democratization reflect objective conditions not yet sufficiently ripe for democracy. It should be noted at the outset of this discussion that an examination of the Soviet Union's relatively unique combination of structural characteristics does not contradict the previous emphasis on the political dynamics common to all liberalizing regimes. The road of liberalization has multiple exits, some leading toward greater democracy, others circling back to (or near) the point of origin. While the USSR has joined other liberalizing regimes in traveling that common road, with all of its predictable twists and turns, the exit it ultimately chooses to take remains a subject of speculation. Consideration of the "preconditions" of democracy may, when applied to the Soviet case from a comparative vantage point, provide some clues.

In the literature on political development and democratic preconditions, the variable that has, perhaps, received the most attention is a country's level of socioeconomic modernization. Reflecting a widely held view among political scientists, Robert Dahl has argued that

> an advanced economy automatically generates many of the conditions required for a pluralistic social order. And as a pluralistic social order evolves . . . some of its members make demands for participating in decisions by means more appropriate to a competitive than to a hegemonic political system.[64]

In terms of this one criterion of socioeconomic modernization, the USSR would certainly seem to be ripe for political reform. Moshe Lewin, Jerry Hough, and other Western students of the USSR have attempted to explain and, in Hough's case, to predict the reforms of the Gorbachev era as a consequence of the increased education, urbanization, and stratification that economic development has produced.[65] However, without denying that those trends have led to strains in communist systems or that they are at the root of recent reform efforts, the fact remains that in other respects the conditions for a successful democratic outcome in the USSR are, at least in the short run, much less favorable.

First, it must be emphasized that while all existing democracies are not equally modern, they are all characterized by largely private enter-

[64] Dahl (fn. 55), 78.
[65] Moshe Lewin, *The Gorbachev Phenomenon: A Historical Interpretation* (Berkeley: University of California Press, 1988); Jerry F. Hough, *The Soviet Leadership in Transition* (Washington, D.C.: Brookings Institution, 1980).

prise, market economies. Charles Lindblom explains this connection between democracy and markets by noting that democratization has historically been the means by which a rising middle class of entrepreneurs and merchants sought to protect its wealth, property, and economic freedom from arbitrary state action.[66] To be sure, it is clear that this middle class does not always commit itself to democratization. There are many existing market systems where the business classes feel their interests are adequately protected from the state without democracy. Indeed, in the twentieth century the business class often feels the need to be protected by the authoritarian regime from leftist and populist movements from below. Nevertheless, successful democratic transitions in Spain, Brazil, and elsewhere have been facilitated, if not determined, by the support of at least some segments of the business community.[67]

Thus, the question is whether it is modernization or, more specifically, capitalist modernization that is most important for the evolution of democracy. While, as previously noted, communist regimes have lacked the ability and desire to eliminate all private economic activity (thereby failing to maintain complete, totalitarian control over the larger society), they have managed to preempt the emergence of any potential political challenge from a rising capitalist elite by effectively monopolizing control of the commanding heights of their industrial economies. Whether a substitute stratum (the managerial class? intellectuals? foreign governments and capital?) can emerge to fill the historic political role of the merchant and entrepreneural classes remains to be seen. In advocating a Chilean or South Korean model of marketization under strong authoritarian guidance, some Soviet observers seem to have concluded that such substitution of roles is impossible and that democracy will, at best, have to await the development of a new stage in the relations of Soviet production.[68] Perhaps the best test case here will be Poland, where an experiment in simultaneous marketization and democratization is currently being pursued most seriously.

---

[66] Charles E. Lindblom, *Politics and Markets* (New York: Basic Books, 1977), 161–69.

[67] O'Donnell and Schmitter (fn. 14), 20. For a more skeptical view of the role of the business community in contemporary transitions to democracy, see Fernando H. Cardoso, "Entrepreneurs and the Transition Process: The Brazilian Case," in O'Donnell et al. (fn. 17), 137–53. Even Cardoso admits, however, that this group gave at least limited support to the transition process.

[68] Yurii Prokofiev, first secretary of the Moscow party organization, is among those reported to favor this model. Sovset Computer Network, *RFE-RL Daily Report* 25 (February 5, 1991). Note that the Chilean reference, although frequently encountered, is a bit of an exaggeration. Not even the strongest advocates of Soviet marketization expect the kind of laissez-faire, Chicago school approach to the market that the Chilean junta attempted. In the Soviet context, therefore, advocates of a Chilean model are simply those who seek marketization now while postponing democracy until some indefinite point in the future.

Whatever the Polish outcome, adding a consideration of "political preconditions" of democracy into the analysis leads one to conclude that Soviet democratization will remain a still more difficult nut to crack. Most importantly, while Poland is an ethnically homogeneous society, the USSR is a state that has not been able to forge a unified Soviet nation. It is difficult to exaggerate the extent to which this factor complicates efforts at democratization.[69] Of greatest significance here is the fact that political energies released by the process of regime liberalization are diverted from the quest for democracy by traveling down the road of national separatism instead. One can even point to cases, such as the Basque separatist movement in Spain, where radical elements, fearing a legitimation of the existing regime, have sought to undermine the democratization process through terror.[70] Even in less extreme situations, independence rather than democracy often comes to be seen as the primary guarantee of protection from the repression of the old regime. In this respect, a transnationally minded capitalist elite driven by the economic logic of economies of scale and the unimpeded movement of goods and capital is particularly missed.

As for the antidemocratic forces of reaction, national strife plays right into their hands. The threat of the country's disintegration not only provides a pretext for renewed repression but also divides the democratic opposition. What O'Donnell and Schmitter refer to as the "popular upsurge"—that fleeting moment that sometimes occurs when a sense of public empowerment and unity arises as the ultimate challenge to the existing order—has difficulty materializing.[71] Moreover, whatever tolerance might once have existed for institutional compromise among conservative and even moderate forces is now undercut. As noted previously, the results of the March 1989 elections, while threatening to the conservative forces in some respects, were sufficiently mixed so as to sustain, perhaps, the institutional compromise Gorbachev had forged. With the strong showing of separatist candidates in local elections in 1990, however, that possibility seemed to evaporate.

Finally, prospects for Soviet democratization are also complicated by the relative lack of a Russian democratic tradition. The problem here involves more than a question of political attitudes and values. In many countries of Latin America, Southern Europe, and even Eastern Europe, the issue on the political agenda is best described not as democratization

[69] Rustow, for example, sees national unity as the single most important background condition for democracy. See Rustow (fn. 40), 350–52.

[70] Donald Share, *The Making of Spanish Democracy* (New York: Praeger, 1986), 170–71.

[71] O'Donnell and Schmitter (fn. 14), 53–56.

but as *re*democratization. In many of those cases, the initial stages of liberalization allowed for long-repressed political organizations to re-emerge in relatively short order. In the USSR, in contrast, building an organized democratic opposition has had to proceed almost from scratch. Unlike neighboring Poland, where a history of challenges to communist governments provided a well-prepared soil for the birth and develop-ment of Solidarity, the USSR lacks a history of even unsuccessful dem-ocratic movements. It is, thus, not surprising that Gorbachev would have had trouble, as noted previously, in finding partners in pact making who could both speak for and restrain a fledgling democratic opposition.

To be sure, in considering the preconditions of democracy, one should avoid extreme determinism insofar as the emergence (or lack thereof) of democracy has not always corresponded to our theoretical understanding of the optimal objective conditions. In Latin America, for example, one can point to a number of exceptions where democratization has either lagged or outpaced expectations generated by an overly deterministic emphasis on structural preconditions.[72] So, too, in the USSR it is at least possible, if not probable, that a combination of skillful political leader-ship, external support, and good fortune may combine to surprise the most pessimistic observers. Taken as a whole, however, this consider-ation of democratic preconditions suggests that in the short run such a surprise remains a long shot, at best.

CONCLUSION

As noted at the outset, this paper had two objectives. The first was to make the case for the profitability of examining the issues of regime transition in the communist world from a comparative perspective. As such, this paper was intended as a beginning more than an end. Many of the topics considered, including the role of the military in the transition process, the relationship between regime hard-liners and soft-liners, and the issue of democratic preconditions, deserve to be examined in the con-text of the Soviet and other post-communist transitions in much more detail than is possible in a single article. For students of communism, these topics represent opportunities to initiate what is, in many cases, a long-postponed reintegration with the field of comparative politics.

At the same time, a second objective has been to provide some im-mediate insights into the political dynamics of Gorbachev-era Soviet pol-itics. Indeed, the two objectives are closely intertwined insofar as the best

[72] See Karl (fn. 45), 4–5.

way to make the case for the utility of comparison is to produce at least a sample of what a comparative analysis can provide. In this instance, the comparison demonstrated that the dynamics of the liberalization process in the USSR adhere to a model of political change previously manifested in other parts of the world. It has, thereby, helped to cast new light on some of the key political and intellectual puzzles of the Gorbachev era.

First, in analyzing the initial strengths of regime reformers, the comparison helps to explain what was for most observers an unexpectedly rapid consolidation of Gorbachev's authority in his first few years in power. Second, the subsequent decline of Gorbachev's centrist political agenda appears, from this broader perspective, not simply, as Martin Malia argues in his well-known "Z" article, a result of a uniquely futile effort to salvage some type of "soft communism," but as a generically similar dilemma of all efforts to reform authoritarian regimes.[73] Third, the comparative analysis suggests that Gorbachev's post-1988 political reform program, harshly criticized by proponents of more rapid and thorough democratic change, was an appropriate step in the process of democratization. Finally, and related to the above, the analysis suggests that the apparent failure of that democratization program was ultimately rooted in structural characteristics of Soviet society that even the wisest leadership would have had difficulty in overcoming.

Beyond the specifics of the Soviet case, the discovery of common patterns *across* such diverse cases may ultimately contribute further to the development of a generalized theory of postauthoritarian transitions. In the interim, students of the communist world, armed with a comparative perspective from the beginning, might not have been so frequently caught off guard by the developments of the last several years. In the early days of reform, when many Western observers questioned the stability of Gorbachev's political position, the literature on regime transitions could have helped point to sources of strength. Likewise, at a point when some began to speak of the irreversibility of reform, a comparative perspective might have provided greater caution.

In conclusion, it must be emphasized that comparison is not meant to substitute for case studies of transition politics. Rather, each approach is most likely to be successful when informed by the other. Nor does comparison imply an expectation of similar outcomes. As was made clear throughout the paper, the purpose of a comparative approach is as much to illuminate differences as it is to confirm similarities. The fact that there were similar political dynamics at work in post-Franco Spain and

[73] Z, "To the Stalin Mausoleum," *Daedalus* 169 (Winter 1990), 295–344.

in the post-Brezhnev USSR does not mean that Spain's present is the Soviet Union's future. Indeed, the ultimate fate of regime transitions has been and will continue to be varied among the nations of both Latin America and Southern Europe. Nevertheless, an examination of the Spanish and other cases does help one to better understand the possibilities and probabilities with which the Soviet Union is faced.

Review Article

THE NATIONAL UPRISINGS IN THE SOVIET UNION

By DAVID D. LAITIN*

Edward A. Allworth. *The Modern Uzbeks: From the Fourteenth Century to the Present, A Cultural History*. Stanford, Calif.: Hoover Institution, 1990, 410 pp.

Robert Conquest, ed. *The Last Empire: Nationality and the Soviet Future*. Stanford, Calif.: Hoover Institution, 1986, 406 pp.

Alan W. Fisher. *The Crimean Tatars*. Stanford, Calif.: Hoover Institution, 1978, 264 pp.

Lubomyr Hajda and Mark Beissinger. *The Nationalities Factor in Soviet Politics and Society*. Boulder, Colo.: Westview Press, 1990, 331 pp.

Martha Brill Olcott. *The Kazakhs*. Stanford, Calif.: Hoover Institution, 1987, 341 pp.

Toivo U. Raun. *Estonia and the Estonians*. Stanford, Calif.: Hoover Institution, 1987, 313 pp.

Azade-Ayşe Rorlich. *The Volga Tatars: A Profile in National Resilience*. Stanford, Calif.: Hoover Institution, 1986, 288 pp.

Orest Subtelny. *Ukraine: A History*. Toronto: University of Toronto Press, 1988, 666 pp.

Ronald Grigor Suny. *The Making of the Georgian Nation*. Bloomington: Indiana University Press, in association with Hoover Institution, 1988, 395 pp.

NATIONALISM is now considered to be the greatest threat to the integrity of the Soviet Union, as well as to any program of political or economic reform. Many analysts believe that in the face of the centrifugal forces of national uprisings, the center will not hold. They therefore

* The author is grateful to John Armstrong, Ellen Comisso, Gerhard Casper, Peter Gourevitch, Ernst Haas, Lubomyr Hajda, Gary Herrigel, Stephen Holmes, Peter Katzenstein, Rasma Karklins, Ian Lustick, Alexander Motyl, Roger Petersen, Tiiu Pohl, Vladimir Razuvaev, Philip Roeder, Brian Silver, John Slocum, and Stephen Walt for their stimulating comments on an earlier draft of this essay. Jerry Hough invited the author to the Center of East-West Trade, Investment, and Communications at Duke University, where Soviet and American scholars commented on this paper. Richard Hellie and Sheila Fitzpatrick invited the author to present the paper to their Russian/Soviet workshop at the University of Chicago. Jean Jackson at MIT provided a similar forum. Many of the participants, and especially the hosts, offered invaluable advice for revision.

foresee in the cumulative logic of these movements the crumbling of a Great Power, with awesome consequences for international stability.[1]

Behind these claims is an unjustifiable assumption that all the national movements currently active in the Soviet Union arise from similar sources and will all lead to movements for national independence. Such an assumption might be justified if there were no available secondary sources on the national movements. But that limitation no longer exists. Over the past decade Wayne S. Vucinich has edited *Studies of Nationalities in the USSR*, a series of books by area specialists (Fisher, Rorlich, Olcott, Raun, Suny, and Allworth) that provides historically sensitive accounts of six nations. These, with the addition of Subtelny's comparable study of the Ukraine, cover a broad range of nationalities from all regions of the Soviet Union: the Baltics (Estonians); the west (Ukrainians, and within the Ukraine, Crimean Tatars); Transcaucasia (Georgians); Central Asia (Uzbeks, Kazakhs); and the Russian federation (Volga Tatars). The books by Conquest (also in the Vucinich series) and Hajda and Beissinger provide useful cross-regional data and interpretations that help supplement the area studies.[2]

These works alone cannot provide an alternative theory or paradigm of Soviet nationality politics. Some are marred by a gratuitous anti-Soviet bias that precludes an accurate assessment of any incentives to integrate with Moscow.[3] Some authors identify so strongly with their subjects that all members of "their" nationality who assimilate into Russian society

[1] See *Nationality Papers*, special issue 18 (Spring 1990), which is a record of discussions among experts at the Harriman Institute for Advanced Study of the Soviet Union at Columbia University. Alexander J. Motyl states the premises of the discussions in the following way: "Gorbachev . . . already has lost control of at least half of the Soviet empire; arguably, control over the other half is slowly slipping out of his hands as well" (p. 6).

[2] Three recent books with findings that bear on nationality politics in the Soviet Union are not under review here, but they have informed my perspective. See Rasma Karklins, *Ethnic Relations in the USSR* (Boston: Allen and Unwin, 1986); Alexander Motyl, *Will the Non-Russians Rebel?* (Ithaca, N.Y.: Cornell University Press, 1987); and Donna Bahry, *Outside Moscow* (New York: Columbia University Press, 1987). See also Motyl, ed., *Thinking Theoretically about Soviet Nationalities* (New York: Columbia University Press, forthcoming). The preliminary draft chapters of this volume have also informed my judgments.

[3] In the Fisher volume, for example, nearly every positive force for the Tatars under Russian/Soviet rule is reluctantly presented only because scholarly objectivity required him to do so. On the question of Nazi collaboration, for example, Fisher argues in two directions at once. In order to exonerate the Tatar people from Soviet charges of collaboration with the Nazis (which was the Soviet excuse for evacuating the entire population from the Crimea in 1944), Fisher points to the Tatars who joined the partisans and who remained loyal. But to explain the joy in the streets during the military defeat of the Red Army, and the collaboration between Ankara exiles from the Crimea and the Nazis, Fisher justifies the Tatars' hatred of the Soviets. A textured social analysis—who among the Tatars collaborated and who became partisans and why—would have served historiography better than an attempt to exonerate the nation from Stalin's charges and simultaneously to excuse them from actions consistent with those charges. The book, replete with grudging admissions of Russian goodwill and excuses for Tatar perfidy, is largely empty of social analysis.

are seen as naïve or emotionally troubled (Subtelny, 352, 524; Allworth, 319–25). And none of the volumes gives a plausible assessment of the economic consequences of political separation from Moscow, in comparison with the payoff for remaining part of the Union.[4]

Also lacking in this series is a shared theoretical thread that would allow for a general interpretation. In fact, the various authors differ in their understanding of even such a basic notion as the meaning of nationality. For Olcott, once national boundaries are historically constituted, they remain relatively fixed; that is, national identifications are eternal. She writes in the Hajda and Beissinger volume that "the Turkmen were known by their *proper* name" (p. 255; emphasis added) as if it had been given by God. Meanwhile Allworth opens his study of the Uzbeks by asking: "How will the creation of a corporate, retrospective nationality where none existed before affect people when it is politically motivated and applied and executed by outsiders?" (p. 4). He answers that a politically imposed category can take on social meaning by virtue of state action (chap. 11) and of the strategic activity of intellectuals who found it useful to call themselves Uzbek (pp. 229–31)—this in combination with a fear of Tatar domination over Central Asia that pushed Uzbek intellectuals away from a broader identity (p. 180). National traditions, that is, are created out of struggle; they are not a primordial given. Finally, Suny looks for answers in social analysis: the various Georgian nationalist movements are seen as the design of particular classes or coalitions of classes, aimed at securing wealth or legitimate domination. In sum, nationalities are variously presented in the volumes as primordially real, historically reconstituted, or socially organized—without any synthesis to reconcile these distinct visions.

The problems with the separate national histories are many: political bias, economic blindness, and lack of a perspective that can explain more than the case at hand. Despite these drawbacks, however, these works are the best historical and contextual accounts of Soviet nationalities available in English. They shed light on important differences between various national uprisings, each with its particular consequences for the integrity of the Union.

Comparativists should seize this opportunity to locate these historical works within a theoretical framework. Just as the breakthrough on superconductivity in the mid-1980s brought euphoria to solid-state physicists, the nationalist uprisings in the Soviet Union and Eastern Europe

---

[4] Gertrude Schroeder's perceptive essays in the Conquest and Hajda and Beissinger volumes analyze economic trends with great perspicacity; one wishes the nationalist historians would make more use of her work.

are a comparativist's dream. The cases are so many and so varied that the possibility for natural experiments abounds. There are many standard variables to account for national revival movements, including (1) a religion and/or a language different from that of the center, (2) economic growth compared with the center, and (3) the degree of cultural homogeneity within the peripheral unit. Yet up until 1989, the number of real-world cases had been limited, exacerbating the normal social science problem of overdetermination, where the number of variables is greater than the number of observations. Under such conditions, isolation of variables becomes a matter of both good judgment and guesswork. For whatever else these nationality movements have given us, they have also provided social scientists with a sufficient range of cases to enable them to do their science better.[5]

I

Conquest's epithet-title obscures far more than it reveals. Virtually all the contributors to his distinguished volume foresaw the growth of national identification that would lead to outright rejection of the Soviet system. Having already surmised by 1983 that considerable nationalist mobilization had already taken place, they envisioned an empire rotting from within.

What makes the Soviet Union an "empire" is not, however, addressed by any author. Is every multinational state an "empire"—for example, Switzerland, India, or Canada—or only those in which the form of domination is particularly egregious? Michael Doyle's monograph, which seeks criteria to label a particular form of domination as "imperial," is plagued by the same problem. The author defines empire as "a relationship, formal or informal, in which one state controls the effective political sovereignty of another political society."[6] Doyle does not resolve the conceptual problem of identifying what is meant by "another political society." Are the Flemish in Belgium, the Catalans in France, the Basques in Spain, the Tamils in India, African-Americans in the United States, or the Chinese in Malaysia "other political societies"? In each case the group in question certainly lacks effective political sovereignty.

More importantly, Doyle's formulation points neither to any theory about the variety of ways rulers have incorporated heterogeneous popu-

---

[5] This is the excuse I give to explain why a scholar who is just beginning to learn his Russian declensions should be writing a review essay concerning affairs about which other scholars are far more competent to make nuanced judgments.

[6] Doyle, *Empires* (Ithaca, N.Y.: Cornell University Press, 1986), 45.

lations into their territorial domains nor to an analysis of the consequences of different forms of incorporation. We know that the Roman
Empire administered its eastern territories through local languages (recognizing that they were other political societies) but ruled in western
Europe through Latin. Similarly just as the French administered Languedoc and Senegal differently, so Spain administered Catalonia and
New Spain differently. All of these cases are imperial, at least from the
point of view of the rulers, but all had very different political implications for state integrity and national separation.

Leaving aside the definitional issue, the problem with calling the Soviet Union an empire today is that by analogy with Austria-Hungary, it
allows one to assume its ultimate decomposition. I do not wish to pre-
suppose the collapse of the Soviet Union. I want to analyze those factors
that can enhance the integrity of the Union, an area shortchanged by the
contributors to the Conquest volume. One gains a sharper understanding
of national uprisings not by comparing "empires" with "states" but
rather by comparing the various methods of incorporation of peripheral
territories into political centers.[7] I will therefore focus on the relationship
of the political center to the nationalities of incorporated territories in the
long process of state building, in order to analyze the countervailing
pressures for state unity and national separation.

More specifically, I propose a model of elite incorporation into a state
and the concomitant national response (for short, the "elite incorporation
model"). This model focuses on the role of elites at the time their territory was first incorporated into the state by the leading social and political strata at the center.[8] If the newly incorporated elites can join high
society at the political center, at more or less the same rank and standing
they had had in their own territory, they are said to enjoy a status of
"most favored lord." By this, I mean that elites in the incorporated region
of a state have rights and privileges equal to those of elites of similar
status and education in the political center.[9]

[7] James Given, *State and Society in Medieval Europe* (Ithaca, N.Y.: Cornell University Press,
1990), is exemplary in its comparative power to analyze the incorporation of Gwynedd into
England and Languedoc into France without presupposing whether the incorporation was
empire or state building.

[8] This key variable was recognized by Rupert Emerson, *From Empire to Nation* (Cambridge: Harvard University Press, 1967), 44–47. The variable is embedded in a model that
relies on the dynamic approach toward nations developed by Karl Deutsch, *Nationalism and
Social Communication* (Cambridge: MIT Press, 1953); but it is more sensitive to the expected
utility of elites and their choices. Gary B. Miles relies heavily on a model of the expected
utility of elites in his "Roman and Modern Imperialism: A Reassessment," *Comparative Studies in Society and History* 32 (October 1990), 629–59, at 638–40.

[9] My concept of most favored lord is borrowed from the notion of most favored nation in
international trade negotiations. Just as it is the case that many of the entities given most-

Under most-favored-lord conditions, there are strong incentives for many of the elites in the incorporated territory to allow themselves to be co-opted into the power establishment at the center. Some elites in the incorporated territory will not take advantage of this opportunity, in large part because of the social pull of their own community. They will seek to build a future in their own region. But intergenerationally, if increasing numbers of the upper strata of society identify culturally with the central elites, the regional language and culture begin to be seen as backward and poor. Over generations, mass education and military conscription will provide inducements to the lower strata to assimilate into the dominant culture.[10] When this process reaches fruition, the imperial state is transformed into a national state—or, in Eugen Weber's oft-quoted image, "peasants" become "Frenchmen."[11]

The construction of a nation-state from the variety of nationalities within a state need not be permanent. Regional cultures tend to preserve the memory of national glory. "The symbols and structures of meaning of the regional language remain," I once posited, "but are carried by half-forgotten poets and lonely philologists."[12] These memories can be reactivated, Peter Gourevitch argues, when the regional bourgeoisie in industrialized capitalist societies exhibits economic dynamism while the political center experiences economic decline.[13] Under these conditions, the bourgeoisie will want rapid changes in tariff polices, capital markets, and corporate laws—changes that will not strike a responsive chord at the center. This dynamic class will patronize and promote the regional poets and philologists, as their symbols will help mobilize the rural folk, whose interests complement those of the bourgeoisie. Although the rural population will not be concerned about capital markets, it will see regional independence as a way to protect its communities from "foreign"

---

favored-nation status are not themselves "nations," in the case at hand, many of the incorporated elites are not "lords."

[10] The most sophisticated elaboration of this pattern, without the focus on most favored lord being a necessary condition for success, is Abram de Swaan, *In Care of the State* (Oxford: Oxford University Press, 1989), chap. 3.

[11] Weber, *Peasants into Frenchmen* (Stanford, Calif.: Stanford University Press, 1976).

[12] Laitin, "Language Games," *Comparative Politics* 20 (April 1988), 289–302, at 293.

[13] Gourevitch, *Paris and the Provinces* (Berkeley: University of California Press, 1980), chap. 10. A distinct identity by the people of a region is a necessary condition for a peripheral nationalist movement to mobilize. Gourevitch does not speculate on the question of how ethnic identities are seen to be distinct. Without independent criteria of ethnic difference (very difficult to establish, given the multiple possibilities of ethnic reidentification), Gourevitch's theory tends toward tautology. In Section III below, I suggest the criterion of perceived ethnic difference at the period of political incorporation. But further work on this point, in light of recent research on identity reconstruction, is clearly necessary if tautology is to be avoided.

encroachment.[14] Nationalism is an ideology—infused as it is with symbols of language and religion, and reinforced through common rituals—that can forge an alliance of peasants and bourgeois. From such an alliance may spring national revivals in economically dynamic but politically peripheral regions. The initial goal will be national separation from the previously consolidated nation-state.

Political movements seeking regional sovereignty in the peripheral regions have achieved considerable successes in our democratic age. Canada, Belgium, Spain, and even France have yielded greater autonomy to their regions in a number of policy domains. The willingness of the political center to be responsive to the appeals from the regions has, however, exposed deep tensions within the elites of the newly revived nations. Those members of the peripheral elites who have fully assimilated into the culture and society of the center—that is, those who took advantage of their most-favored-lord status—saw the nationalist symbols of the revival as antiquated and provincial. Unable to compete in the language of their own ancestors, they feared the consequences of the full realization of their national dream. Symbolic nationalism would have sufficed for them. The most bitter tensions of national revival under conditions of previous incorporation through most-favored-lord status have thus been the tensions *within* the new national elites.[15] In the cases of revival politics in Western democracies in the 1970s, the apparently rapid movement toward full independence was slowed not so much by central resistance as by the conflict of interest within each of the national elites.[16]

This situation of ethnic difference crossed with economic dynamism is not, as Gourevitch recognizes, the only route to national revival.[17] Suppose, for example, that in the period of political incorporation, elites from

[14] Rural populations in Catalonia, for example, blamed Madrid for extortionist taxes and for forcing them to billet troops. When "Spain" was in trouble in the seventeenth century, and in need of new taxes, rural folk at the peripheries saw local nobles as potentially more benign than those at the center. See J. H. Elliott, *The Revolt of the Catalans* (Cambridge: Cambridge University Press, 1963). The Catalan national revivals in the 1920s and 1970s relied on an alliance between the rural folk and the rising bourgeoisie.

[15] This is the argument in my study of the Catalan revival in Spain; see Laitin, "Linguistic Revival: Politics and Culture in Catalonia," *Comparative Studies in Society and History* 31 (April 1989), 297–317.

[16] Hudson Meadwell, "A Rational Choice Approach to Political Regionalism," *Comparative Politics* (forthcoming). Meadwell's discussion of national revival politics in Brittany is a sophisticated analysis of the internal dynamics of nationalism among elites from the periphery.

[17] Gourevitch (fn. 13) points to Ireland as the principal exception of his model for Western Europe (pp. 209–10). The alternative path I propose can, I believe, explain the Irish case. I doubt, however, that the two paths described in this paper account for the full range of incorporative strategies. I make no claim for completeness.

the region do not receive most-favored-lord status, as was the norm for Indian and African royalty during the era of European expansion. Control from the center will then require mediators from the elite strata of the "titular" nationality.[18] For the native elites, to serve as mediators between the center and their own masses yields rich payoffs, and many will be co-opted for sure. But even so they will not be able to translate their economic rewards into social status at the center. Suppose those elites who learn the language of the political center, and even convert to its religion, still face status deprivation and are not accepted as elites with a status similar to those who trace their ancestry to the culture of the ruling classes. Under these conditions, the most ambitious and powerful members of the periphery will operate with an eye to their homeland, rather than to the state that controls it. Economic dynamism is constrained under these conditions because indigenous elites tend to suppress the activities of entrepreneurs whose economic successes might challenge their status in society. And without economic dynamism, the logic of the first model will not hold.

When national independence movements develop in the wake of political incorporation that has been achieved without granting most-favored-lord status to elites, the following broad outlines are discernible. Younger generations of subject nationalities, educated in the schools built by the political center, face many barriers to mobility: the ruling native elites do not have incentives to turn over power across generations; and by definition the opportunities at the center are equally constrained. The idea of full political independence is attractive to these "new men." It would give them access to all the sensitive jobs currently held by nationals from the center, and this would benefit both the older and the younger generation. The strategy for seeking sovereignty has a political twist—it places the co-opted native elites in a bind. On the one hand, the status quo protects their welfare; on the other hand, they cannot be seen as opponents of independence—that would cost them their credibility as "natural" leaders of the region. They are therefore compelled to support, albeit unenthusiastically, a national-independence coalition with the "new men," with the goal of full national sovereignty.

Pressure by the new men is not the only possible motor that will propel a movement for national sovereignty in a subject territory. The lower strata of these societies pay heavily for having to rely on their elites for any communication with the political center; they will have uncountable grievances about the corruption of their leadership and their own inabil-

[18] In Soviet studies the "titulars" are those people who live in a republic named for their nationality.

ity to communicate directly with political authority. Furthermore, they will surely take note of neighboring regions or countries that are mobilized into national action: nationalism is "contagious" in this situation. And once the lower strata are mobilized, the titular rulers, fearful of being supplanted by the new men, find themselves leading the movement for national sovereignty.

Whichever the motor—the new men or contagion—the ensuing national independence movement will follow a script different from that of the national uprisings in areas where elites "enjoyed" most-favored-lord status. Here, the alliance between the established titular elites and the new men (or the mobilized lower strata) must rely on notions of cultural distance from the center, out of a belief that they represent (in Doyle's words) "another political society." This alliance will muzzle the antagonisms between social strata within the periphery for the duration of the struggle. (These will reappear after independence, though.) But there is another, concomitant conflict associated with nationalist movements of this type—that between the "authentic" nationals of the periphery and minority populations. An exclusivist nationalist ideology will be attractive to the new men and the lower strata of the titular nationality. The potentially oppressed minority peoples will likely see their only chance for a better life to be based upon continued rule by the center. Since the national cause is built upon the indignities suffered by the authentic cultural group, nonmembers who live within its designated boundaries will become forgotten people—or worse, they will face discrimination. Since non-most-favored-lord situations offer few incentives for minority groups within the territory to assimilate into the larger groups, and since central rulers often appoint minorities to subaltern positions, peripheral regions tend to be multiethnic. The titular groups, especially the new men seeking social mobility, will have an incentive to exclude minorities from government jobs. The hidden struggle for independence in regions that were incorporated without receiving most-favored-lord status is therefore the one between the titular nationals and minority peoples.

An important corollary of the elite incorporation model differentiates the political situation of rural minority nationalities in non-most-favored-lord regions from that of working-class immigrants in peripheral regions that are economically dynamic. Unlike the settled nationalities, the urban migrants play only a limited role in the regionalist drama. Working-class migrants come to the region for the sake of their families and not their cultures. They and their children will learn the language of the region to the extent necessary for economic advance. They will be mobilized more readily by political elites providing them with individual benefits (an apartment, a job) than by those offering them group benefits (education in one's ancestral language). Essential though they are to the region's industrial development, these migrants inevitably face discrimination and prejudice. But they nevertheless have incentives to assimilate, and the leading economic strata of the region have incentives to give them protection. They are therefore spectators at, rather than participants in, the drama of national revival.

Applying these models to the Soviet case will require substantial reformulation. But at this point I shall state boldly, without qualification, the implications of the elite incorporation model for interpreting the national uprisings in the Soviet Union. In the Soviet republics that were incorporated with elites receiving most-favored-lord status, the deepest tensions in the glasnost-inspired national uprisings will be within the elite strata of the titular nationals. Here Moscow's allies are those titulars who would confine the claims for national sovereignty to the symbolic level. In those republics that were incorporated without elites receiving such status, the deepest tensions will be between the titular nationals and the settled minority populations within the republics (that is, those who are not recent migrants). Here Moscow's allies are the minority populations within the republics. Conquest's vision of the collapse of the Soviet "empire" in a torrent of sovereignty-hungry nationality movements underestimates both the sources of support for the Union and the variation in the political makeup of the nationalist revivals.

II

The rise of nationality politics might lead one to conclude that attempts to create a "Soviet" citizen or a merged culture in the Soviet Union were founded upon delusions about the plasticity of national identification. But the books under review show that there was considerable plasticity in Russia and in the Soviet Union—and that under certain conditions reidentification and melding did occur.

The cultural boundaries between Soviet peoples—reified by both the Stalinist state *and* the organization of the Hoover monograph series under review—may now appear eternal and fixed. But the data show otherwise. In a marvelous discussion of elite identity in Uzbekistan, Allworth reproduces satiric journalistic material from 1924. In one cartoon, a man in Kazakh costume writes "Uzbek" on his nationality form while a Tajik-appearing man declares "Kazakh." In another plate, a man advises a friend, "From your fair skin and black eyes, you belong precisely to the Tajik nationality. Why be an Uzbek?" Or, in the words of a satiric writer, "Before the partition into nationality republics, we got so completely befuddled that we couldn't figure out which of the nationalities we ourselves might belong to" (p. 189). And this boundary quandary is not just between Central Asians and other Central Asians. After 1924 it became fashionable in Uzbek society to assume Russian patronymics (Allworth, 291–93); and in Uzbek writing today, an increasing number of root words are Russian.[19]

If the books under review paint a picture of the melding of languages and cultures throughout the "empire," they also provide significant evidence of people assimilating into foreign cultures for instrumental reasons. Consider the case of the *jadid* (Islamic reformer) Mahmud Khoja from Samarkand (Allworth, 138). He finished his Muslim education in 1894 and mastered Arabic and Farsi in addition to his native Turki. "Unlike many," Allworth speculates, "he also taught himself Russian. After madrassah he married, had a family, and sent his son to Russian-Native School, where he could learn Russian and some secular subjects." Khoja is well known for opening the first free library and reading room in Turkistan for Turki speakers. Allworth also describes a dramatic episode in the play *The Addict* by Hajji Muin ibn Shukrullah: a group of addicts in an insouciant stupor are finally aroused when they hear a "rumor that a few Turkistanian young people were learning to speak Russian." For these men of the lower strata, the subversion of Turkic culture by the upper classes was outrageous (p. 150).

Or consider this example from the Volga Tatars. Kayyum Nasire is known as the "Tatar Encyclopedist" for his efforts to preserve and standardize the Tatar language. Yet he secretly learned Russian, which enabled him to read modern mathematics and to land a position at the University of Kazan (Rorlich, 65–68). After 1870 in Kazakhstan, according to Olcott, "many *biis* [aristocrats] and tribal elders sent their children to [Russian] schools for a few years . . . in order better to represent their people upon assuming their fathers' positions" (pp. 104–5). The members of this first generation of Kazakh elites who experienced a Western-type education wrote exclusively in Russian for the remainder of their careers.

In Estonia, during the period of Polish and Swedish hegemony in the

---

[19] For evidence that in a variety of language domains, especially in science and technology, Asian languages of the Soviet Union rely almost totally on Russian roots, see Wolf Moskovich, "Planned Language Change in Russian since 1917," in Michael Kirkwood, ed., *Language Planning in the Soviet Union* (New York: St. Martin's Press, 1990), 87–88. Use of Russian root words is not evidence of assimilation. But as Deutsch's work teaches (fn. 8), it is a good indicator of high levels of transactions, a necessary condition for a new national identification.

seventeenth century, many peasants escaped to freedom in Russia, a pattern that continued well into the nineteenth century. By the end of the nineteenth century most Estonians (not from the German aristocracy, but from the Estonian peasantry and lower bourgeoisie) who had received higher education earned their degrees in Russia (Raun, 30–31, 61–73). Even today, the Estonians' knowledge of Russian is probably greater than what they report to census takers. While the census data suggest a secular decline in knowledge of Russian among Estonians, reports from the Soviet military journals suggest that Estonian recruits have had little trouble understanding Russian.[20]

These examples from the books under review reveal a universal assimilationist dynamic. Under conditions of conquest, those individuals who learn the conqueror's language, convert to the conqueror's religion, or participate in the conqueror's markets gain access to some of the resources that permitted the conqueror to defeat the colony. While it may be a public good (from the point of view of the elites in the incorporated territory) to resist any cultural accommodation, those individuals who "cheat" will benefit themselves and their families. The first to learn the language of the center—if they are not heavily sanctioned by their own society (and that is why they often learn the language of the center secretly)—will by their success invite others to follow in their paths. Perhaps the first generation learns Russian and attends Orthodox churches for purely instrumental reasons; but if incentives remain the same, their descendants will begin to see the Russian language or the Orthodox church as "theirs." The books under review show the dynamic of intergenerational cultural assimilation to be as strong in territories conquered by Russia in the sixteenth to nineteenth centuries as it was in territories conquered by France in the sixteenth and seventeenth centuries.

The data reported by Anderson and Silver (for example, in their paper published in Hajda and Beissinger) confirm this view. They show that the historical dynamic of rapid expansion in the percentage of the population that has a working knowledge of Russian (unassimilated bilingualism) remains powerful. The major factor hindering full assimilation (where Russian becomes the primary language of everyday life) in the Soviet Union is political. Where territorial jurisdiction gives recognition to titular nationals, Anderson and Silver's data show that most nationals remain unassimilated bilinguals. Political jurisdiction rather than impenetrable cultural boundaries explain why the processes of cultural assimi-

[20] See Karklins (fn. 2), 59–60. On the military, see Martha Brill Olcott and William Fierman, "Soviet Youth and the Military," U.S. Department of State Contract #1724-620124, pp. 30–31.

NATIONAL UPRISINGS IN THE SOVIET UNION

lation of subject peoples has not advanced as far as in other state-building experiences.

In light of this, we can see how misguided are the ideological attempts by the Soviets to induce Central Asians to migrate into areas in the RSFSR that suffer from labor shortages. The core symbol here is that of *sliianie*, the merging of Soviet cultures (Dunlop, in Conquest, 265–69). The unwillingness of Central Asians to migrate to "better" jobs in mineral- and capital-rich areas of the Soviet Union cannot be adequately explained by a cultural rejection of *sliianie*. My hypothesis is that Central Asians have not accepted jobs outside their region because under Soviet rule, geographical mobility (especially leaving one's titular republic) necessarily entails the loss of the support network that helps people get their apartments repaired or obtain basic foodstuffs. The benefits of knowing the local police officer or party official are exceedingly high and probably outweigh the salary differential offered in a different republic. After Brezhnev, there was yet another reason. The opportunities in the gray market in Uzbekistan are far more attractive than are those of the red market in Sverdlovsk. Huge wage differentials are hardly an incentive when rubles buy almost nothing. During the war in Afghanistan a significant number of Central Asians picked up and moved to the U.S., where indeed jobs and opportunities *were* available. Not lack of desire to be abroad, then, but lack of real opportunity in Russia is what has limited Central Asian migration within the Soviet Union.

Each of the volumes under review is sensitive to the special characteristics of its respective Soviet nationality. The authors know the relevant languages, and some of them have an emotional investment in the future of the peoples about whom they write. Yet all are well aware that Moscow was a powerful magnet for both elites and masses and that processes of assimilation were always present. We cannot then attribute the uprising of the nationalities in the 1990s to an immutable unwillingness of the peoples of the periphery to merge into a common national identity. For this reason I focus on the elites at the center and on their willingness to allow conquered elites to climb their social ladders.

III

If nationality is plastic, what has restricted the full development of a new Soviet nationality, with Russian language as the key to internationality communication? The volumes from the Studies of Nationalities in the USSR Series are at least suggestive in this regard. Where language or religion was similar to that of Russia, elites were more likely to receive most-favored-lord status than were elites coming from territories that were non-Slavic in language and/or non-Orthodox in religion. Where most-favored-lord was granted, the elite incorporation model predicts greater plasticity of cultural reidentification in the incorporated region, first among elites and then spilling over to the lower strata.

Historians will rightfully be skeptical of the proposition concerning cultural similarity and the probability of getting most-favored-lord status. More than a decade ago S. Frederick Starr, in a masterful review of imperial policy, found considerable similarities across regions. One important similarity was that elites from each of the subject territories had easy access to Russian high society. "One will not find among the aristocracy of any other European state," he argues, "so many great families tracing their ancestry to the subject areas." And he is careful to note that Muslim Kazan was no exception.[21]

And the historians disagree among themselves. According to Bennigsen, Russian state expansion had no such synoptic vision (Conquest, 134–36). Perhaps Bennigsen would agree with Starr's formulation for the reign of Ivan the Terrible. Accordingly, Bennigsen points out that Muslim subjects at that time were permitted to intermingle freely in the empire—Ivan even married a Muslim woman. But the continuity ends there. Ivan's son Feder began to reverse his father's cultural pluralism, and until the time of Catherine II, Muslims were systematically persecuted. Orientation toward Muslims changed once again under Alexander II, who attempted to incorporate Muslims through religious conversion and linguistic Russification. Bennigsen's paper is a reminder that all patterns in Russian state building can be erased by exceptions. One should therefore be wary of generalizing about any state policy that sought to induce national elites to become equal members of Russian society.

Furthermore, as Hugh Seton-Watson demonstrates, the nineteenth century rewarded peripheral elites more for political loyalty than for cultural proximity (Conquest, 20). Nicholas I and Alexander II cultivated the Baltic Germans, Finlanders, and the Armenians because they were loyal; they hated the Poles because they rebelled. According to Seton-Watson, it was not until Alexander III that cultural assimilation became a prerequisite for political or social incorporation.

Nonetheless, there are generalizations that can be sustained. Cultural similarity favored the successful administration of a most-favored-lord

[21] Starr, "Tsarist Government: The Imperial Dimension," in Jeremy Azrael, *Soviet Nationality Policies and Practices* (New York: Praeger, 1978), 18–19.

program. The Ukraine is the model most-favored-lord republic. Ukrainians speak an East Slavic language closely related to Russian. As for religion, under Vladimir the Great in the late tenth century, paganism was outlawed and the Orthodox Christianity of Constantinople became the state religion (Subtelny, 33–34). Although there was extensive Jesuit influence in the East in the sixteenth century, as well as the creation of a unified Catholic/Orthodox church in the seventeenth century and the emergence of an autocephalous Orthodox church in the twentieth century, it is fair to say that Russia and the Ukraine share a common Orthodox tradition. It would be going too far to claim cultural harmony between Russia and the Ukraine; I argue only cultural similarity.

What about the granting of most-favored-lord status? The notion of most favored lord may seem out of place in a region in which the Ukrainians were the peasants serving Russian and Polish landlords. At the time of the conquest in the mid-seventeenth century, the eastern Ukraine was ruled by cossacks—basically "runaway peasants . . . burghers, defrocked priests, and impecunious or adventure-seeking noblemen" who moved from the Polish-Lithuanian commonwealth to recapture the eastern part of their land from the Golden Horde (Subtelny, 108, 149). Yet Russian officials created Ukrainian lords and gave them most-favored status.

In the early years of its overrule, Moscow had had to contend with a succession battle for the position of hetman, the leader of the cossacks. The lower-class Ivan Briukhovetsky challenged a cossack of nobler stock who had already been incorporated into the Polish aristocracy. Moscow sided with Briukhovetsky. State officials conferred on him the rank of a Muscovite boyar and found him a Russian wife from a noble family. This was the beginning of Moscow's policies of elevating the status of the cossacks, even to the point of ennobling them.

This orientation toward the Ukraine continued under Catherine II in the late eighteenth century. The 1785 Charter of Nobility exempted Ukrainian nobles from all government and military service. The hetman was encouraged to compile lists of potential nobles. "Because St. Petersburg was unsure of how to define nobility in the Hetmanate," Subtelny reports, "thousands of Ukrainian petty officers and wealthier Cossacks claimed noble status, many using falsified documents" (p. 181). Data from A. Romanovich-Slavatinskii's encyclopedic study of the Russian nobility support this point. Ukrainian assimilation into the Russian nobility was largely completed in the eighteenth century, although disappointed applicants for noble status continued to make claims for redress well into the nineteenth century.[22] Ukrainians filled high positions in the Russian Orthodox church and in state service.[23] The Russian state, then, created and legitimated a Ukrainian nobility in order to give its lords most-favored status in the empire.

Why were these rights denied elsewhere? Consider Rorlich's account of the incorporation of the Volga Tatars into the Russian state. Before the conquest of Kazan (Muscovy's first non-Slavic and non-Christian subject population) by Ivan IV in 1552, members of the Kazan court were visible and active in the highest aristocratic circles in Muscovy. But once incorporated politically, and despite continued trade and intellectual dynamism in Kazan, princes and pretenders began to be treated as "unclean" in Moscow (p. 38). All sorts of restrictions were put upon their access to power in Russia. Into the early twentieth century, there still remained on the books laws limiting their right to enter the Russian civil service, the legal profession, and publishing. Restrictions existed as well on Tatar trade, ownership of real estate, and migration east of the Urals (Rorlich, 108). Indeed, in 1906 the tsar opened the Duma to Turkestanian representatives but in 1907 reneged by disenfranchising Central Asia and relying instead on emirs as natural intermediaries (Allworth, 157–60). What were "rights" in Orthodox and Slavic areas were "privileges" in Central Asia. The opportunities for Tatar elites to achieve social and economic mobility within the tsarist empire were sharply circumscribed.

Even under liberal tsars who sought to give most-favored-lord status to elites in all subject areas, the policy was extremely difficult to implement. Fisher discusses the case of the Crimean Tatars after Catherine's 1775 Charter of Nobility, which gave Russian nobles limited self-government (pp. 75, 84–86). At this time, Tatar nobles were to be made members of the newly constituted Crimean Assembly. The Russian government found that it was hard to give Tatars noble status when the nobles (*mirzas*) had no papers establishing their landholdings. (They evidently had fewer problems doing so for Orthodox cossacks.) The division of clan lands that distinguished Tatar from Russian society made it infeasible to apply the same decrees on noble status to both societies. Eventually, a Tatar commission was set up, and verbal testimony was permitted

[22] Romanovich-Slavatinskii, *Dvorianstvo v Rossii ot nachala XVII veka do otmeny kreposnago prava* (Nobility in Russia from the seventeenth century until emancipation of the serfs) (St. Petersburg: Tipografiia Ministerstva Vnutrennikh Del, 1870), 87–112.

[23] Lubomyr Hajda (in comments on my presentation at MIT, February 21, 1991) pointed out that while Ukrainians did get most-favored-lord rights, they could not exercise those rights anywhere in the empire. Notably, their successes were greater in Russia than in the Ukraine, suggesting tsarist fear of fifth columnists. Greater mobility at the center than at the periphery should make the national dynamic outlined in this paper even more pronounced.

in lieu of written records of nobility. With this change, 334 Tatar *mirzas* were assigned the rank of Russian noble (*dvoriane*). To make their testimony credible, the *mirzas* had to pay a high cost. They were expected to ape the life-style of the Russian nobility, something that lowered them in the estimation of their own society. Yet their apparent reluctance to act like Russians or to learn the Russian language was of minor importance in comparison with the administrative barriers preventing them from taking advantage of *dvoriane* status. Crimean governors, most notably Semen Zhegulin, periodically requested that Moscow reaffirm their noble privileges, largely in reaction to policies that threatened their regional supremacy, such as those rewarding Russian nobles with lands in the Crimea for service to the tsar. These policies forced many noble Tatars into either exile or poverty. In 1802 Zhegulin's successor, Grigorii Miloradovich, constituted a commission of Russian bureaucrats and *mirzas* to attempt to resolve these problems. For eight years the commission could do no more than reaffirm verbally the commitment to equal rights for *mirzas*. But Fisher concludes:

> Although Russian laws of that century give the impression that the rights and privileges granted to the *mirzas* after 1783 were preserved and constantly reaffirmed, the fact that one edict after another called for the introduction of *dvoriane* rights for them indicates that they either had not received or were unable to retain these rights. (p. 86)

And Fisher goes on to show how a string of Russian noble rights came to Tatars as "privileges granted only by special governmental decree." These include the right to take part in *dvorianstvo* elections and the right to register one's children in *dvoriane* rank before they had performed any state service.

The Estonian case is an intermediate one. The Estonian language is from the Finno-Ugric group, which is neither Slavic nor a member of the wider Indo-European language family. The Estonians are Christians, mostly Lutherans. In the seventeenth century, under Polish and then Swedish hegemony, many peasants were sold into permanent bondage under German lords (Raun, 30–31). As serfs, about 17 percent of the Estonian peasants converted to the "tsar's faith," in the hope that the political protection of the tsar would eventually release them from their bondage (Raun, 45). Many peasants even fled to Russia, seeking the tsar's protection. They were largely rebuffed when a self-proclaimed prophet attempted to deliver his following to the Crimea; but Estonians were able to get their own land around St. Petersburg. These émigrés generally learned the Russian language, in hopes that it would open the way to employment in the Russian state service.

Estonians took strategic advantage of their potential alliance with Russia. In the late nineteenth century many of the freed serfs who had migrated to the city celebrated the Russification policies of the Russian administration of Estonia, because it meant that they would be able to replace the Germans, who refused to learn Russian, as state bureaucrats. Raun reports that the percentage of Estonians in the state bureaucracy increased from about 5 percent in 1881 to 52 percent in 1897. Although it would be inaccurate to claim that Estonians received most-favored-lord status (there had been no Estonian lords, after all; Estonians had been peasants under the suzerainty of German nobles), it is fair to say that due to a Christianity in common with Russians, they were able to receive land and state positions that allowed them considerable social mobility (Raun, 59, 61, 73).

Georgians, who are Orthodox[24] but do not speak a Slavic language, are another intermediary category between the Tatars and the Ukrainians. Through successive bargains and deals with the Georgian nobility, the Russian crown was able to incorporate Georgia into the empire by the early nineteenth century (Suny, chap. 4). Under Alexander I, Georgian nobles were given key roles in the courts under the guidance of the Russian administrator. By 1827 Alexander had issued a ukase that declared that all Georgian nobles, whether in state service or not, were to receive status and privilege equal to that received by Russian nobles. But the implementation of this decree, whether under the imperialistic governor Pavl Vasil'evich Hahn (sent out by Nicholas I to redesign the territorial administration along Russian lines) or his more accommodating successor Mikhail Semenovich Vorontsov, was fraught with technical difficulties, basically concerning the need to furnish proof of one's Georgian noble status. Eventually Georgian nobles were satisfied, and in 1848 the nobles of Tbilisi pledged their support to the tsar and their willingness to fight for him during the European revolutions. Only in 1850 was a final survey of Georgian noble families conducted.[25] Cultural distance between Russia and Georgia made the path to most-favored-lord status somewhat slower and more complicated than it was for subjects in Slavic areas.

[24] Under the Georgian king Erekle II (1762–98), an agreement of protection with Russia permitted the Georgian Orthodox church to remain autocephalic, yet with representation in the Holy Synod of the Russian church. In 1811 the Georgian church was brutally incorporated into the Russian church, and the churches were forced to employ the Slavonic liturgy. It was not until 1943, under Stalin, that autocephaly was restored (Suny, 64, 84–85, 284).

[25] Romanovich-Slavatinskii (fn. 22).

Many analysts have assumed far too much variation in the intensity of the desire of peoples of the incorporated regions to assimilate into the dominant Russian society. By contrast, the variation in the status granted by central elites to assimilators from the incorporated regions is significant and historically consequential.

IV

I have argued that the historical dimension that accounts for distinctions between the national movements in the Soviet Union is based upon a single variable—the degree to which elites in the peripheral nationalities received most-favored-lord status in Russia. The historical data show that in the territories west of Moscow, most-favored-lord status was readily granted, even when there were no indigenous lords. Lords in the Turkic areas were often given elite privileges, but they were not given access to positions of high status by right. In intermediate cases like Georgia and Estonia, elite mobility was possible but circumscribed.[26] Certain predictions follow from this: (1) in the most-favored-lord regions there would be powerful symbolic unity among titulars for full independence but a waning of resolve as the conflict of interest among two branches of the titular elites begins to manifest itself; and (2) in the non-most-favored-lord regions, the pressure for independence would come more slowly (but once set in motion, there would be unity among the titular elites, with only settled minority populations seeking to slow the process down).

Testing the theory against the nationalist outpourings since the end of the Brezhnev era is fraught with difficulty, despite what I stated earlier about the possibility of overcoming the problem of overdetermination. For one, the Russian Revolution and the vast modernization project under Stalin brought class politics into play in a way that vastly altered the structure of society. The Gourevitch model was designed for social classes under capitalism, and the correspondence between cadres and bourgeoisie is weak. The big problem here is that without capitalism, the Soviet republics do not have rising bourgeois elites to trigger peripheral nationalism, as specified in Gourevitch's model. However, there is a related trigger in the Soviet case today. It is consistent with the thrust of the model to posit that the economic catastrophe brought about by pere-

[26] In his discussion of Soviet "semicolonies," Michael Voslensky differentiates between Russian and Soviet rule along the same geographical divide; see Voslensky, *Nomenklatura: The Soviet Ruling Class*, trans. Eric Mosbacher (Garden City, N.Y.: Doubleday, 1984), 285–86.

stroika has made cadres in the republics believe that there is no longer a "center" capable of governing the Union. These cadres recognize that they could take advantage of a newly formed market by buying ownership of state factories and turning them into profitable concerns, unshackled by the Moscow bureaucracy. These cadres will see themselves as a rising bourgeoisie, and the chaos at the center gives them the confidence that republican independence would be economically advantageous. Decline of the center rather than the economic rise of the periphery is the triggering mechanism for the most-favored-lord republics.

There have been discontinuities in the Soviet period as well, making a test of a model that posits a continuous effect of a historical variable precarious. By 1959 high-level jobs as cadres, available through a Russian-dominated system called *nomenklatura*, kept non-Russians (except possibly Ukrainians) out of virtually all sensitive positions in the all-Union service. Teresa Rakowska-Harmstone argues (in Hajda and Beissinger, 84), based on interviews with émigrés, that in the Soviet military the top security jobs are invariably reserved for Russians. "The KGB Border Troops," she reports, "are said to be staffed almost exclusively by Slavs. . . . The Strategic Rocket Forces, the Air Force, and the Navy are reported to be composed mostly of Slavs. . . . The airborne units are also predominantly Russian." Meanwhile the construction brigades employ mostly Muslims.[27] But one should not conclude on the basis of these data that the overall status of non-Russians vis-à-vis the center is uniform: while mobility for non-Russians in the Union *nomenklatura* is in general blocked, there are probably closer career links to central authorities in the most-favored-lord republics than in the non-most-favored-lord republics.[28]

The possibility that there are other variables or alternative explanations poses a third methodological difficulty. The focus on a single historical phenomenon—the nature of elite incorporation into the state—can help isolate a variable, but it cannot adequately control for a number of other variables that might have influenced the pattern of outcomes. Perhaps some factors previous to the choice of providing most-favored-lord status (such as level of economic development) can explain both the granting of most-favored-lord status and the pattern of national uprisings as well. Perhaps the economic potential of the West (the Ukraine

[27] This view is amply supported by the quantitative data presented by Grey Hodnett, *Leadership in the Soviet National Republics* (Oakville, Ontario: Mosaic Press, 1978), 309, Table 6.2.

[28] This is the assessment of Rasma Karklins, in a personal communication to the author, November 11, 1990.

and the Baltics) can explain the social acceptance of minorities, while the fight for basic resources (including water) in Central Asia explains the intense interethnic tensions. Perhaps the interwar experience of administrative separation from the Soviet Union in the Baltics and West Ukraine explains the special nature of nationality politics that I attribute to the most-favored-lord phenomenon. These alternative hypotheses cannot be discounted; further research using strategic comparisons will be able to put them to the test. The large number of potential cases, however, makes testing possible, and social scientists should mine these cases to modify the proposed elite incorporation model.

Finally, the nuances in the different nationality scripts presented herein might disappear in the face of cataclysmic events. (Buildings relying on standards designed to withstand structural damage from earthquakes should show their relative strength in withstanding the power of moderate tremors; an earthquake of devastating proportions would render differences between buildings that met or did not meet those standards largely irrelevant.) If the economic and political crises of the Soviet state lead to complete anarchy, the differences in response by most-favored-lord and non-most-favored-lord republics would be inconsequential.

Despite these formidable challenges to the model, there is some order to the scraps of evidence now accumulating—many of them from the books under review—about regional variations in the nature of the national uprisings.

Consider the case of the Ukraine. Its elites enjoyed most-favored-lord status, and consequently it fits the west European pattern of peripheral nationalism. During the Brezhnev years Ukrainian elites were angered that industrial investments made in Siberia would have had higher marginal returns if they had instead been made in the Ukraine, with its more highly educated work force and better industrial infrastructure. This discontent fed the belief that the Ukraine could have advanced more rapidly if it were free from all-Union control. This feeling of economic loss as the price for being part of the Union was too vague to impel cadres to seek autonomy. It took the collapse of the Soviet economy under Gorbachev for the Ukrainian national front, the Rukh, to become a major force for separation.

Because of the most-favored-lord status, we should expect to find significant tensions within Ukrainian society between those who have Russified and those who have banked on their Ukrainian identity. Indeed, we find some support in the reported division between East and West Ukraine. The West was ruled by Poland and Austria through the eighteenth century; Russian rule was not a factor there until the Second World War, however. Consequently, the West has had few Russian assimilators. The East Ukraine, which was treated as "Little Russia" from the seventeenth century onward, has a large population of Ukrainian nationals who do not have full fluency in Ukrainian. Beginning in the 1920s East Ukrainians entered the Ukrainian Communist Party in record numbers, received appointments in prestigious Russian academic institutes, and felt that assimilation had paid off reasonably well.[29] Bialer points out that in the late 1970s only in the Ukraine was the KGB chief a member of the titular nationality, and he provides a long list of Ukrainians who have secured excellent positions outside the borders of their own republic.[30] Assimilation has been so great, complains Ukrainian writer Dmytro Pavlichko, that unless the Khrushchev rule of free choice in the language of school education is changed, "the Ukrainian language will remain in Canada only."[31]

Although I have not systematically examined the politics within the Rukh, I would hypothesize that the East Ukrainians feel threatened by the radical calls for making Ukrainian the sole official language of the republic. This would give West Ukrainians a better chance to succeed in the reconstituted civil service, the teaching profession, journalism, and other arenas where the quality of one's literacy determines occupational success; and this would undermine the tremendous advantages now enjoyed by East Ukrainians in the republican *nomenklatura*.[32]

What does this intraethnic political cleavage mean? To be sure, East Ukrainians will need to come out publicly as nationalists, since nationalism is the only framework for radical protest against the centralization of power in Moscow. However, it is in their interest to work privately to slow the process down, by seeking to bargain with Soviet authorities (for example, by showing greater willingness to accept Gorbachev's offer for a new Union treaty) and by pushing for bilingual administration and education. Motyl analyzes this fissure well. East Ukrainians, he reports, seek merely a "symbolic sovereignty," whereas West Ukrainians see the symbolic sovereignty of the 1990s as a step down. They still cling to the

[29] See Motyl (fn. 2, 1987), chap. 4. Motyl's interpretation of these data differs from mine.
[30] Seweryn Bialer, *Stalin's Successors* (Cambridge: Cambridge University Press, 1980), 219, 223–24.
[31] Isabelle T. Kreindler, "Soviet Language Planning since 1953," in Kirkwood (fn. 19), 48–49.
[32] See Mark Beissinger and Lubomyr Hajda, "Nationalism and Reform in Soviet Politics," in Hajda and Beissinger, 308. The authors argue that the ethnic division of political labor is characteristic of politics at all levels. But their data suggest that in the western republics the division of political labor is intraethnic—as would be predicted by the most-favored-lord model.

myth that the Ukraine earned its sovereignty during the Second World War, and that this process culminated in its recognition by the United Nations as a sovereign state.[33] To the extent that Moscow ceases to resist national popular movements and thereby ceases to be a common enemy to all social groups in the Ukraine, these fissures within Ukrainian society should become more visible still.

If the dominant tensions within republics whose titulars are favored lords are between segments of the titular nationality, then we should expect fewer tensions between the titular nationals and the minorities within the republic, who become spectators to a subtle intranational conflict. Consequently, although the Ukraine has had a history of brutal anti-Semitism and although its national revival owes a good deal to Hitler's machinations, the Rukh has been insistent about recognizing the rights of minorities and has explicitly mentioned the Jews (Solchanyk, in Hajda and Beissinger, 192). Furthermore, minorities in the Crimea have apparently been less nervous about the implications of possible Ukrainian sovereignty than have the Armenians in Azerbaidjan.

Let us now move from the Ukraine, where most-favored-lord status was easily granted, to Estonia, where there were no Estonian lords, just a sector of Estonians from peasant and trader backgrounds that worked its way up in the Russian state service. While not most favored *lords*, Estonians rose to a reasonably high status among Russia's bureaucratic elites. In consequence, according to Raun, a key cultural divide in the Soviet era has been between Russian/Estonians (those Estonians who had migrated to Russia) and local Estonians, with the former getting most of the important positions requiring Moscow's trust (pp. 191–93). An exemplary figure here is Johannes Käbin, a Russian Estonian called "Ivan" by the local Estonians. He served as first secretary during Stalin's rule, learned his ancestral language, and was able to secure limited rights for Estonians during Stalin's rule (Shtromas, in Conquest, 199). For the past generation, Russian/Estonians have received most of the political benefits of Soviet rule. But the number of these Russified Estonians is shrinking; in the Gorbachev period they have practically disappeared. Recognizing that they had become "history," most strategically reidentified themselves or openly repented their past collaboration and therefore play no role as Russian/Estonians in the current period.

Limited social mobility for elite Estonians in Russian society surely narrowed the divide between Russified Estonians and Estonian Estonians. Yet even without unambiguous most-favored-lord status, the Bal-

---

[33] Motyl (fn. 2, 1987), 85–86.

tics' contacts with and proximity to industrial Europe afforded them the opportunity to expand faster economically than could the rest of the Soviet Union (Schroeder, in Conquest, 304). More importantly, many Estonians are familiar with life in Western Europe (via Finnish TV), which opened them earlier than elites in other regions to the possibility of joining the world capitalist economy. The Estonian national movement was propelled not only by the collapse of the Soviet center but also by the expectation of rapid growth under capitalism in an independent state. (In this sense, the mechanism triggering the nationalist uprising in Estonia is similar to what Gourevitch found in his European cases.) Estonian peripheral nationalism consequently developed early and was much stronger than peripheral nationalism in the Ukraine.[34]

The combination of economic dynamism and very low elite co-optation into the center makes it likely that the Estonian roller-coaster ride toward independence can only be braked by military action from the center. There are few internal elites who will have an interest in promoting mere symbolic sovereignty in order to amortize their investment in Russian assimilation. Few in the Baltics see any long-term advantage to becoming a special economic zone, the "Hong Kong" of the Union. Massive Soviet military action indeed could put a halt to the process; but it will be nearly impossible for Russian politicians to find a sector of the Estonian population willing to negotiate new terms for continued membership in the Union.

Finally, what about the large non-Estonian working-class population? Due in part to Estonia's economic dynamism and all-Union policies, which brought many military and heavy industrial units to Estonia, Russians now constitute some 30 percent of the population of Estonia. In Estonia's industrial sector 60 percent of the output in 1980 was in union-republic ministries and in oil-shale mining entirely managed from Moscow. These are the industries that attracted Russian workers, and the high turnover rate among workers offers Russian families little incentive to assimilate into Baltic life.[35] Typical of working-class migrations, the host nationality, especially the lower social strata, tends to develop nativist hostilities toward the migrants. This has undoubtedly occurred in Estonia: the tensions between Estonians and Russians are real though by no means a signal that an ethnic time bomb is ticking.

[34] John A. Armstrong points to the relatively moderate level of nationalist activity in the Ukraine; see Armstrong, *Ukrainian Nationalism*, 3d ed. (Englewood, Colo.: Ukrainian Academic Press, 1990), 238.

[35] See Rein Taagepera, "Baltic Population Changes, 1950–1980," *Journal of Baltic Studies* 12 (Spring 1981), discussed in Karklins (fn. 2), 35–57, at 54–55.

The strikes by the Russian workers against proposed discriminatory legislation in Estonia tell a more ominous story, however. The Estonians sought to intimidate the Russians by requiring them to send their children to Estonian language schools and to fulfill residency requirements before they can vote. (Under pressure from Moscow, these regulations were modified, providing for implementation over a five-year period.) The rapid mobilization of working-class migrants for organized protest against these provocations and in support of group rights is theoretically surprising, in terms of the elite incorporation model. One could argue that the militant protests organized by Interfront expressed the outrage of Russians who had been recruited by Moscow to serve in the Baltics and who had no interest in assimilating into Estonian society. My surmise is that the Russian workers were induced to strike by Russian managers in Moscow, who saw a threat to their control over industries in the Baltics. It is these directors and the secretaries of the plan party committees who were, according to Priit Jarve of the Estonian Academy of Sciences, the first to speak at the strike organization meetings and the ones who gave explicit instructions to the workers in stage-managing the strikes. If this is correct, then political and economic decentralization in Estonia should reduce the nationalist organization of Russians in Estonia. Under economic decentralization, should it come, unassimilated workers who lose their jobs at all-Union factories would vote with their feet and return to Russia. With political decentralization, the Russians who remain in Estonia will do as working-class migrants everywhere have done: they will seek a better life for their families by accommodating to the local culture. The vast enrollments by non-Estonians in the five hundred Estonian language classes set up by the republican government in 1990 suggest a greater willingness on the part of immigrants to assimilate than on the part of the autochthonous populations to have them assimilate.[36]

If the model developed herein has explanatory power, Estonia will present a united front to Moscow in the cause of independence. Minorities, however much they support the Interfront program, will have strong incentives to assimilate into Estonian society and few incentives to organize against independence.

Georgia is the other intermediary case. Unlike the Ukraine, it had indigenous nobles, but they faced considerable bureaucratic resistance to

[36] Jarve spoke on this issue at the East-West Center, Duke University, April 13, 1991. On Russians learning Estonian, I rely on Toivo Miljan, who spoke at a panel discussion on Comparing the Democratic Movements in the Baltics at the University of Illinois, Chicago, October 6, 1990.

their claims for the privileges of nobility. The many contradictions and counterpressures in Georgian history are filled with irony and drama, as is evident from Ronald Suny's nuanced and perceptive national history. On the one hand, Georgian nobles took the initiative and joined the Russian empire; on the other hand, they were partially rebuffed. Although bureaucratic procedures well into the nineteenth century slowed considerably the access of Georgians to noble privileges, many Georgians were nevertheless active in Russian social and cultural life.

The incorporation of Georgia into the Russian state is similar in a number of its characteristics to the incorporation of Alsace into France or of Scotland into Great Britain. Economic interdependence developed quickly. Beginning in the nineteenth century trade with Russia created many jobs for a Georgian service gentry (but perhaps too much wealth for urban Armenians in Georgia, at least for Georgian tastes). Also in the nineteenth century the Georgian language "gradually lost significance in the eyes of Georgians themselves" (Pilipe Makharadze, quoted in Suny, 128). The first generation of educated Georgians entered the Russian state service. The second generation was known as the *tergdaleulni*, literally, "those who drank the water of the Terek," meaning those who crossed the Terek River to study in Russia. They were liberals who favored emancipation (to the chagrin of their fathers) and were completely at home in Russian intellectual life (Suny, 125–28).

Suny observes that despite a century of elite assimilation, by the late twentieth century "Russification is simply not evident in Transcaucasia. . . . [W]hat is evident is the strengthening of the local ethnic groups as self-conscious nationalities even as they are educated in Soviet schools" (in Hajda and Beissinger, 248). Rapid elite assimilation in the nineteenth century and resistance to Russification on the mass level in the twentieth century are the principal contradictory trends.

Georgia's 5.7 percent annual rate of growth per capita between 1960 and 1980 is by far the most dynamic of all the republics considered in this essay (Schroeder, in Conquest, 297–304). Yet because the west European scene was less well known to Georgians, the impetus for national sovereignty has been slower than in Estonia, with a 5.1 percent growth rate. In the 1970s Georgia had low levels of dissident nationalism and hardly any mobilization—until the 1978 decree attempting to remove official recognition of the Georgian language (Suny, 308–9). It took a massacre by Soviet security forces in Tbilisi in April 1989—an overreaction to a peaceful demonstration—to radicalize the national autonomy movement. It was not economic dynamism that pushed Georgia into the politics of autonomy; thus for the Georgian case, the west European model of peripheral nationalism does not hold.

Finally, given the high level of Georgian noble collusion with Russian elites dating back more than a century, Georgia exhibits a tight titular family circle of rule, consistent with the republics whose lords had little status in Russian society. The nineteen-year rule by Mzhavanadze, built upon national pride, has been pointed to as the exemplary "family circle" (Suny, 306–7). (Yet the power of the Mzhavanadze machine is hard to explain given the rapidity with which his successor, Eduard Shevardnadze, was able to emasculate it and collaborate with central authorities.) And as expected with nationally defined family circles, its treatment of minorities, whether of Armenians[37] or smaller minority language groups (the Mingrelians, Svans, and the Abkhazis),[38] is that of explicit discrimination justified on national grounds. In the wake of the March 1991 poll in which Georgians voted overwhelmingly for independence, the Ossetian population in Georgia took up arms in fear of being ruled by Georgians without protection from Moscow. In Suny's sardonic summary: "National autonomy in Georgia had come to mean . . . resistance to central Russian authorities and . . . the exercise of local power against the unrepresented local minorities" (p. 305). Georgian nationalism—on two paths at the same time—will continue to exhibit qualities consistent with ethnic nationalism in Europe (with a divided elite, many of whom symbolically support independence but have an interest in union with Russia) and consistent as well with the non-most-favored-lord regions (with the titulars protecting their turf through discrimination and intimidation of minorities).

In Central Asia, where there has been neither economic dynamism nor most-favored-lord status, the revised model holds less ambiguously. Here, our authors have observed "welfare colonialism" (Bernstam, in Conquest, 326–27), where titular elites administer social service programs (in health, education, and industrial development) organized from the center and also collect rents for the administration of the programs and for assuring political quiescence. Under these circumstances, the titulars in Uzbekistan and Kazakhstan would not favor independence from Soviet Union. To the extent they have supported national fronts, it is to maintain their leadership as lower strata respond to the contagion

[37] Barbara Anderson and Brian Silver report rapid Armenian out-migration from Georgia in the 1960s and 1970s; see Anderson and Silver, "Demographic Sources of the Changing Ethnic Composition of the Soviet Union," *Population and Development Review* 15 (December 1989), 638.
[38] See B. G. Hewitt "Aspects of Language Planning in Georgia," in Kirkwood (fn. 19).

effects from elsewhere in the Union. By developing fluency in Russian (but maintaining the titular language as the dominant one), these elites have monopolized mediation services with Soviet authorities. It is the new generation trying to crack the family circles of rule that has an interest in pushing for sovereignty. In the period from 1955 to 1972 Kazakh nationals had only 46.6 percent of the top cadre positions in Kazakhstan, and Uzbeks had 76.3 percent in Uzbekistan; both of these are lower than the 83.7 percent in Estonia, 85.3 percent in the Ukraine, and 97.2 percent in Georgia.[39] Those in the new generation of technocratically trained personnel surely see the most sensitive jobs in their region as theirs should the region achieve sovereignty. And the technocrats in the center need hardly object. As with other cases of welfare colonialism in Africa and Asia, economic considerations suggest to rulers at the center the rationality of accepting separation and national sovereignty. The resistance from the center to these movements will be far less than it is to the popular fronts in the Ukraine and even Georgia.

If the movement toward national sovereignty in Central Asia is slow but inexorable, the tensions between titulars and minorities have been quick to flare and violent. Titulars in the non-most-favored-lord regions have systematically discriminated against minority populations within their republics as well. Data on the percentage of secondary school graduates in the urban work force in 1970, by republic, show that in only five republics have the titular nationals had more than a one percentage advantage over the population at large: Uzbekistan, Kazakhstan, Georgia, Azerbaidjan, and Kirghizia (Schroeder, in Conquest, 297). These are the republics whose elites were least likely to receive most-favored-lord status. Let us examine the political dynamic that lies behind these data in the two Central Asian republics under review.

Consider Uzbekistan. *Birlik* (Unity), the Uzbek popular front, was constructed on the Baltic model, with demands similar to those voted in the Baltic assemblies. In this sense, the outpouring of national movements appears to be homologous, with all taking advantage of a rotting empire. But, as I have argued, the dynamics are distinct. First, Uzbekistan did not experience dynamic economic growth relative to Moscow that would impel an emergent bourgeois class to ally with peasants in

---

[39] The percentage of the titular population having these jobs (which is quite high for the Kazakhs) is not relevant here. Titular nationals seeking social mobility will seek a near monopoly on high-status cadre jobs even if they have only a plurality of the republican population. The data here are from Hodnett (fn. 27), 108, Table 2.14. Excellent general discussions of the role of the new men in the Soviet context are available in Bialer (fn. 30), chap. 6; and Jerry Hough, "In Whose Hands the Future," in *Problems of Communism* 16 (March–April 1967), 18–25.

the rural areas. Its rate of growth has been behind that of the RSFSR, and its rate of savings considerably lower, suggesting little opportunity for massive internal investments should the republic achieve freedom from the center. Second, there is not a solid core of Russified Uzbeks whose future depends upon continued collaboration with the Soviet state. In the Ukraine, by contrast, there is an abundant core of Russified Ukrainians. Uzbek elites did not enjoy the most-favored-lord status that would have allowed such a core to develop.

The political dynamic of national uprisings in Uzbekistan thus conforms to the non-most-favored-lord model. Here we expect nationalism to be based on a reified definition of the culture of the republic. Jobs and opportunities that will aid in the amortization of their investment in independence—especially those jobs that were associated with all-Union ministries and had been in the hands of Slavs—can go principally to Uzbeks. Data from Nancy Lubin support this. "Professionally," she concludes, "an Uzbek can go farther the more he asserts himself *as an Uzbek*."[40] This pressure for jobs, coming from the younger and better trained Uzbeks against their own seniors, is reflected in tensions within *Birlik*. The "new men" have broken away into a parallel movement, called *Erk* (Freedom), and its leaders complain that the old Uzbek family circles have not been forthcoming with the new generation.[41]

The most-favored-lord model should further lead us to expect that the nationalist movement would unleash a counternationalism by the ethnic minorities who live within the boundaries of the republic. Indeed, the dominant political tensions within Uzbekistan are apparently between "genuine" Uzbeks and ethnic minorities within the republic. Lubin reports anger by Russians over affirmative action programs favoring the Uzbeks.[42] Uzbek discrimination against the Crimean Tatars who were "resettled" around Tashkent has raised fears among the Tatars that if they become subjects of an autonomous Uzbek state, their position will be worse than it has been since their deportation from the Crimea (Allworth, 314). Violence has already broken out with another deported nationality, the Meshketians. "The Meshketians are seen by the Uzbeks as troublemakers," reports the *Economist*, "and, even more, competitors for

[40] Lubin, "Assimilation and Retention of Ethnic Identity in Uzbekistan," *Asian Affairs* (London) 12, pt. III (October 1981), 277–85, at 283–84. See also idem, *Labour and Nationality in Soviet Central Asia* (Princeton: Princeton University Press, 1984). This extremely astute volume focuses on Russian/Asian ethnic relations in the economy, not on Uzbeks versus other Asian minorities within Uzbekistan.

[41] My analysis of *Erk* is based upon remarks made by James Critchlow of the Russian Research Center, Harvard University, at the East-West Center, Duke University, April 13, 1991.

[42] Lubin (fn. 40, 1984).

scarce jobs in a republic whose population is soaring."[43] Indications that the Kazakh population in Tashkent—a city that could well have been "awarded" to Kazakhstan—is also restive, fearing Uzbek independence and what it would mean for them (Allworth, 198–202). In the 1920s in Samarkand, Tajiks were strongly pressured to declare themselves as Uzbeks. In the 1989 census, however, already mobilized in an underground movement, they have begun to redefine their national identification as Tajiks. Tajik-Uzbek enmity in Uzbekistan is a bomb waiting to be detonated.[44] The Karakalpak minority (with its own ASSR) in Uzbekistan would also be threatened by Uzbek autonomy. And looking at the border from the other side, the Uzbek minority in the Kirghiz SSR has resorted to violence to protect itself in the wake of greater Kirghiz autonomy.

Kazakh nationalism is similar to that in Uzbekistan and is built upon family circles of ethnic Kazakhs.[45] Mikhail Cheifets, a Russian dissident writer in exile in Kazakhstan, was reported to have said the following by Radio Liberty in 1980: "The question of nationality doesn't arise . . . in Leningrad and Moscow," but "Kazakhstan . . . is riddled with ethnic barriers, although authorities fail to acknowledge it. . . . The support of one's 'clan' is considered the ethical basis of life, and to violate this is a moral transgression even in the eyes of the passive members of an ethnic community."[46] Violence instigated by Kazakhs at Kazakhstan State University at Alma-Ata in 1978 was directed against Russians, whom young Kazakhs felt were too heavily represented in the student body; this resulted in a tighter family circle of university admissions in Kazakhstan.[47] In 1986 Gorbachev sought to replace the Brezhnev protégé Dinmukhamed Kunaev as first secretary. Kunaev had restored a Kazakh family circle in positions of leadership after Khrushchev tried to open up the *nomenklatura* system. Gorbachev chose a Russian, Gennadii Kolbin, and riots ensued in Alma-Ata. (These riots were likely organized by Kunaev's henchmen; the protesters nevertheless responded enthusiastically.) Even though Kolbin pushed through legislation making Kazakh one of the two official languages of the republic (and used it in his public appearances), he was replaced in 1989 with Nursultan Nazarbaev, a titular

[43] *Economist*, June 10, 1989, p. 44.

[44] This is the view of Alexander Zevelev, of the Historical Archives Institute, Moscow, expressed at the East-West Center, Duke University, April 13, 1991.

[45] Olcott (pp. 25ff.) presents data suggesting that Kazakh elites received most-favored-lord privileges more often than my model would suggest. Tsarina Anna gave Russian citizenship to the khan of the Small Horde, to protect him against the Kalmyks. But whether this bargain enabled Kazakh khans to claim equal rights with *dvoriane* is doubtful.

[46] Cheifets, quoted in Karklins (fn. 2), 29.

[47] Karklins (fn. 2), 65.

national who was a Gorbachev loyalist (Olcott, in Hajda and Beissinger, 257–61).

The most extreme ethnic violence in the post-glasnost period has occurred in republics whose elites did not receive most-favored-lord status: this violence originated among groups that are territorial or displaced minorities threatened by the possibility of titular sovereignty.[48] An egregious example has been in Azerbaidjan, where the Armenian minority living (as a majority) in Nagorno-Karabakh, protected under Soviet rule, would be left to the mercy of the Azeri nationalists should the Soviet empire disintegrate into its constituent republics.[49] The greatest challenge for those who accept the "collapsing empire" paradigm is to recognize that among the Meshketians and Karakalpaks in Uzbekistan, the Armenians in Azerbaidjan, and the Uzbeks in Kirghizia, there is an interest in allying with Moscow to redraw boundaries of existing republics, create new republics, and protect minorities within republics. Regardless of whether they have historical memories of exile and extermination, the logic of their situation points them toward an alliance with a reforming Soviet state.

V

The series under review concentrates on the non-Russians, but Russian nationalism is also a force to be reckoned with. Frederick Barghoorn foresaw the rise of Russian nationalism and predicted that it would grow in inverse proportion to the collapse of Marxism-Leninism as an official ideology. Paraphrasing Vladimir Bukovsky, a Soviet civil rights advocate, Barghoorn suggests that "from the point of view of Russian chau-

[48] Some analysts suggest that the causes of titular/minority violence lie in the arbitrariness of the boundaries—an explanation often used to explain ethnic violence in postcolonial Africa. Olcott accepts this view in arguing that the Central Asian republics had an especial problem with arbitrary boundaries and therefore are more subject to conflicts with ethnic minorities. But this logic does not hold. I concur with E. Glyn Lewis that the Soviet jurisdictional boundaries in Central Asia were remarkably sensitive to cultural boundaries, and with James Dingley that the real boundary hodgepodge is in the west, especially in Belorussia, in which four major language groups (Belorussian, Polish, Russian, and Yiddish) were put into a single republic. Most-favored-lord dynamics, rather than the nature of the boundary mechanisms, will best explain minority politics within the union republics. See Lewis, *Multilingualism in the Soviet Union* (The Hague: Mouton, 1972), 58–59; and Dingley, "Ukrainian and Belorussian: A Testing Ground," in Kirkwood (fn. 19).

[49] A comparison of the Azeris in Armenia with the Armenians in Azerbaidjan would constitute a critical test of the model proposed in this paper. Suppose the Armenians have had greater opportunity to become most favored lords but, nevertheless, in the current nationalist ferment discriminate against Azeri citizens as much as Azeri titulars discriminate against Armenians. Such evidence would constitute disconfirming evidence for the model. My surmise is that intra-Armenian conflict of interest is sufficiently strong to mute efforts to terrorize minorities in Armenia.

vinists the only thing missing in official Soviet policy today is a pogrom" (Barghoorn, in Conquest, 72).[50] How, then, does Russian chauvinism "fit" into the model proposed here? I offer some suggestions, but future work on Russian nationalism is obviously required to flesh out these skeletal points.

Consistent with the elite incorporation model is the enthusiastic support given to Boris N. Yeltsin, president of the Russian Republic, for his message that the Russian Republic has been victimized by the unfair redistribution of wealth made possible by centralized rule. Russian technocrats of the post-Stalin generation have held that the redistributive policies of the Brezhnev era have caused Russia's economic misery. They hold to a myth of Russian vitality within a context of *Soviet* decline. Separation from Central Asia would be a blessing for many Russians who would like a smaller Russia to become part of the west European political economy. Russian willingness to loosen ties with the Soviet Union reflects the perception that Russia would experience great economic growth if the Union were to break apart.

What about the minorities within the RSFSR? Here the data are clear (Anderson and Silver, in Hajda and Beissinger, 116). The ethnic groups estimated to have the largest percentage of people who reidentified themselves as "Russians" in the censuses between 1959 and 1970 are the ASSR nationalities whose official territories are in the RSFSR. Of the Karelians between the ages of 0 and 38 in 1959, about 17 percent are estimated to have reidentified as Russians by 1970. The figure for the Mordvinians is similar. Anderson and Silver see intermarriage and the high status of Russian administrators as the catalyst of the switch.

Do these data disconfirm the most-favored-lord model? Should not those ethnic minorities whose leaders did not get most-favored-lord status consolidate around titular leadership in their ASSRs, autonomous oblasts, or national okrugs, as seems to have been the case with the Volga Tatars? Perhaps not. A special relationship with Russians enables them to achieve social mobility within the Soviet hierarchy. By contrast, the prospects for mobility as a minority within a union republic or even as a majority within an ASSR do not hold out the promise of sufficient rewards for ambitious families. Some good census data supporting this proposition show the remarkable achievements in higher education made by minorities such as the Buryats, Ossetians, Circassians, and Balkars, all of whom have a significantly higher percentage of their popu-

---

[50] Vladislav Krasnov in his "Russian National Feeling" (in Conquest) picks up from samizdat comments made by visitors at a Russian chauvinist art exhibit; these express deep longing for symbols glorifying the Russian spirit.

lations in institutes of higher education than do the Russians, Ukrainians, Estonians, or Lithuanians.[51]

Rorlich's juxtaposition of the Volga Tatars and the Bashkirs demonstrates this point (chap. 12). The Tatars, with a chance of one day becoming a union republic, have organized to maintain literacy in their own language and have de-emphasized the learning of Russian. The Bashkirs, who are outnumbered by the Tatars even in the Bashkir Autonomous Soviet Socialist Republic, have assimilated the Russian language more quickly than have the Tatars. The Tatars, although they have done slightly better than the Bashkirs in gaining admission to universities, have still done far worse than the average for their republic (Rorlich, 174, 160).[52] Clearly there is a conjunction of interests here: the Soviet authorities want to buy the support of non-Russians, and it is convenient to lure small minority groups into the central net while giving autonomy to larger groups; meanwhile, given the paltry resources available to jurisdictions smaller than union republics, individuals from smaller groups will perceive the relative advantages of assimilating into Russia over maintaining a cohesive titular family. My model would argue that one can explain the fact that minority revivals have been relatively weak within the RSFSR by noting the limited resources available to the "titular" role and the far greater possibilities for individuals to achieve moderate successes climbing the Soviet mobility ladder, however unfavored they might be as they approach the top.

Moving from growing Russian nationalism and weak minority revivals within the RSFSR, let us now consider Russian nationalism among Russian migrants now living in the national republics. Russian working-class communities labor under constraints very different from those of territorially based minority communities in the national republics.[53] Migrants come for individual or family benefits and have little motivation to fight for group rights. Though they live in neighborhoods with ethnic kin, they rarely fight to maintain their "culture" in their new home. Most often it is second- or third-generation assimilated descendants of migrants who seek to reclaim the "lost" culture.

The data on Russian migrants into the non-Russian republics show that assimilation correlates well with the economic dynamism of the region of migration. Consider Table 1, which juxtaposes levels of linguistic

[51] See Robert A. Lewis, Richard H. Rowland, and Ralph S. Clem, *Nationality and Population Change in Russia and the USSR: An Evaluation of Census Data, 1897–1970* (New York: Praeger, 1976), 137.

[52] On university admissions, see ibid., 137.

[53] See Laitin (fn. 12), 297–99, for a formal demonstration of the difference between migrant and territorial minority incentives to fight for language revival.

TABLE 1

RUSSIAN MIGRATION AND THE ECONOMIC DYNAMISM OF THE REPUBLICS

Percentage of Russsian Migrants Learning the Language of the Republic		Growth of GNP/CAP, 1961–85, by Republic (Russia = 4.4)	
Lithuania	37.9	Belorussia	6.3
Ukraine	34.4	Georgia	5.4
Belorussia	24.8	Armenia	5.2
Georgia	31.8	Lithuania	5.0
Estonia	15.1	Latvia	4.9
Azerbaidjan	14.5	Moldavia	4.8
Moldavia	12.1	Estonia	4.7
[No more significant cases]		Ukraine	4.2

SOURCES: Left-hand column: Anderson and Silver, in Hajda and Beissinger, 647; the percentages are from Silver, personal communication, from his culling of the 1989 census data. These figures are not commensurate with the published ordering. Right-hand column: Schroeder, in Hadja and Beissinger, 47.

assimilation by Russians with the level of economic dynamism of the region of migration. One infers that "language distance" does not act as an impediment to Russians learning the language of their new home, as the first and fourth languages on the list are non-Slavic. Russian working-class migrants into Lithuania, the Ukraine, Belorussia, and Georgia are like working-class migrants elsewhere in the world—in a couple of generations children become fluent in the language of political, economic, and social power.[54] In a democratic arena migrants are more likely to be recruited by "titular" elites giving individual payoffs for political loyalty (for example, jobs) than by migrant elites offering symbolic support for cultural retention. Even without the democratic arena, levels of Russian migrant assimilation appear to be consistent with this model. We should of course expect ethnic tensions, induced especially by titulars who fear ethnic contamination by the migrants; but this should not significantly slow down rates of ethnic assimilation.

The other form of Russian migration into foreign republics is that of Russian colonial "settlers" into regions of economic weakness, for example, to the virgin lands of Kazakhstan. Here we should expect low levels of assimilation, as has been the case of French settlers in Algeria,

[54] Catalonia is actually a better example. There, Spanish-speaking migrants from Andalusia speak the language of the central state but not the language of the region. Language assimilation is consequently slower than for, say, Italian migrants to New York. But in the past fifteen years (since Franco, who repressed the use of Catalan) most second-generation migrants into Catalonia are fully bilingual. See Laitin (fn. 15).

Protestant settlers in Ireland, and Jewish settlers in the West Bank.[55] These settlers comprise the social strata most threatened by movements for national sovereignty in the republics, and they have generally allied themselves with the most nationalist forces in the center to put down nationalism at the periphery. Spechler suggests that Russian nationalism is fanned in part by these Russians residing in the national republics and facing growing nationalist demands of the titulars (Hajda and Beissinger, 292). But so far Russian settlers in the Central Asian areas have tended to migrate back to Russia rather than defend their nationality in their regions of settlement. To the extent that the rise of the popular fronts in Central Asia accelerates the trend of Russian settlers returning to their region of origin, there will be little violence. But if the national movements continue to snowball and the Russian settlers remain and seek to cultivate a special relationship with the center, then the situation is ripe for ethnic violence. The settlers will have a strong incentive to ally with the most chauvinist elements in Russian society.

VI

The major finding of this essay is that it is historically inaccurate to identify the incorporation of Estonia, the Ukraine, Georgia, Uzbekistan, Kazan, and Kazakhstan as examples of the construction of the "last empire" and to juxtapose Russian imperial expansion categorically to French state building. Through a discussion of the granting of most-favored-lord status to incorporated elites, I distinguish two strategies of elite incorporation for imperial rulers. I then delineate a pattern of national revivals that differentiates between republics according to whether their elites enjoyed most-favored-lord status.

The two political dynamics can be summarized as follows. Where elites received most-favored-lord status (the Ukraine), the popular fronts supporting national revivals mask a conflict of interest between national elites who have identified themselves culturally as Russians and those who have not. The former group, in the name of prudence and realism, will advocate sovereignty but will surreptitiously seek to limit its fulfillment; the latter group, in the name of self-determination, will not only

[55] I owe this interpretation to the work of Ian Lustick; see Lustick, *State-Building Failure in British Ireland and French Algeria* (Berkeley: Institute of International Studies, 1985). One crucial way in which the Russian case differs from Lustick's cases of Algeria, Ireland, and Israel is that "the Russians who live in the republics enjoy no privileges and are merely a minority against whom the hostility felt by the local populations for their nomenklatura masters in Moscow is often directed. . . . The life led by Russians in the national republics is, generally speaking, not very agreeable"; see Voslensky (fn. 26), 286.

call for complete sovereignty but will also work to bring it to fruition. In the regions where elites did not receive most-favored-lord status (Uzbekistan and Kazakhstan), the action of the popular front obscures the lack of interest by the titular elites in secession from the Soviet Union. But as they must not be seen as trying surreptitiously to subvert the calls of the "new men" for independence, they have an incentive to remain in the nationalist vanguard. Those who will suffer most from increased autonomy for these republics will be the indigenous minority populations. If the principal source of support for the Soviet "Union" in the republics whose elites were granted most-favored-lord status are those whose families took advantage of it, the principal source of support for the Union in the republics whose elites had no such opportunity are the national minorities, who have already assimilated to Russian at a faster rate than have the titulars. With different sorts of political cleavages, the unfolding of the national dramas will have distinct plots.

This finding has implications for policy, although of course those implications would depend on the political goals of the analyst. Suppose, for example, the analyst were interested in the evolution of the Union into a liberal state. Rather than recommending the undifferentiated strategy of a new all-Union treaty, the analyst might advise leadership to develop a different nationality policy for each type of republic. For the non-most-favored-lord republics, central leadership might be advised to set up bureaucratic mechanisms to hear appeals for new boundaries, holding open the possibility of the creation of new union republics. The bureaucratic processes will relieve the pressure on Moscow and instead increase the pressure on the titular nationals to defend their current boundaries. This would give Moscow a strategic advantage in its dealings with the titular elites. It would also give minorities within the present republics a chance to challenge titular power.

For the most-favored-lord republics, the key would be to grant ever-new levels of autonomy to these republics, recognizing that each concession by the center will provide new incentives for the Russianized titulars to slow the process down. Not Moscow, but the cautious titulars, will be subjected to nationalist scorn. Meanwhile, the center might be advised not to incite minorities, especially working-class immigrants, to any sort of collective action against autonomy. Although these immigrants face discrimination, they will most likely assimilate into the republican nationality over a few generations. At most, the center might provide an all-Union commission of human rights to hear cases of minority discrimination within republics.

These recommendations are based upon the assumption that the center will hold. The March 1991 all-Union referendum and the ability of the center to deploy troops to intimidate—even murder—nationalist demonstrators in Lithuania suggest that Gorbachev may still have some latitude to refashion the Union. If he does, he would be wise to handle the nationality issue in a more differentiated way than he has up through the referendum. The center has potential support among minorities in the non-most-favored-lord republics, among majority assimilators in the most-favored-lord republics, and among the Russian settlers in the virgin lands. Exploiting these potential allies and seeking to deflect potential violence over boundary issues to independent commissions could buy him even more time. Inciting Russian migrant workers against titulars would, however, be counterproductive. Understanding the logic of elite incorporation could help Moscow preserve much of the present Union within a democratic framework.

POSTSCRIPT

The events of August 1991 highlight the image of the earthquake portrayed in this essay. If an earthquake of moderate force hits a city, one can discern the effects of stricter building standards and codes. But with an earthquake of devastating proportions—when all structures collapse—the distinction between buildings constructed under different zoning regimes is washed out. The failure of the anti-Gorbachev coup in the face of KGB defections and democratic resistance was a political earthquake that registered at the upper limits of the Richter scale! Many of the nuanced differences between nationality groups—consequential when this essay was initially drafted in August 1990—seem similarly to have been washed away.[56]

Clearly the events following the coup of August 19–21, 1991, will have powerful consequences for the nationalities issue; some of these will override the trends outlined in these pages. First, the framework of the all-Union treaty (based upon the so-called 9 + 1 negotiations, between nine republics and the center) has been disassembled. The coup occurred shortly before the ceremonial signing of the treaty was to take place. Even though six republics refused to take part in the extensive negotiations that went into the draft, their leaders had been attentive to its provisions. These leaders felt it necessary to compromise with those forces within their societies that had come to terms with what they saw as the

---

[56] I have nevertheless chosen, on September 4, to leave the manuscript intact, exactly as it stood in April, when I added material on the all-Union referendum. I write this postscript not to correct errors but to reflect on the overall argument in light of historic events.

practical reality of a viable Union. The failure of the coup, which had been carried out in the name of the integrity of the center, shifted the balance of power away from the center and toward the republics. Politicians in the republics who had been talking the language of pragmatism felt compelled to do a quick volte-face, demanding far higher levels of republican sovereignty than they had before the coup. Consequently, the suggestion in the conclusion of this essay that Moscow could work to preserve the Union has been overtaken by events. The preservation of the Union relies far more heavily on initiatives taken by republican politicians than compromises designed by Gorbachev's allies at the center.

Second, the chaos in late August gave European states the courage to recognize Baltic independence. International recognition is a key element that differentiates the Baltic republics from the Ukraine, Moldavia, and Georgia. This essay correctly saw the route toward Estonian independence as smoother than that of the Ukraine, though it focused on co-opted elites rather than on international support. While further research is needed to sort out which of these two factors was the more consequential, the essay was insufficiently attuned to distinctions between republics drawn by foreign countries.

Third, the contagion effects alluded to in the essay appear now to be more powerful than had been assessed, making the image of the rotting empire, discredited in this essay, seem intuitively correct. The independence of the Baltics is now a riveting model for all republican leaders, even those who would pay dearly for following a similar course. In the wake of the failed coup, it will be very difficult for the leaders in the Central Asian republics to bargain for greater economic transfers from Moscow as the price for their acceptance of a centralized Union. The immediate effect of the political earthquake was to give all republican forces the feeling that they would be buried in the debris if they held back from demanding full republican sovereignty.

Longer-term trends, however, may well reemerge once the initial shocks of the political events begin to dissipate and the dust settles. Policies and positions have been toppled, but many underlying structures have been preserved. And we may yet again observe the guiding principles of those structures. For example, already in the early days of September interests in preserving the Union have begun to surface. Presidents Yeltsin and Gorbachev, with the complicity of Nursultan Nazarbaev, mooted the idea of a loose confederation. If Nazarbaev can withstand the pressures for sovereignty within Kazakhstan, other republican leaders may see that symbolic independence within a decentralized union is a viable option. With the Baltics out of the Union and with

Moldavia and Georgia in limbo, ten union-republics supported the idea, and a two-thirds majority of voting delegates of the Congress of People's Deputies approved the idea in principle on September 4, with details still to be debated. The former Union may be changing radically, but social forces interested in maintaining some common structures have withstood the initial deluge that was overwhelming the center.

In regard to the republics, independent or not, the underlying trends identified in this essay remain discernible, and the predictions should be put to test. Stated baldly, the predicted trends are as follws: (1) There will be pressures for continued ties with Russia from the republics that enjoyed most-favored-lord status. Within those republics, the tensions between those who are oriented toward Russia and those who are oriented toward national autonomy will reflect a major line of cleavage. (2) In the republics that did not enjoy most-favored-lord status, the principal tensions will be between the titulars and the national minorities. These tensions will be exacerbated to the extent that republican sovereignty is achieved. Violence between minorities and titulars, with the minorities demanding sovereignty, will mark political life in these republics. (3) Russian minorities in the most-favored-lord republics will begin to assimilate into the new national cultures, although the process will generate social tensions and will take generations. (4) Russian minorities in the non-most-favored-lord republics will not assimilate into the new republican cultures, and their leaders will seek alliances of protection from the leadership of Russia. (5) The less populous minorities in the Russian Republic will not take advantage of the instability of the state to press for independence; the assimilationist logic will draw many of their most talented young people into Russian society.

The establishment of greater republican sovereignty, and perhaps independence for some republics beyond the Baltics, will not eliminate the national cleavages that have become institutionalized within the republics—and to identify those cleavages was the principal goal of this essay. Despite the colossal changes engendered by the failed coup, the books under review remain a useful background for scholars seeking to ascertain the dynamics of nationality politics in the republics of the now defunct Union of Soviet Socialist Republics.

SURPRISE, SURPRISE
Lessons from 1989 and 1991

By NANCY BERMEO*

O N August 18, 1991, just as the social science community was beginning to recover from the shock of communist disintegration in Eastern Europe, the world was shaken by the news of an attempted coup in Moscow. The August coup was, in many ways, a unique event. To begin with, the perpetrators called themselves an "Emergency Committee" rather than a junta or an interim government, and they denied that their seizure of power constituted a coup at all.[1] They inititially sought Gorbachev's support for their declaration of a state of emergency (and presumably for their assumption of power) and when Gorbachev refused, they stopped short of doing what so many coup-makers do elsewhere; they never killed their adversary. In fact, only three people were killed during the heady days before August 22, when the coup was finally scotched, and these were ordinary citizens who were crushed by a tank as they tried to defend democratic forces in Moscow.

If the attempted coup was unique in seeming comparatively reluctant and relatively bloodless, it was also unique in its composition. The intervention was less a military coup than a coup by remnants of the "military society" described so eloquently by Andrew Janos. Each of the most important members of the Emergency Committee was directly linked to the threatened military society. Yazov, of the Defense Ministry, Pugo, of the Interior Ministry, and Kriuchkov, of the Security Police, were all part of the forces of coercion that sustained this society, and Pavlov, Baklanov, and Tiyakov were linked to the military-industrial complex that formed its essence. Yanayev represented those elements of the Communist party who most feared the dismantling of the military society that perestroika entailed.

The efforts of these conspirators failed, of course, but their actions were momentous, nevertheless, because they led to the further empowerment of Boris Yeltsin, the breakup of the Soviet Union, and the resignation of Gorbachev himself. With the August coup attempt, Moscow became the

* The author thanks Henry Bienen, Richard Thypin, and especially Robert C. Tucker for help with an earlier version of this manuscript. Lori McGill and Ilene Cohen also deserve thanks.

[1] I owe this insight on the reluctant nature of the Soviet coup to Professor Robert C. Tucker. For further substantiation of this point, see Foreign Broadcast and Information Service [FBIS] Daily Report-Soviet Union, August 20, 1991 p. 9.

"city of surprises," upstaging Berlin, Warsaw, and even Washington, D.C.[2]

Having introduced this volume of essays with a discussion of political surprise, I find it fitting that such a coup would occur between the editing of the articles and their initial publication as a special issue of *World Politics*. This postscript analyzes the surprises of 1989 and 1991 in light of some of the themes raised in the preceding chapters and discusses how these events might be integrated into debates within comparative politics in general.

The collapse of communism in Eastern Europe involved not one surprise but many. First, scholars and policymakers were shocked by the fact that the old orders in the Central European states had so few domestic defenders. Then, they were shocked by the passivity of the Soviet Union. Throughout the drama, many were surprised at the speed and size of popular mobilization. At borders, in city squares, in factories and shipyards, wherever the curtain of oppression showed signs of wear, throngs of people jammed through the opening—tearing the old fabric of the state beyond repair.

The Soviet coup of August 1991 also involved several surprises, though these varied from one set of observers to another. Some observers, notably Gorbachev and Bush, were surprised by the coup itself.[3] Most were surprised, as in the East European case, by the speed of popular mobilization. Many were surprised by the success of popular resistance. The initiating actions of elites, the speed of the mobilization against anti-democratic forces and the success of popular resistance each provide bases for comparing the surprises of 1989 and 1991. They also provide the bases of important lessons for future research.

The Initiating Actions of Elites

At a very general level, our surprise at the initiating events in Eastern Europe was understandable. No communist system of rule had ever collapsed, and, since forecasts are built on precedents, we seemed to lack the basic building materials for theories of regime change in the communist world. The cases that provided the basis for the speculations that Juan Linz and Alfred Stepan offered us in *The Breakdown of Democratic Regimes* in 1978 had no counterpart in the literature on the communist bloc. Indeed, Linz introduced his discussion of democratic breakdown with the reminder that no communist, Nazi, or fascist system had ever "broken down through internal causes."[4]

---

[2] The phrase is from Zbigniew Brzezinski, "Toward a Common European Home," *Problems of Communism* 38 (November–December 1989), 1.

[3] See *New York Times*, August 19, 1991, A 1:4.

[4] Juan Linz, *Crisis, Breakdown and Reequilibration: The Breakdown of Democratic Regimes* (Baltimore: Johns Hopkins University Press, 1978), 7.

As Linz's statement implies, nondemocratic regimes *had* been transformed through "external" causes (namely, wartime defeat by the democratic allies), but few could have anticipated that the Soviets would be a force for democratization in the 1980s. For this type of forecast, there were precedents, most of which led to the opposite conclusion. From East Germany in 1953, from Hungary in 1956, from Czechoslovakia in 1968 and from Poland in 1956, 1970, 1976, and 1981, we inferred that the Soviet Union would always defend its hegemony in its European satellites. We forgot about the ambiguous cases of Romania and Yugoslavia. We did not reckon with the appearance of a Gorbachev, and many refused to believe it when he did appear. As late as November 1989, Jeane Kirkpatrick was stating categorically, "the Soviet Union is not going to withdraw from Europe."[5]

Social scientists tend to confuse the probable with the historical. We speculate about what will happen on the basis of what has happened. For Eastern Europe in 1989, "the predictive power of political science" was indeed "a dismal failure,"[6] but it was also a predictable failure. It was predictable because there were no clear precedents for either the actions of the Soviets or the actions of domestic elites. But it was also predictable because we are very poor at anticipating regime change anywhere. Russell Bova is correct in asserting that we have much to gain from comparing transitions in postauthoritarian and postcommunist regimes, but we must remember that scholars of authoritarianism proved no more prescient than scholars of communism when the first authoritarian regimes collapsed.[7] No one predicted the Portuguese revolution in 1974, or the collapse of the colonels' regime in Greece in the same year, or the nature of democratization in Spain in 1976. Instead, scholars who studied authoritarian regimes wrote of "their impressive policy flexibility," "their extraordinary persistence," and their capacity not only to "adapt to" but to "determine the course of" social change.[8] Southern Europe provided the same surprises in the mid-1970s as Eastern Europe did in 1989.

The Soviet coup of August 1991 was, in certain respects, much less

---

[5] Jeane Kirkpatrick interview, quoted in Alan F. Pater and Jason R. Pater, eds., *What They Said* (Palm Springs, Calif.: Monitor Books, 1990), 284.

[6] Adam Przeworski, "The 'East' Becomes the 'South'? The 'Autumn of the People' and the Future of Eastern Europe," *PS XXIV* (March 1991), 20.

[7] I am distinguishing authoritarian regimes from communist regimes throughout this essay. The former are typically demobilizing and not guided by an explicit and codified ideology. The overwhelming majority of these regimes are right wing.

[8] See Philippe Schmitter, "Liberation by Golpe: Retrospective Thoughts on the Demise of Authoritarian Rule in Portugal," *Armed Forces and Society* 5 (November 1975), 7; and Susan Kaufman Purcell, "Authoritarianism," *Comparative Politics* 5 (January 1973), 4. I first discussed our early inattention to authoritarian regime breakdown in Bermeo, "Redemocratization and Transition Elections: A Comparison of Spain and Portugal," in *Comparative Politics* 19 (January 1987).

surprising than the Eastern European revolutions. A reactionary seizure of power had already been forecast by several Soviet political leaders; Eduard Shevardnadze's address to the Congress of People's Deputies warned of an impending intervention as early as December 20, 1990. Party organs had publicly investigated one coup attempt already, and on July 23, 1991, twelve Communist Party hard-liners appealed to the military to rescue the nation from "humiliation" and those "who enslave themselves to foreign patrons." Finally, on August 16, 1991, Alexsandr Yakovlev warned that hard-liners were preparing a coup when he resigned from the Communist party.[9]

Scholars who chose to ignore these and other warnings might still have gleaned the same message from two related literatures in comparative politics. The literature on regime change addressed by Bova warns that liberalization is very likely to be reversed if national integrity is challenged, if the military as an institution is threatened, or if widespread violence occurs.[10] All three of these conditions obtained in the Soviet Union on the eve of the coup. In this sense, then, the coup attempt was quite predictable.

The literature on military interventions would have led analysts to predict a coup as well. As I have already stated, the failed coup of August 18 was not an exclusively military intervention. It was a reactionary intervention with a large military component. Yet, if we combine our knowledge of what had happened to the Soviet military since Gorbachev had come to power with what comparativists have written on the causes of military coups more generally, some sort of offensive from some elements within the Soviet military seemed very likely indeed.

Though explanations vary, most analysts who offer predictions of coups d'état agree that "when there is both the *disposition* and the *opportunity* to intervene, intervention will occur."[11] The *disposition* to intervene derives, we are told, from challenges to the "military's corporate interests,"[12] namely, budget cuts, threats to military autonomy, or any developments that create an "acute feeling of injured self-respect" among military officials.[13] Extensive

[9] The Soviet press itself was full of warnings. See, e.g., the interview with the right wing Russian nationalist Vladimir Zhirinovsky in FBIS Daily Report-Soviet Union, July 30, 1991, 54.

[10] Guillermo O'Donnell and Phillipe Schmitter, *Tentative Conclusions about Uncertain Democracies* (Baltimore: Johns Hopkins University Press, 1986).

[11] Samuel Finer, *The Man on Horseback: The Role of the Military in Politics* (Boulder, Colo.: Westview Press, 1988), 74. Emphasis mine.

[12] Eric Nordlinger, *Soldiers in Politics, Military Coups and Governments* (Englewood Cliffs, N.J.: Prentice-Hall, 1977), 78. See also William R. Thompson, "Regime Vulnerability and the Military Coup," *Comparative Politics* 7, (July 1975).

[13] The quotation is from Finer (fn. 11), 55. The general argument about the military's corporate interests is presented in Nordlinger (fn. 12), 78; Samuel DeCalo, *Coups and Army Rule in Africa: Motivations and Constraints* (New Haven: Yale University Press, 1990), 4.

social turbulence and violence[14] and the emergence of violent "rival political forces" provide especially potent stimuli for action.[15]

The Soviet military had literally all these motives for intervention by August 18, 1991. The most reactionary elements of the old order shared these motives, for they recognized that their tenure in office required a strong coercive apparatus. Gorbachev was set to sign the new Union Treaty on August 20. This would have given the various republics substantial independent power, not simply over natural resources but also over taxes and state security. These latter two provisions were a clear and severe threat both to the military budget and to the autonomy of the military as an institution.

Threats of a similar nature had already materialized. The military budget had already declined, and Soviet officials were openly discussing further cuts of 16 to 30 percent. Gorbachev's foreign policy initiatives meant that "millions of men and tens of thousands of tanks, armored vehicles and aircraft would be removed from the Soviet inventory."[16] Perestroika meant that the vast military-industrial complex that lay at the foundation of what Janos called the military society would be dismantled and restructured for civilian needs.[17] Institutional autonomy was threatened by the official prediction of an 83,000-person cut in the officer corps and by the fact that Gorbachev had already replaced 50 percent of all military district commanders, "three out of five commanders of military services and eleven out of sixteen deputy ministers of defense."[18] There was much evidence of wounded institutional pride. Rampant draft evasion and increasing incidents of desertion were a source of great embarrassment.[19]

If it is true that "social mobilization favors coup decisions," there were many reasons to expect a coup in August of 1991. There were reportedly seventeen thousand men in a paramilitary organization in Georgia; Azerbaijan and Armenia were on the verge of civil war; and the crackdown in the Baltic republics had brought the death toll from ethnic violence to over one thousand. The military's actions in Tbilisi and Baku had done great damage to the public image of the armed forces.[20]

The *opportunities* for intervention described in the literature were present

[14] Nordlinger, (fn. 12), 92.

[15] Finer, 66. See also DeCalo, (fn. 13), 4.

[16] Paula Dobriansky and David Rivkin, Jr., "Does the Soviet Military Oppose Perestroika?" *Orbis* 35 (Spring 1991), 169.

[17] It was Oleg Baklanov, the head of this complex, who helped launch the coup—precisely as Janos's argument would have led us to expect.

[18] *New York Times*, December 23, 1988, from Dobriansky and Rivkin (fn. 16), 175, 173.

[19] See, e.g., Yazov's discussion of military issues in FBIS Daily Report-Soviet Union, February 7, 1990.

[20] The first quotation is from Thomas Johnson, Robert Slater, and Pat McGowan, "Explaining African Military Coups d'Etat, 1960–1982," *American Political Science Review* 78 (September 1984), 636.

as well. Dramatic performance failures (usually of an economic nature) are thought to provide the essential opportunity for intervention because they are associated with a deflation of the regime's legitimacy and a related decrease in the costs of a coup.[21] There was little doubt that the Gorbachev regime was in fact performing very badly on the eve of the intervention. Industrial output had actually dropped since the previous year, as had labor productivity and national income. Production of a variety of food products (including meat, fish, cheeses, and sugar) had also dropped. Prices rose 48 percent in the six months preceding the coup, while the Soviet Academy of Sciences was forecasting an annual drop of 10 percent in GNP. The state's own report on the economy concluded: "The socioeconomic situation in the country deteriorated significantly in 1990. . . . Crises continued to grow, encompassing all spheres of the economy."[22]

In the general literature on military interventions, performance failures are thought to provide coup makers with an opportunity to rationalize their actions in positive terms. Predictably, the official rationalization of the coup was a textbook amalgamation of the themes summarized above: The Emergency Committee announced that it was "forced" to take power "by the vital need to save the economy from ruin" and by the fact that "authority at all levels has lost the confidence of the population." "The country," they asserted, "is sinking into an abyss of violence and lawlessness," and the various crises were "undermining the position of the Soviet Union in the world."[23] Put in the context of the literature on military intervention, what was surprising about the Soviet coup attempt was not that it occurred but that it took so long in coming.

Thus, from at least one perspective, the initiating phases of the 1989 and 1991 events were markedly different: in Eastern Europe, Soviet and domestic elites took actions that were largely unprecedented and probably unpredictable. In the Soviet Union, the coup makers acted much as our literature predicted they would. What makes the events similar is the role played by popular forces in the defense of democracy and our surprise at both the nature and the success of popular mobilization. Let us consider each of these features in turn and try to derive some lessons for comparativists in general.

The other material is from Martha Brill Olcott, "The Soviet Disunion" *Foreign Policy* (Spring 1991), 134; and from Dale Herspring, "The Soviet Military Reshapes in Response to Malaise," *Orbis* (Spring 1991), 180.

[21] Rosemary O'Kane. "A Probabilistic Approach to the Causes of Coup d'Etat," *British Journal of Political Science* 2, pt. 3 (July 1981), 289; and DeCalo (fn. 13), 14.

[22] The figure from the Academy of Sciences appears in FBIS Daily Report-Soviet Union, July 30, 1991, p. 58. The other materials are from FBIS Daily Report-Soviet Union, February 4, 1991, pp. 39–40, 44.

[23] See Yanayev's message to the United Nations and heads of state and the official "Emergency Committee Message of August 19," FBIS Daily Report-Soviet Union, August 19, 1991.

The Actions of Popular Forces

Coping with Hidden Preferences

Why are we caught off guard when people take to the streets? Kuran's discussion of hidden preferences provides a compelling answer and a consoling excuse. If citizens in highly coercive societies always hide their true preferences, how can we possibly anticipate their actions when the balance of coercion changes?

Rather than end with a rhetorical question, we might ask how we can cope with the implications of Kuran's argument. There are at least three possible reactions. One would be simply to direct our attention to other, more easily researchable issues. We might ignore popular preferences in highly coercive regimes and focus on studies of elites and policy-making instead. This was in fact the option most frequently chosen by students of dictatorship in Latin America before the liberalization of these regimes. The selection of this particular option derives in part from a notion similar to Kuran's. Where Kuran wrote of citizens hiding their preferences, the Latin Americanist Guillermo O'Donnell wrote of citizens being deprived of "voice"—vertical voice, which allowed them to express their will to political superiors, and horizontal voice, which allowed them to express themselves to those with whom they shared some potential "collective identity."[24]

If the people are truly silenced by dictatorship, how can we possibly assess the popular will? What becomes of civil society? Much of the literature written during the dictatorial period in Latin America assumed that it lay dead or dormant. This is why we read so much of the "rebirth" and "resurrection" of civil society when Latin dictatorships finally started to collapse.

But is civil society ever obliterated by coercion? The vast literature on dissent in Eastern Europe and the Soviet Union illustrates that civil society survives, even in highly coercive settings. The problem is how to go about assessing the preferences of people who have been deprived of public voice.

James Scott's recent work provides a solution to the problem posed above, and a second option for those who recognize the problem of falsified preferences. Rather than neglecting or misreading the consciousness of the common citizenry, Scott urges us to look behind the public stage (on which the weak will inevitably dissimulate) and look instead to "off-stage" forms

---

[24] Guillermo O'Donnell, "On the Fruitful Convergences of Hirschman's Exit, Voice and Loyalty: Reflections from the Recent Argentine Experience" in Alejandro Foxley, Michael S. McPherson, and Guillermo O'Donnell, eds., *Development, Democracy and the Art of Trespassing* (Notre Dame, Ind.: University of Notre Dame Press, 1986), 251, 256.

of struggle. His emphasis on "everyday forms of resistance" offers us a useful alternative perspective on how the preferences of oppressed peoples can be understood.[25] These forms of struggle "stop well short of outright collective defiance" (precisely because of the costs that Kuran details), but they are eloquent nonetheless. Comprised of "foot-dragging, dissimulation, desertion, false compliance, pilfering . . . sabotage and so on,"[26] these mundane and relatively safe forms of resistance send out clear signals about the illegitimate nature of existing authority. The signaling is done *within* the communities of the oppressed, but the messages can be read by outsiders.

Readers with even a remote familiarity with Eastern Europe and the Soviet Union know that the use of everyday forms of resistance was widespread. The literature on East Europeans and Soviets in the workplace paints a vivid picture of a resisting population. Even in Hungary, where labor-state relations were thought to be relatively good, scholars wrote that the predemocracy workforce "wanted to get by with as little work as possible, steal as much as they could, drink as much as allowed and rip-off . . . the workers' state, their own state, whenever possible."[27] Another author concluded that "the essence" of the working class in Hungary, Czechoslovakia, and Poland was "a strategy of maximizing benefits while circumventing regulations without openly challenging state power."[28].

In the Soviet Union the situation was similar. There, too, we read that worker "dissatisfaction . . . takes the form of spontaneous and individualized actions which result in a significant negative control of the labour process," that "drunkeness, loafing and other violations of labor discipline are impressive [for] their ubiquity and persistence," and that "everything is permitted as an excuse for not working."[29] The saying, "They pretend to pay us and we pretend to work" was common throughout these regimes and

---

[25] James C. Scott, *Weapons of the Weak: Everyday Forms of Peasant Resistance* (New Haven: Yale University Press, 1985).

[26] Ibid., xvii. Scott's insights have not been integrated into our thinking about the experiences of workers in communist regimes. Roman Laba's superb study is the only example I have found, and even he mentions the work only briefly. See Laba, *The Roots of Solidarity: A Political Sociology of Poland's Working Class Democratization* (Princeton: Princeton University Press, 1991). Scott himself uses examples from the East European and Soviet experiences to legitimate related theoretical points in his most recent book. I discovered this after the present essay was completed. See Scott, *Domination and the Arts of Resistance Hidden Transcripts* (New Haven: Yale University Press, 1990).

[27] Ivan Volgyes, "Hungary: The Lumpenproletarianization of the Working Class," in Jan Triska and Charles Gati, eds., *Blue Collar Workers in Eastern Europe* (London: Allen and Unwin, 1981), 228–29.

[28] Alex Pravda, "Political Attitudes and Activity," in *Blue Collar Workers in Eastern Europe*, 48.

[29] A 1983 survey of 800 Moscow factories found that in several firms, less than 10% of the labor force was present during the hour before the official end of the workday. The evidence for the more general argument is from Bob Arnot, *Controlling Soviet Labour* (Armonk, N.Y.: M. E. Sharpe, 1988), 79; Walter D. Connor, *The Accidental Proletariat* (Princeton: Princeton University Press, 1991), 174; and Mark Harrison, "Lessons of Soviet Planning for Full Employment," in David Lane, ed., *Labour and Employment in the USSR* (Brighton, England: Wheatsheaf Books, 1986), 77. See also Murray

captures one of the principal means of citizen resistance. "Pretending to work" has especially weighty political implications in a command economy. First, it sends a clear signal that the commanders are somehow illegitimate. Second, it undercuts the whole idea of legitimation through economic growth: when people are only pretending to work, productivity and quality suffer greatly. Thus, the legitimating myths that Di Palma and Janos wrote about became openly mythical because a satisfactory level of growth became unattainable. Worker productivity in Eastern Europe and the Soviet Union was in fact notoriously low—approximately 25 to 34 percent below levels in the West (even after allowing for differences in capital investment).[30] A vast amount of literature suggests that low productivity was due in part to the deliberate action and inaction of the common citizenry.

What is the connection between the everyday forms of struggle sketched above and the extraordinary struggles we saw in 1989 and 1991? Both are eloquent manifestations of hostility to the existing order. Silence should never be mistaken for willing submission. For the weak, silence is merely a means of surviving on one front while battles are waged on others. We shall never understand those relatively rare moments when the people confront the powerful in the streets unless we understand the mundane battles waged elsewhere. Perhaps we are taken aback by regime change not because oppressed people always hide their preferences but because we look for the expression of preferences in too narrow a political space. Whether we speak of "preferences" as Kuran does or of the "popular will" as Scott does, we will benefit from listening for the voice of the people in new settings and in new ways.

We will also benefit from listening more carefully on those occasions when a dictatorship allows an imposed public silence to be broken. The study of dictatorially sponsored elections and referenda offers a third option for coping with the problem of hidden preferences. Elections that involve choice (and I am deliberately dismissing those that do not) provide a fertile arena for discovering the sorts of leaders that the citizenry prefers. Elections are not perfect indicators of preferences, because options are always limited, but scholars of regime change can learn a great deal from analyzing the

---

Yanovitch, *Work in the Soviet Union* (Armonk, N.Y.: M. E. Sharpe, 1985), 7; and David Lane, *Soviet Labour and the Ethic of Communism* (Brighton, England: Wheatsheaf Books, 1987), 111. Lane points out that indiscipline was not the only factor hampering Soviet productivity. This is undoubtedly true though the fact that Andropov and Gorbachev put a great verbal if not policy emphasis on these issues indicates that in one respect at least, the "preferences" of the Soviet working class were not "hidden" from the leadership at all.

[30] Abram Bergson, "Comparative Productivity: The USSR, Eastern Europe and the West," *American Economic Review* 77 (June 1987), 342–57. The author compared output per worker in four socialist economies and seven Western economies and obtained this figure after controlling for differences in capital per worker and land per worker.

elections that precede the actual collapse of dictatorship. With the possible exception of Poland, the type of election I am discussing never occurred in Eastern Europe, but the East European chronology of regime change is relatively rare. Many dictatorships allow some sort of competitive electoral contestation before they collapse, and these contests can be important in-dicators of future shifts in power. Brazil, Chile, South Korea, the Philip-pines, and Nigeria offer just a sample of the types of dictatorial regime that have sponsored competitive (usually regional) elections while nondemocratic forces still maintained control of the central government.

The Soviet Union—prior to the August coup attempt—fitted squarely into this latter category of state, and the popular mobilization against the coup was not at all surprising if the implications of the various Soviet elections are taken into account.

It is fruitful to inquire about the sorts of leaders the various peoples of the Soviet Union were supporting on the eve of August 18. There was little doubt that Gorbachev himself had lost credibility, but the political reforms he had initiated had produced an array of new leaders who had all the legitimacy that competitive elections confer. Many of these leaders were openly anticommunist. The Soviet citizenry had been given the opportunity to voice its preferences in a wide variety of elections, and it used that opportunity to send a seemingly unambiguous message about their dissat-isfaction with communist rule.[31]

The signals sent in the Russian Republic itself were clearly the most important. There, where the coup was centered, the people had gone to the polls less than nine weeks before, in presidential elections, and had given the hard-line communist candidate a mere 3.74 percent of the vote. As Table 1 indicates, over seventy-nine million citizens participated in the elections and over 57 percent of them voted for Boris Yeltsin—despite the fact that there were five other candidates from which to chose. Yeltsin won clear majorities in eighty of the republic's eighty-eight electoral districts, and, although his majority was narrower in rural areas than in urban ones, he won sweeping victories in Moscow, Leningrad, and all other cities. Is it really so surprising that the man who had won the endorsement of over forty-five million people in June would be able to rally the open support of several thousand in August? The coup makers seemed to have ignored the implications of the Soviet elections, but social scientists should not make the same mistake. Where preferences were hidden at all, they were not well hidden. They were simply ignored, misread, or overlooked.

[31] Many elected rulers were outspoken if newly transformed anti-communists. Some were even former political prisoners. The mayors of Moscow and Leningrad and the elected heads of Russia, Armenia, Georgia, Moldavia, and the Baltic republics are examples. Dimitri Simes, "Gorbachev's Time of Troubles," *Foreign Policy*, Spring 1991.

TABLE 1
RUSSIAN PRESIDENTIAL ELECTION CANDIDATES AND RESULTS (1991)

Candidates	Political Leaning	Votes	%
Boris Yeltsin	Liberal-Radical	45,552,041	57.30
Nikolai Ryzhkov	Center-Conservative Communist	18,395,335	16.85
Vadim Bakatin	Center-Liberal	2,719,757	3.42
Albert Makashov	Hard-line communist	2,969,511	3.74
Vladimir Zhirinovsky	Russian nationalist	6,211,007	7.81
Aman-Sledy Tuleyey	unclear	5,417,464	6.81

SOURCE: *Kessing's Record of World Events*, (June 1991), 38273.

THE SUCCESS OF POPULAR RESISTANCE

Our mention of the popular support for Yeltsin brings us to the intriguing issue of why the resistance to the August coup proved triumphant. The triumph of antidictatorial forces in Eastern Europe is less difficult to explain; outside of Romania, they faced almost no resistance. Most of the East European communist regimes simply had no defenders, but the old order in the Soviet Union clearly did. These defenders represented powerful organizations within the Soviet state. The Ministry of the Interior, the Ministry of Defense, and the KGB certainly seemed to be formidable foes for the democratic opposition on August 19, 1991. This is probably why many outside observers (including Helmut Kohl of Germany and François Mitterrand of France) came to the premature conclusion that the coup attempt would succeed.[32] Yet there were two sets of reasons to argue otherwise, and both emerge if we put the Soviet coup in comparative perspective.

The first set of reasons for expecting the coup attempt to fail emerges from the literature on military intervention cited earlier. Just as the literature on military intervention would have led us to expect a coup, so it would have led us to predict that this particular attempt would fail. The coup makers violated all the major guidelines for successful assaults. To begin with, they failed to marshal the support of strategically situated, middle level troop commanders. Several troop commanders defected to Yeltsin immediately, and the air force as a whole refused to participate in the coup at all.

The coup makers also failed to arrest all the powerful opponents of the coup. Putting Gorbachev under house arrest in the Crimea was a reasonable

[32] *Le Monde*, August 20, 1991, p. 5, August 21, 1991, pp. 8a and 9a, and August 23, 1991, p. 1d.

start, but leaving Boris Yeltsin and all the other major elected officials of the new order free to galvanize opposition was a fatal error. The coup makers' attempts to correct their mistake and seize Yeltsin came too late. The literature tells us that communications, strategic positions, and incumbent leaders must be seized "in a single well-coordinated stroke.[33] The reactionary forces in the Soviet Union did too little too late.

The coup makers also failed to understand just whose legitimacy had been undermined by the policy failures they used to rationalize their actions. There was little doubt that the Soviet state had failed to solve an ever-increasing range of problems, but the people seemed to attribute this failure to Gorbachev rather than to officials such as Yeltsin who had just won popular endorsement. These freely elected officials were thought to be part of the *solution* to the problems that Gorbachev had proved incapable of solving. Yet the coup was made against both sets of leaders—one, embodied by Gorbachev, who had never been subject to popular elections and had held power long enough to be deemed responsible for a whole range of maladies, and another, embodied by Yeltsin, who had just assumed office and who had recently gained the unambiguous endorsement of popular majorities. In moving against the latter, the coup makers moved against truly popular representatives and thus against the Soviet people themselves. It is possible that a coup against Gorbachev alone might have succeeded, but a televised assault on elected officials in parliamentary institutions had much higher costs.

This brings us to the second reason to believe that a comparative perspective would have led us to predict the success of popular mobilization in the Soviet case. It is increasingly rare for freely elected officials to be ousted by reactionary coups. Based on data from Southern Europe, Latin America, the Caribbean, and Asia, Table 2 lists the very wide range of states that have instituted electoral democracy since 1974. Remarkably, only three out of a possible eighteen transitions have been reversed, and one of these three (Bolivia) has already reinstituted democratic elections. The democracies created since 1974 have shown a greater longevity than any of their predecessors. The odds for successful coups seem especially poor these days.

The Soviet coup makers might have succeeded against the odds, but there are major differences between the two "successful" coups and the August attempt in Moscow. In Thailand, the military acted with the endorsement of the most popular figure in Thai politics—the monarch—and the ousted government was so riddled with military officials that many

---

[33] This phrase and the "guidelines" referred to in the two previous paragraphs are from Nordlinger, 102–5.

TABLE 2

ELECTORAL DEMOCRACIES ESTABLISHED SINCE 1974: ASIA, THE CARIBBEAN,
SOUTHERN EUROPE, SOUTH AMERICA

Nation	Year of Transition[a]	Successful Coup Attempts
Argentina	Oct. 30, 1983	none[b]
Bolivia	Aug. 6, 1979	November 1, 1979[c]
	Oct. 5, 1982	none
Brazil	Dec. 12, 1982	none
	Jan. 15, 1985[d]	
Chile	Dec. 14, 1989	none
Dominican Republic	Apr. 16, 1978	none
Ecuador	July 16, 1978	none[e]
Greece	Nov. 17, 1974	none[f]
Haiti	Dec. 16, 1990	September 30, 1991
Pakistan	Nov. 16, 1988	none[g]
Paraguay	May 1, 1989	none
Peru	June 22, 1978	none
	May 18, 1980[h]	
Philippines	Feb. 7, 1986	none[i]
Portugal	Apr. 25, 1975	none
South Korea	Dec. 16, 1987	none
Spain	June 15, 1977	none[j]
Taiwan	*Apr. 22, 1991[k]	none
Thailand	July 24, 1988	Feb. 23, 1991
Uruguay	Nov. 25, 1984	none

SOURCE: Dorothy Kattleman, ed., *Facts on File* (New York: Facts on File), 1974–1991.
[a] The year of transition is defined conservatively here. The dates cited are the dates on which the first competitive national elections were held. Thus, the longevity of these systems is in many cases more impressive than these dates indicate. In many cases, the actual transition to democracy began before elections were held.
[b] Several barracks revolts have taken place but all have been controlled.
[c] The military government restored democracy in October 1982.
[d] These figures are for state and presidential elections, respectively.
[e] A military coup was attempted in March 1986 but was scotched by the military itself.
[f] A coup was attempted on February 24, 1975, but was foiled immediately.
[g] The military has increased its power in Pakistan but stopped short of an outright coup. Prime Minister Bhutto was dismissed by President Ghulam Ishaq Khan on August 6, 1990, on charges of corruption. The dismissal was upheld in court twice, and elections were held on October 24, 1990. Bhutto's party was roundly defeated by the Islamic Democratic Alliance, a party with close ties to the military.
[h] These dates are for the constitutional assembly and presidential elections, respectively.
[i] The government of Corazon Aquino has been the target of several coup attempts.
[j] There was a coup attempt in Spain on February 23–24, 1981. It was immediately foiled by the center-right civilian government and the king himself.
[k] As this chapter goes to press, Taiwan seems to be in a process of transition. The date cited is the date on which a forty-three-year period of emergency rule was lifted. Selection of candidates to the National Assembly is now more democratic. Martial law ended in 1987.

question whether it was a civilian democracy at all.[34] In Haiti, the military took on Aristide, a leader who clearly had widespread legitimacy, but there, the coup makers drew on a bizarre reserve of uniformed thugs who simply murdered anyone who took to the street in Aristide's defense. This reserve of killers never materialized in the Soviet case.

If we follow Bova's lead and look to the more developed Latin American and Southern European cases as our reference points, Table 2 yields two important facts. First, coups in these states are very rare. Most countries had none at all. Second, the coups that have taken place have at least until now, *all* been unmitigated failures. Spain's electoral democracy was the target of a reactionary coup in 1981, and Argentina was the scene of three barracks rebellions in 1987 and 1988. Despite dramatically different levels of governmental "efficacy," popularly elected officials survived each assault.

In each of these cases, the people filled the streets in massive demonstrations against the forces of reaction. The early coup attempts against the government of Corazon Aquino provoked the same response. In all of these cases, citizens who had recently been granted public voice showed no hesitation in using it against the forces of the old order. In all of these cases, the coup makers failed. What happened in the Soviet Union in August 1991 seems to be part of a more general pattern.

What sustains this pattern? What caused the reactionary forces in the Soviet Union to back down in 1991? We cannot conclude that reactionary forces are simply overpowered by the sheer number of people who are now willing to take to the streets in democracy's defense. As many commentators have already remarked, only a small percentage of the Soviet population actually participated in the protests when the coup was launched. We can guess (given recent electoral results and most eyewitness accounts) that millions of cautious citizens cheered the opposition from behind closed doors, and we know that thousands joined mobilizations in all the major political centers—but military forces might have gunned them down anyway. One need only recall the events in Tiananmen Square in 1989 to recognize this possibility. Events in the Baltic republics (just eight months before the coup attempt) illustrated that the possibilities of Soviet soldiers firing on unarmed civilians were very real indeed. So why did the Soviet coup makers (like their counterparts elsewhere) fail to make use of their full coercive potential?

Part of the answer is straightforward. The soldiers sent in to crush the opposition were simply not willing to shoot. (The unwillingness of the OMON special forces of the Interior Ministry was especially important.) Showing remarkable naïveté, the men who organized the coup relied on

---

[34] On the Thai case, see *Far East Economic Review*, March 7, 1991, and May 2, 1991.

192 LIBERALIZATION AND DEMOCRATIZATION

only locally garrisoned troops. These were mostly young ethnic Russians and mostly conscripts. Their association with what social scientists rather awkwardly refer to as "the coercive apparatus of the state" was neither voluntary nor long-standing. Ten tank units and five-hundred paratroopers joined Yeltsin's side immediately. Even the soldiers who did not risk mutiny eagerly displayed the fact that their weapons were unloaded. When the three civilian resistors were crushed to death in Moscow, soldiers emerged from nearby tanks with tear-stained faces. The problems of discipline did not end with the regular troops. The KGB's Alpha Group—an elite two-hundred-man commando unit—simply refused to obey the order to raid the Russian parliament.

The most significant domestic factor contributing to the failure of the coup was probably not the number of people who took to the streets but the number of soldiers who refused to shoot the people who did.[35] The coup makers might have marshaled other forces, but by the time they had recognized the need to do so, a different set of factors had altered the costs of continuing the struggle. These came from the international arena.

The international community made it very clear that insurgent forces would govern (if they won the struggle at all) without material assistance from the West. The European Community immediately froze over $1.1 billion of promised aid, including funds for much-needed foodstuffs. Great Britain froze $80 million in technical assistance, and Canada froze $131 million in food credits. The United States froze all its support—totaling some 900 million dollars in agricultural assistance alone.

The fact that the Soviet Union is (or at least aspires to be) a European state matters greatly. The essay by Andrew Janos in this volume makes the point that European aspirations were critical in distinguishing the Soviet liberalization from the Chinese. The Soviet coup attempt of 1991 bears this out. When the coup makers recognized that their actions would deprive them of the aid deemed essential for the restoration of the Soviet economy, the costs of continued belligerence soared.

It is important to remember that the coup makers acted principally against Gorbachev and not against Europe or the West in general. Western journalists and politicians were subject to very little coercion, and the public statements of the Emergency Committee emphasized legality and democracy; both curious facts suggest that this was not a wholly isolationist group. There were probably elements within the coup coalition who were willing

[35] Colonel-General Gennadiy Stefanovskiy, deputy commander of the Main-Military Political Administration of the USSR, had predicted this in an interview published on August 15, 1991, stating "only someone who knows absolutely nothing about the mentality of our soldiers and officers can expect their readiness to stage a coup and give themselves up to dictatorship." FBIS Daily Report-Soviet Union, August 19, 1991.

to go it alone and pay the costs of international censure, but as soon as the ambivalence of the armed forces became manifest that option appeared unrealistic. Who would control the inevitable rise in opposition as the economic crisis worsened? The civilians who were willing to side openly with Yeltsin were filling the streets and visible to the whole world. But where was the civilian support for the Emergency Committee?

Here, we come up against the problem of hidden preferences once again—and it is not just a problem for social scientists. Uncertain about how many citizens actually supported their cause, knowing that the armed forces were far from united behind them, and learning that they would be forced to proceed without desperately needed foreign aid, a civil war was the *best* the reactionary forces could hope for by August 20.

The contemporary international community seems to have developed a new way of reacting to assaults on democratizing and democratic states. One need only contrast the response to the Soviet coup with the response to the reactionary coups in Greece in 1967 or in Czechoslovakia in 1968 to see the point. In both of these historical cases, the reactionary forces were verbally condemned. (Greece was even expelled by the Council of Europe.) But in neither case were the coup makers deprived of significant material resources from the West. Today, in the United States, aid to any sort of government that replaces a democracy by force is legally forbidden. The European Community's de facto policy is the same.[36]

This does not mean that reactionaries will no longer be willing to pay the costs of a coup—the recent events in Haiti provide a case in point— but the fact that these costs are higher than ever before may act as a significant deterrent. Just as it is helpful to see the Soviet coup in comparative context, so it is helpful to see it in historical context.

Could the positive effects of a newly supportive international arena be outweighed by negative factors emanating from other sources? If we believe in a connection between regime performance and regime stability, the answer may be yes. No one knows how the breakup of what was once the Soviet Union will affect domestic economies in the long run. Indeed, no one even knows how the final borders of these economies will be defined. But there can be little doubt that there will be massive economic problems including food and fuel shortages in the short run. We can be certain that restructuring will create confusion and chaos for some time to come.

---

[36] A series of amendments to the U.S. Foreign Assistance Act makes overt aid illegal. The European Community has no precisely comparable legislation but executes a similar policy de facto. At present, for example, the EC's recognition of the breakaway republics of Yugoslavia depends on their commitment to human rights and democratic freedoms. If these republics are not officially recognized, they have no access to loans or most assistance.

Will the seemingly inevitable performance failures that accompany restructuring mean an end to democratic initiatives throughout the new
commonwealth? Given that the very identities of our subjects are shifting,
any prediction would be foolhardy at the present time, but if we analyze
how the connection between performance and stability has fared in general
lately, there are two reasons to be optimistic.

First, none of the successful challenges to democracy detailed in Table
2 was related to economic performance. Thailand's economy was doing
well when the military moved in, and the governments of Bolivia and Haiti
were doing no worse than usual when their democracies were challenged.
Second, the long list of electoral democracies that have managed to endure
since the "third wave" of democracy started includes several in which
economic performance has not been simply abysmal but in a state of seemingly permanent crisis. Peru has been struggling with a declining growth
rate and four-digit inflation for years.[37] Brazil is also battling four-digit
inflation, and what are often characterized as unresolvable economic dis-
tortions as well.[38] The Philippines are still struggling to resolve the grave
economic crisis that contributed to the Marcos ouster in 1986.[39] Even in a
case such as Argentina, where a long economic crisis seems to have at least
temporarily abated, electoral democracy endured dramatic economic strains
in the recent past. When Carlos Menem replaced Raul Alfonsín through
free elections in 1989, inflation stood at a full 12,000 percent, fifteen people
had been killed in food rioting, and the country's hard currency reserves
were sufficient to cover only two weeks of imports.[40]

What has enabled these democracies to endure despite desperate economic performance problems? The answer varies somewhat from case to
case, and the question deserves much more attention than I can give it
here. However, part of the answer is directly relevant to the emerging
democracies in formerly communist Europe. First, the figures indicate that
a regime's endurance is not based on economic performance alone. New
democracies can buy themselves time and maintain support through "performance" in other areas. The provision of basic human rights for the
politicized part of the population is an achievement in itself that should
not be discounted.[41] The provision of formal independence, that is, the
association with a historical moment in which a nation is liberated from
control by a foreign power, is also a great asset. The new democracies in

[37] Inflation in 1990 reached 8,292 percent, though it is now declining. Economist Intelligence Unit
(EIU) Country Report Peru and Bolivia no. 3 (1991), 7.
[38] EIU Country Report Brazil no. 3 (1991) reports 1990 inflation at 1,795 percent.
[39] EIU Country Report Philippines no. 4 (1990), 6.
[40] New York Times, May 31, 1989, p. A1, and June 12, 1989, p. D1.
[41] See O'Donnell (fn. 24) on the euphoria of regaining voice (p. 266).

Eastern Europe and the emerging regimes in what was once the Soviet Union both have these very substantial advantages.

They also have the advantage of coming into being at a time when the credibility of *non*democratic formulas for legitimation is at a new low. Legitimacy is always a relative term, in that a regime has legitimacy if it is thought to be the best of the alternatives available. Legitimacy, as Seymour Lipset reminded us long ago, derives from a state's capacity "to engender and maintain the belief that the existing political institutions are the most appropriate ones for the society.[42] Engendering and maintaining the belief that democratic institutions *are* the most appropriate (or "the least evil")[43] options available is easier now because there is so much negative evidence on the alternatives. The articles by Janos and Di Palma are part of a vast literature that focuses on the relatively poor performance of left-wing dictatorships.

The performance problems of *right*-wing dictatorships have also been amply documented. Although this latter category seems to be a mixture of failures and occasional successes, the consensus in the literature is that right-wing dictatorships have not been any better at promoting economic growth than their democratic counterparts.[44] The fact that even economically successful right-wing dictatorships (such as South Korea and Taiwan) have themselves turned in the direction of democratization illustrates that the argument for dictatorship is increasingly difficult to formulate. According to Lucian Pye, "the idea that centralized authority enhances the state's ability to shape society has been dealt a devastating blow" by the very performance of the dictatorships themselves.[45]

Many of the more urbane political elites in the new democracies are probably aware of these trends. For them, the appeal of nondemocratic formulas for legitimacy will therefore be limited. But we know little about whether this awareness has penetrated either the popular sectors of these societies or the remnants of what was once the Soviet military. Both these sets of actors, i.e. the people at the base of these societies and the people who will be part of their radically restructured armed forces, deserve our most careful attention.

Given recent electoral and mobilizational behavior, we can guess that the people at the base of these societies will not be easily seduced by a

[42] Seymour Lipset, *Political Man* (New York: Doubleday, 1963), 64.

[43] Linz (fn. 4), 18.

[44] See, e.g., Henry Bienen, "Armed Forces and National Modernization: Continuing the Debate," *Comparative Politics* (October 1983); Robert Kaufman's essay in *The New Authoritarianism in Latin America* (Princeton: Princeton University Press, 1979); and Karen Kemmer, "Democracy and Economic Crisis: The Latin American Experience," *World Politics* 42 (April 1990).

[45] Lucian Pye, "Political Science and the Crisis of Authoritariansim," *American Political Science Review* 84 (March 1990), 9.

dictatorial alternative that duplicates what they have experienced in the recent past. But we do not know if their rejection of *communist* dictatorship is a rejection of dictatorship in general. Nor do we know that the popular resistance to the August coup was based on a support for democracy per se. Perhaps it derived from a more personalized support for Yeltsin and his counterparts elsewhere—a very different and much more ominous phenomenon.

The popular defense of Gamsakhurdia in Georgia suggests that there is still broad support for ethnocentric tyranny and, more distressingly, that this tyranny can triumph, at least temporarily, *through* rather than *against* a competitive electoral process. Given the power of ethnicity as an identity in this part of the world (and the long history of scapegoating in times of scarcity that has accompanied it), it is likely that electoral democracy will, in some regions at least, legitimate other leaders like Gamsakhurdia and therefore be no democracy at all. The civil war in what was once Yugoslavia suggests that violence borne of ethnic hostility can preempt movements for democracy altogether.

The fact that the Soviet Union has now disintegrated into separate republics makes the likelihood of ethnically based tyrannies even greater, for there will be no third party to protect the interests of minorities. We do not know the extent to which ethnic rivalry will work against the process of democratization, although we can guess, given David Laitin's essay, that its salience will vary from region to region.

We also do not know how the people will rank the desire for order and predictability against the desire for civil liberties and economic modernization. For all their performance failures in the realm of individual rights and economic growth, dictatorships that have the backing of their armed forces are generally very good at providing order.[46] Will the people of these new states opt for order over other values? Will their soldiers opt to enforce a dictatorial order? The fact that so many rank and file soldiers and their officers chose to side with the forces of democracy during the August coup gives us reason for hope. The fact that this same military disintegrated in December 1991 gives us reason to be extremely wary.

The Future and the Lessons for Comparativists

How shall we, as social scientists, cope with all this uncertainty? Where shall we go for guidance in charting a sea change never seen before? Bova

---

[46] I use the term generally here because there are many examples of dictatorships that have failed to perform on this dimension as well. Marcos's inability to control the communist guerrilla army in the Philippines and Franco's failure to control ETA in Spain are cases in point.

is right to direct our attention to the merits of looking at the literature on earlier transitions from authoritarian rule. There is much we can learn from this literature, and it can itself be improved by the incorporation of the East European and Soviet cases. However, there are several reasons to avoid relying too heavily on this literature for guidance about the future of the formerly communist states.

To begin with, the literature that focuses on the last wave of authoritarian transitions says little indeed about the role of ethnicity or national identity as either a stimulus or a barrier to successful democratization. These issues are clearly very important in the post-communist regimes, but with few exceptions they are not addressed directly in the mainstream transitions literature.[47]

Secondly, most of the best-known literature on transitions from authoritarian rule focuses on the role of civilian political elites.[48] There are parallels to be drawn between civilian elites in transitions from noncommunist and communist regimes, but there are dramatic and possibly decisive differences as well. Civilian elites in most of the noncommunist transitions emerged from societies with some historical experience with electoral democracy. These elites led processes of redemocratization that were informed and assisted by political learning, that is, by the lesson learned when previous democracies collapsed.[49] With few exceptions, the elites who are struggling with transitions in Eastern Europe and the new commonwealth are emerging from situations in which neither they nor their followers can draw lessons from a democratic past. They have probably learned a great deal from their experience with communist dictatorship, but they have no direct experiences with either the failure of democracy or with the costs of right-wing dictatorship. Ironically, it is often this very experience that lays the foundation for the conciliatory behavior that consolidating a new and troubled democracy requires.

Whatever the similarities and differences between civilian elites in post-authoritarian and postcommunist regimes, these elites are only one of several

[47] In South America and Southern Europe, these questions of identity did not figure in the transition processes in a major way, so it is understandable that they attracted little discussion. The emerging literature on democratization in Africa provides a different and perhaps more comparable perspective. See Donald Horowitz, *A Democratic South Africa? Constitutional Engineering in a Divided Society* (Berkeley: University of California Press, 1991).

[48] The work of O'Donnell and Schmitter, as well as the emphasis given by Larry Diamond, Juan Linz, and Seymour Lipset in *Democracy in Developing Countries* (Boulder, Colo.: Lynne Reinner, 1989), provide the leading examples. Giuseppe Di Palma, *To Craft Democracy* (Berkeley: University of California Press, 1990) and John Higley and Richard Gunther, eds., *Elites and Democratic Consolidation in Latin America and Southern Europe* (New York: Cambridge University Press, 1991) provide further examples of the point.

[49] For a more detailed discussion of political learning, see Nancy Bermeo, "Democracy and the Lessons of Dictatorship," *Comparative Politics*, forthcoming in 1992.

sets of actors who affect the course of any transition. The August coup attempt in the Soviet Union is a vivid illustration of this fact, and it provides a clear incentive to look for guidance not only in the literature on regime transitions in general but also in the literature on specific political actors—most notably the military and the common citizenry.

We can debate about the future of formerly communist regimes with a variety of scenarios. Some scholars will insist that the transitions in Southern Europe provide the proper reference point. Others will argue that the closest parallel is with the revolutions that swept Europe in the mid-nineteenth century. Others will claim that the troubled democracies of Latin America in the 1960s are the proper reference points, while still others will argue that comparisons with ethnically divided and tragic cases such as Sri Lanka are the most appropriate.

It is likely that none of these historical parallels will be appropriate across this very heterogeneous region. It is also highly unlikely that all of the new regimes will make the transition to democracy on their first try.

Whatever the historical or regional cases we use to guide us, we must never lose sight of the fact that the future of formerly communist states depends largely upon what the people at their base will tolerate and defend. Common citizens in civilian clothes or in the rank and file of the armed forces have a great deal to do with political development in this region.

The Soviet coup attempt offers many reminders for scholars of comparative politics. One is that civilian elites can be challenged at a moment's notice by military elites, even if the latter represent only a faction within the military establishment. Gorbachev had gone very far to appease the old order and its military allies,[50] but his position was challenged anyway. Whatever their dedication to compromise, civilians rule only if armed men allow them to. Thus, the study of the military as an institution must be more carefully and deliberately integrated into our studies of postcommunist regimes and into our work on transitions to democracy in general.[51]

The second reminder provided by the August takeover attempt is that all elites—both civilian and military—are powerless without the ability to command *some* popular support. The coup makers were undone in part

---

[50] Gorbachev deliberately named some of the most conservative members of his opposition to pivotal positions in the state apparatus months before the coup attempt. Ironically, these were the men who moved against him on August 18th.

[51] The study of the military has received surprisingly little attention in the transitions literature thus far. The exceptions to this generalization seem to come most often from Africa and Africanists. See Claude Welch, *No Farewell to Arms?* (Boulder, Colo.: Westview, 1987); and Henry Bienen and Jeffrey Herbst, "Authoritarianism and Democracy in Africa" in Kenneth Erikson and Dankwart Rustow, *Comparative Political Dynamics* (New York: HarperCollins, 1991). For evidence see Alfred Stepan, *Rethinking Military Politics: Brazil and the Southern Cone* (Princeton: Princeton University Press, 1988), pp. 8–9, 129–30.

by Yeltsin and other reformist civilians. But who allowed these civilian elites to mobilize support? Ultimately, the coup makers were undone by the fact that key people in the massive coercive apparatus of the state were unwilling and unable to shoot (or even arrest) the pivotal civilian elites. Men at the very top of what seemed to be the most powerful (and ruthless) sectors of the Soviet state were defeated because many of their underlings simply refused to follow their lead.

The fact that Yeltsin mobilized resistance from atop a tank and not from a balcony was of great symbolic importance. It showed the Soviet people and the world that the Soviet military, the bastion of the old order, might defend a new order instead. At that moment, the "possible" was redefined. Sidney Tarrow has written that "states" define "the boundaries of the permissible."[52] There is much truth to this, but we must think harder about just how these boundaries are set. The August coup and its surprising aftermath illustrate that "states" define the boundaries only in the abstract. In the real world of politics, the boundaries of the permissible are defined by one set of human beings in uniform facing another set of human beings in civilian clothes. No states (and no reactionary movements) survive unless simple soldiers are willing to shoot and kill in their defense.

When we turn our attention to the military as an institution, we must remember that the people at the base of these institutions are as important as their officers, if not more. Adam Przeworski provides evidence for this assertion in his work on the revolutions in Eastern Europe in 1989. There, the old regimes fell, he writes, "because they did not have the guns. In no country did the army . . . come to the rescue. In Poland, the army led the reforms; in all other countries, including Romania, they refused to repress."[53] This is precisely what happened in the Soviet Union in August 1991.

We must never forget that the "forces of coercion" have human faces.[54] The abstractions that concern us as social scientists are experienced only through human interactions in the real world. We must also remember that the terms we use to describe the states and the societies we study sometimes set boundaries that are wholly artificial when seen in the light of daily life. During the August coup attempt, the "coercive apparatus" of the Soviet state was shown to be a set of individual officers who refused to side with their minister of defense and a set of enlisted men who refused to shoot or even harm unarmed civilians.

Our theoretical constructs view these soldiers as part of "the state ap-

[52] Sidney Tarrow, "Aiming at a Moving Target: Social Science and the Recent Rebellions in Eastern Europe," *PS* (March 1991) 17.
[53] Przeworksi (fn. 4), 22.
[54] Scott (fn. 23) makes a related point about the forces of exploitation in *Weapons of the Weak*.

paratus," but they clearly saw themselves as connected to "civil society" as well. This sort of ambiguity is often forgotten by social scientists, but it was foremost in the minds of the civilian elites who proved triumphant in August of 1991. Eyewitnesses report that the resistance leaders constantly urged the people to "talk to the soldiers"—to make the human connections that would highlight the soldiers' ambiguous identity.[55] When it was learned that troops from the Asian regions were approaching the White House area, the resistance leaders collected people who spoke Asian languages. The main goal, a participant recalled, "was to establish contact with the troops so that they knew that we were brothers."[56] The women who marched through Moscow streets with banners reading "Soldiers: Don't Shoot Mothers and Sisters" also recognized that it was the soldiers' identities as sons and brothers—that is, their very real connection with civil society— that could eventually undo the forces of dictatorship.

Of course, soldiers do not always act against dictatorship. The East European revolutions and the August coup attempt are not the only cases in which troops proved reluctant to fire on civilians,[57] but soldiers *do* shoot mothers, and sisters and brothers in the service of widely varied regimes. Will the shooting start again in the region that concerns us here?

This essay suggests that the international community has raised the costs of such action to a new high. It also suggests that global trends are running in the direction of democracy as various forms of dictatorship discredit themselves. On the negative side, we know that democratic elites in many of these states will encounter grave difficulties with their economies and also with ethnic divisions. Whether the people of these regions will abandon their democratic leaders and follow alternative elites depends, of course, on popular preferences and, therefore, on the puzzle with which this essay began. No matter what literatures or examples we draw on to understand the future of these regimes, we will always be taken by surprise if we do not seek a better understanding of the people and the preferences at their base. Now that these states are at least temporarily liberalized societies, our capacities for understanding popular preferences are greater than ever before.

---

[55] Personal interviews, Radio Moscow journalists, C-Span 91-11-29-1503-1, Purdue University Public Affairs Video Archives.

[56] Ibid. According to Radio Moscow journalists, this maneuver was itself the result of political learning from the Tallin massacres.

[57] The fall of the Shah of Iran and the fall of Marcos in the Philippines immediately come to mind.

Index